THE ROAD TO KILIMANJARO

Geoffrey Salisbury MBE

MINERVA PRESS
LONDON
MONTREUX LOS ANGELES SYDNEY

THE ROAD TO KILIMANJARO
Copyright © Geoffrey Salisbury 1997

ISBN 1 86106 232 X

First Published 1997 by
MINERVA PRESS
195 Knightsbridge
London SW7 1RE.

Printed in Great Britain for Minerva Press

THE ROAD TO KILIMANJARO

A Traditional Tribal Greeting

Cease oh winds from the west
Cease oh winds from the south
Let gentle breezes blow o'er the lands
Let calm seas flow o'er the oceans
Let the red tipped dawn come with a sharpened air
A touch of frost and the promise of a glorious day
Behold 'tis life! I live!

Acknowledgements

The origins of this work and its companion volume, *Yesterday's Flight Path* can be traced back to the interest and encouragement of that brilliant journalist and author, the late T.E. (Peter) Utley. Peter, in his capacity as a former Deputy Editor of the *Daily Telegraph*, was a man of wide interests and original ideas. He was intrigued that men and women who survived some of the most vicious experiences in the last war, including the Nazi death camps such as Dachau and Ravensbruck, could play a leading role in the fight against disability in distant lands. I suspect that this may have been one of the reasons that he found time to go through the original manuscript of this work. Subsequently he made some invaluable suggestions which helped enormously.

I am also grateful to former colleagues and to many friends for their assistance in writing this book. These companions represent a diversity of experience and disciplines. There are some who played a significant, if unobtrusive role in the transition of their respective homelands from colonial rule to independence. There are others from both sides of the warring 'divides' of the Forties era who took on momentous humanitarian tasks in Africa and Asia. There are a few who escaped oblivion at Ravensbruck or less well known hell holes like Neuengamme, Drancy, and the 'den of the Executioners' located almost under the shadow of Rheims Cathedral. I am indebted to them all for allowing me to draw on their personal memories, both for this work and for its companion volume, *Yesterday's Flight Path*.

In deference to them I hesitate to single out individuals and do so only where they are representative of specific areas of activities. In this respect I think of Tom Wijenjie of East Africa and his work amongst blind Africans which culminated in the Kilimanjaro climb; of Monica Fisher, a medical doctor with a long tradition of service to the handicapped in central Africa, and of Sir John Wilson whose wide-ranging work in organising sight saving missions and services in

v

distant lands for those who are already blind, is legendary. There is also a new generation of professionals and executives who have taken over from the pioneers of the early Fifties. It is these men and women, adventurers in the best sense of the word, who are manning lonely outposts and mobile clinics, sometimes in hazardous circumstances, whose courage and skill have contributed in full measure to this book. Now, far out on distant horizons are my 'helpers' of French Maquis days, people like Simone Poupart and other personalities, who, in their own way, made history. They kindly supplied material used in this work and its companion volume.

In Britain I am indebted to the Royal Commonwealth Society for the Blind under whose auspices I first set foot in Africa. Amongst the sterling team which ventured out from its headquarters, then located in Westminster, I include my wife Cathleen, who nursed her way across some of Africa's wildest terrain and still managed to enjoy life, and raise two robust infants. I acknowledge with much appreciation the untiring work of Mrs Betty Biss who typed the manuscripts of both volumes and, with Miss Doris Webb, advised me on a number of aspects of the work. Mrs Elizabeth Lucas-Harrison kindly assisted me with material drawn from RAFES records.

I was fortunate to have the support and advice of two international authorities on visual disability and Down's syndrome, respectively, Sir John Wilson CBE and Professor Peter Mittler CBE. Their commentaries are much appreciated.

In Northern Ireland I acknowledge with gratitude the help of my neighbour Mrs Audrey MaVitty in connection with communications problems.

I am especially grateful to Lord Hunt of Llanfair Waterdine, KG, CBE, DSO, who amongst his numerous duties and commitments found time to write a deeply thought-provoking foreword.

Finally, may I record my sincere thanks to my publishers, Minerva Press and all their staff for their co-operation and help.

Abbreviations Used in Text

SOE	Special Operations Executive
CO	Commanding Officer
DC/DO	District Commissioner/District Officer
RAFES	Royal Air Force Escaping Society
RCSB	Royal Commonwealth Society for the Blind
SHAEF	Staff Headquarters Allied Expeditionary Force
TAF	Tactical Air Force
UAS	University Air Squadron
WAAF	Women's Auxiliary Air Force
WI	Women's Institute

Photographic Material and Maps

Photographs and maps are gratefully acknowledged to the following agencies, government offices and persons:

Mohinder Dhillon	Africapix (K) Ltd. Nairobi
V. Clark	Topkim Productions, Johannesburg
Arthur Jones	Claverley, Shropshire
Jeremy Salisbury	Dubai, UAE
Frank Dolan	Westport
Foreign & Commonwealth Office	London
St Helena Administration	Jamestown, St Helena
Royal Commonwealth Society for the Blind (Sightsavers)	Haywards Heath, England
United Nations, (mandated territories division)	New York
International Centre for Eye Health	London
Ministry of Defence (Air)	London
Anne Chambers	Castlebar
Agnes Corcoran	Westport
Zambia Information Service	Lusaka
Mohamed Amin	Camerapix Ltd., Nairobi
Archives du Journal L'Union	Rheims
Yvonne Salisbury	Dubai, UAE

About this Book

Prior to setting foot in Africa the author, by the time he was twenty-two, had survived some of the bloodiest air-battles of 1944. This was followed by a stay with the French Maquis. His *dizaine* or cell was penetrated by the Gestapo and SS counter-intelligence. Eleven of his comrades were executed on the spot. He survived thanks to families who at great personal risk hid him.

At the end of the war he returned home, in his own words, "suitably chastened". He took up a teaching post at King's College, Taunton, and later at Wells Cathedral School. Congenial though these surroundings may have been they were no solution to his turbulent past. Like so many others from both sides of the warring factions of the Forties era he turned to Africa. Here he found it possible to erase some of the terrifying memories of the past and divert his energies to humanitarian challenges of considerable magnitude.

In a wide-ranging scenario he picks up the threads of a very different type of war, a 'timeless' one in which the author and his wife, (a trained nurse), come face to face with the appalling incidence of unnecessary blindness. The Valley of the Blind where visual impairment equates with death is the initial focal point of their work.

Against often beautiful but uncompromisingly harsh and rugged landscapes the author brings back to life the magic of Africa, a place where nature still ruled, where tribal customs were still respected and where the village 'herbalist' or 'witchdoctor' could destroy the eyes of a child with his vile concoctions in hours. It is here in the remote Luapala Valley and along the shores of Lake Mweru that much of the action took place, saving sight and helping those who had needlessly been blinded.

But the traumas of lost sight, both here and in other regions including another Valley of the Blind in Mali, hung heavily. Traditional apathy and indifference linked with the taunts of the able-bodied had conditioned the blind into 'accepting' that they really were 'the dead people who walked'.

It was from this appalling starting point that a triumphant finale is eventually reached. The author with his colleagues demonstrates that when the blind are given the right help and training they can overcome formidable obstacles. These same young people, classed as 'the living dead' by their families and villages, made up the team of eight totally blind men who climbed to the summit of the nineteen thousand, three hundred and forty foot Kilimanjaro. This is just one of the fascinating glimpses of encounters with an Africa which is fast disappearing.

Geoffrey Salisbury is an international authority on the handicapped in Third World nations whose papers delivered at conferences in Europe, America, New Zealand and Asia have been widely acclaimed.[1] He was an inspector of Special Services and eventually a consultant to a large number of overseas countries.

Geoffrey Salisbury MBE was 'mentioned in despatches' and was one of the first members of the RAF Escaping Society.

---

[1] Geoffrey Salisbury's previous works include 'Amongst Rhodesia's Blind' and 'Reports on Blindness in Mali and The Ivory Coast' (RCSB, Haywards Heath, UK).

Foreword

If you are born blind, how do you perceive a world which you have never seen? If you were once blessed with the precious gift of vision, how do you face up to a life of total darkness? These are questions which I, who only suffer from glaucoma, have tried to imagine, as must every caring person.

The quality of courage has many aspects. In my book, the courage to accept a life without sight, in which visual communication is denied, beauty shut out, and the joys of reading and recreation severely limited, ranks very high among human virtues.

This book, through living examples of African people who are blind, helps to answer my questions. It leaves me with a deep sense of wonder at such fortitude, such initiative and enterprise, such brotherhood in adversity.

I remember my astonishment, twenty years ago, when Geoffrey Salisbury wrote to tell me of his plan to accompany a group of blind young Africans to the summit of Kilimanjaro. It was a privilege to be invited to be the Patron of the expedition, and I rejoiced in its success.

Climbing a mountain is as much a challenge to the mind as to the body and the physical skills involved. Many times, while on a climb, I have been aware of how the visible technical details have served to absorb my total attention, shutting out awareness of fatigue. On a rock face or a steep ice slope, my thoughts are focussed on the next move up to some small ledge or crack, the next step to be cut, or pe͏
hammered into the ice. On a scramble or a simple plod uphill
is usually the view and a foreground of vegetation to deli͏
But without these things, how soon one becomes aw͏
effort! That effort of will and limb, that triumph
was what made those boys on Kilimanjaro
an inner vision, very special people.

I hope that this book will help others as fortunate as myself to understand better the quality of courage of the blind, and to appreciate the understanding and patience of those who support them.

Lord John Hunt KG, CBE, DSO

Commentary

Along the rutted roads of northern Zambia, Geoffrey Salisbury drove his jeep with the same panache with which, a few years earlier, he had piloted his bomber.

"That escarpment is going to be tricky," he said. "We'll take it fast – gives us power to handle the curve."

We went down on an avalanche of stones, slithering, sliding, lurching with the engine racing. The escarpment drops in five miles, with a lethal plank bridge half way down, to the peaceful shore of Lake Mweru. "Hold on to the bar of the dashboard," Geoffrey said. "When the bumps come watch out for the tool box. If it cracks you on the head, push it back. If we damage those tools, we'll really be in trouble." We were visiting village schools for the blind, which Geoffrey had established in the Luapula Valley on the Congo border. We were trying to find the cause of the excessive prevalence of blindness in that area where one child in thirty was totally blind.

That was one of a score of journeys Geoffrey and I made together, in Tanzania, Zambia, Nigeria and, later, in Arabia, Bangladesh and India.

I first met Geoffrey in 1952, in a prosaic café in Bristol. That was two years after the Royal Commonwealth Society for the Blind had been formed with vast objectives but little money, to take action against the formidable task of blindness in Commonwealth countries. This was the sort of challenge Geoffrey had been looking for: "It's a different sort of war," he said.

So Geoffrey joined the small pioneer staff of our Society which, overworked and underpaid, laid the foundations of a Commonwealth, and later a global, attack on blindness and its consequences in developing countries. In those first fifteen years, 1950-1965, the Society established organisations in most of the developing countries of the Commonwealth, with fifty new schools and twenty-eight training centres. Its mobile teams travelled across Africa to reveal the extent of blindness and to attack its main causes. It was a time of exciting new ideas and new methods to which Geoffrey, schooled in improvisation in the underground war of northern France, made an invaluable contribution.

We sent a research team to West Africa to those 'villages of the blind' where a fly-borne scourge, 'river blindness', darkened the lives of whole communities. At the time we had just enough money to pay salaries for the first six months and I remember Geoffrey saying, at the meeting when we made that decision,

"If this is where we go bankrupt, at least it will be in a good cause."

Our first school for the blind, which Geoffrey built on sixty acres of overgrown swamp in the Zambian copper belt, was an extraordinary place. I visited it whilst the building was in progress and was met at the gate by three energetic blind youngsters who took me on a clambering tour of the place, talking volubly about everything from drains to roof. They knew every inch of the place, because they had helped to build it, beating the paths, moulding the bricks, thatching roofs, helping to dig the well. The school cook was a redundant local witch doctor. In that unpromising setting, Geoffrey created a school and teacher training centre which was a model for central Africa.

Special schools could not cope with the numbers of blind children coming forward for education. We switched the emphasis to the training of teachers who, travelling on bicycles, helped blind children to enter ordinary village schools. Geoffrey developed a model system of 'open education' in northern Nigeria. With the help of UNESCO, the Braille alphabet was adapted to the tones and clicks of African languages.

We had to adjust the techniques of rehabilitation to the realities of life in an African village or Asian city. Geoffrey established a training centre and co-operative for blind village farmers in Tanzania. Blind people cultivated and harvested tobacco and coffee, grew cash crops and learnt to make a living as village craftsmen.

I well remember visiting that centre one night when Geoffrey, with some of the senior students, was hunting a lion which had raided the cattle kraal.

It is difficult to change immemorial attitudes to disability. As an African Chief once told me, "We are practical people; if you say goats can fly, we would first like to see one of them doing it."

It was against that background that Geoffrey led a group of blind youngsters to climb Kilimanjaro, Africa's highest mountain. As they reached the summit, an East African Airways plane dipped in salute with a message from the Queen.

The Road to Kilimanjaro tells this story against the panorama of Africa's transition from colonialism to self-government. It is a fitting sequel to *Yesterday's Flight Path*, describing how the faith and courage learnt in a war against Fascism in Europe survived to make its invaluable contribution to the very different war against the tyranny of avoidable blindness in Africa and Asia.

Sir John Wilson, CBE
Roedean

Commentary

Geoffrey Salisbury is a pioneer in every sense. His work in Africa with people with visual impairments was carried out at a time of limited knowledge and great superstition. The causes of blindness were not understood, there were few programmes of prevention, treatment or rehabilitation and the attitudes of the local community were characterised by fear and ignorance. The expedition of blind men to climb Mount Kilimanjaro which he led helped to change public attitudes by showing that blindness need not be an obstacle to participation in the life of the community and that blind people were capable of achievements which were beyond the reach of most sighted people.

Despite rapid advances in our knowledge of blindness, more recent testimonies by blind and visually impaired people make it clear that negative attitudes, based on fear and prejudice, are still widespread. For example, Joseph Kisanji, a Tanzanian writing as a university lecturer in 'special needs' who has himself experienced periods of blindness, describes how he was patronised and victimised both by the general public and by professionals and overprotected by his family. But he has also made a detailed study of local proverbs and sayings about disability which reflect positive, humanitarian and caring attitudes towards disabled people in community settings (Kisanji, 1995). Because disability is a fact of everyday life, disabled people are seen as the responsibility of the community.

Some disabilities are more easily accepted than others. While in Africa, Geoffrey Salisbury became the parent of a child with an intellectual disability caused by Down's syndrome. He was thus confronted in his personal and family life by negative community attitudes to people with an intellectual disability and continued to encounter such attitudes on his return to Europe.

I first met Geoffrey Salisbury at a conference in India. My contacts with him were based on his pioneering work for people with an intellectual disability and their families in small, rural and maritime communities in the west of Ireland. Working with other parents and with the local community, he established what seemed to me to be a model service in which support was available to a family from the first moment a child was born or identified as having a disability and continued in one form or another as long as it was necessary. Here again, local attitudes were not always positive and there was initial opposition to proposals to extend community facilities to people with intellectual disabilities.

Geoffrey Salisbury's life and work reflect a total commitment to the rights of people with disabilities to take their place in the life of their local community and to receive whatever professional and personal support they need in doing so. His book is an eloquent testimony to what can be achieved with courage and determination and to the similarity of the struggle in different cultures and continents.

Professor Peter Mittler, CBE
University of Manchester, July 1996

References

Kisanji, J., 'Attitudes and Beliefs about Disability in Tanzania', in: O'Toole, B. and McConkey, R. (eds.), *Innovations in Developing Countries for People with Disabilities*, Chorley, Lancs., Lisieux Hall Press, 1995.

List of Maps

Zambia   95

Uganda, Kenya, Tanganyika   172

Republic of Malawi   193

Kayes Region in Republic of Mali   250

Bangladesh: Satellite Hospitals   251

Contents

Acknowledgements   v

Abbreviations Used in Text   vii

Photographic Material and Maps   viii

About this Book   ix

Foreword by Lord John Hunt, KG, CBE, DSO   xi

Commentary by Sir John Wilson, CBE   xiii

Commentary by Professor Peter Mittler, CBE   xvi

List of Maps   xviii

Introduction   xxi

One   29

Two   41

Three   53

Four   73

Five   91

Six   116

Seven   133

Eight   158

Nine	170
Ten	186
Eleven	199
Twelve	210
Thirteen	220
Fourteen	240
Epilogue	254
Appendix I	273
Appendix II	275
Appendix III	277
Bibliography	279
Index	281

Introduction

I can well remember the first day I set eyes on the Valley of the Blind. It was in early 1953 in what is now Zambia. The rains were late that year but on the afternoon of my visit, following an oppressive sultry morning, they chose to break with a violence and ferocity rarely experienced in this part of tropical Africa. The towering black storm clouds which had built up earlier in the day out of an azure blue sky melted away as soon as the rain ceased. The storm had lasted less than twenty minutes. It left behind the sweet earthy tang of freshly damp soil. The parched earth had already absorbed every droplet of moisture and the sun was again unleashing a searing heat, the kind which within ten degrees of the equator can be devastatingly enervating for the unwary.

I viewed the scene which had unfolded before me from the summit of a desolate rock-strewn escarpment. Set out almost two thousand feet below and approached by a steep zigzag stony trackway lay a verdant carpet of jungle stretching as far as the eye could see. Winding through it and at times quite indiscernible was a slim silver thread of water, the crocodile infested Luapula river which flowed along the valley basin into Lake Mweru: to many people in Europe in the Fifties, a largely unknown inland sea. It lay glistening and shimmering in the powerful sunlight, at least sixty or seventy miles to the east of my vantage point. This was Chief Kasembe's country. Here before me lay the land of the Lunda tribe – a remote and hauntingly mysterious savage landscape touching the borders of the Congo, now renamed Zaire. But to some of us destined to spend much of our lives in this region, in spite of its traditionally bad reputation for disease, and some might claim 'witchcraft', it had an almost magnetic and insidious attraction. Such was the spell of Africa where the past still mingled with the present in those days.

But why did it appeal to me? I suppose that there were many reasons, some logical and valid but others unconvincing and hollow.

Perhaps after the traumas of war with their inevitable 'hang ups', the sheer isolation and wildness of the region offered a refuge, a haven of peace – some have said even an escape to sanity from a war-torn Europe whose wounds were still deep and festering. Perhaps, and I like to think that this is so, there were challenges, the opportunity to create, to build something out of nothing for a humanity which, a few years earlier, was bent on destroying itself. Maybe a crowded listless Britain, insipid (and some might have claimed rudderless) was an incentive to move on. I suspect that the real reason was the prospect indeed a galling one, of being tied to the tread-mill of an unimaginative teaching profession. Probably this was the catalyst which provoked me to escape the unsustainable frustrations of the late Forties. Be that as it may, it was an era of restlessness not only for the young but for the not so young as well. Sometimes it is forgotten that war shatters not only bodies, but minds, family ties, long standing values and standards. Things we never questioned are scrutinised. Youngsters who had been taught to kill had now found time to ask questions, some of which I suspect were unanswerable. Meanwhile amidst this inner turmoil I had found for myself a comfortable niche in a West Country cathedral school where I could quite happily have remained for the rest of my working life until, in a suitably anaesthetised condition, old age would beckon me out to the tranquil pastures of retirement. The warning bells must have sounded just in time and I escaped, albeit with considerable reluctance and with not a little trepidation. There were many others of my generation with whom I met up later who also had decided that it was time to stretch and test themselves in outlandish places.

I have never had any regrets about my decision though financially and socially it could have been disastrous. On reflection it seems that the mental and psychological treasures I may have garnered on the way have far out-weighed the inhibitions and inertia of boarding school life in the late Forties. The memories of nightmarish wartime flights bent on destruction have largely receded and, equally, the intensity of life with a Maquis *reseau* or network, playing hide and seek with a Gestapo Chief, Captain Josef Weisensee, and his men who have slipped quietly into perspective. I find no solace or comfort in revenge or recrimination for, at the end of the day, Captain Weisensee and three of his junior officers were sentenced to death after being found guilty of crimes against humanity by a military tribunal sitting at Metz.

Significantly it was in the Luapula and Lake Mweru regions that I was forcefully reminded that crimes against humanity had, until very recently, been part and parcel of the local scenario of where I had been designated to work. Scenes of the formidable Arab slave trains were memories a few of the elderly still recalled with clarity. The slavers herded their captives: men, women and children, along a fifteen hundred mile route to the coast. The death rate was quite appalling. It was here that history almost touched the hand of the present. As a new era swept its way across much of central Africa in the mid-Fifties, one could still talk with a few who remembered those frightful days; the old man who, as a child saw his sisters and father taken; the missionary who described to me vividly the columns of manacled captives wending their way to Mbala and on to Tabora, the main slave market in East Africa, and then down to the ancient slaving port on the Indian ocean of Bagamovo. As the sun set on this gloomy period of suffering there were still a few old men, both European and African who, at tremendous risk to themselves, had driven the last of the slaving elements out of business; an elite band of pioneers and askari who, though largely unknown and undervalued, did much to rid central Africa of an obscene trade.

When I first arrived in the valley it still basked in an aura of sinister history. Livingstone noted this when he visited Chief Kasembe and found the palisades around the village decked with the skulls of his enemies. Of course there have been massive changes but, nevertheless, the ravages of man-eating lions in this area are fact not fiction. Some authorities consider them more sensational than the episodes which cost nearly one hundred and forty lives when the Mombasa-Nairobi rail line was being built. One brute, *Chiengi Chali*[2], has been credited with ninety human kills. But there were other hazards which gave the area a bad name, like disease: leprosy and sleeping sickness were endemic. In addition the whole valley had suffered from a highly virulent type of measles which coupled with a poor diet and unskilled treatment by local 'herbalists' had led to a high incidence of blindness, hence the name – the Valley of the Blind. It was here that some of the first organised research took place. The

---

[2]*Chiengi Chali*: Chiengi refers to the area where the lion roamed and *Chali* indicates that he is an angry dangerous animal.

region is now with the support of the Government medical service, an area where blindness is no longer an overwhelming problem. Over the years I 'criss-crossed' the whole of Africa very many times but it was only in the mid-Seventies that I came across another and more horrendous Valley of the Blind. It was in a lonely region of Mali on the banks of a series of fast flowing streams where the land is good, but quite deserted except by those who are blind or are in the process of going blind. I had never seen anything quite like it. Whole villages lay decimated by onchocerciasis – commonly known as river blindness. It is spread by a small black fly much smaller than a mosquito. I had seen the destruction the disease had wrought in other parts of West Africa, but was now quite appalled at the intensity of its onslaught.

The Military Governor at Kayes had invited me to accompany him to some of the worst regions in his province. In a letter to me he wrote... "the direct consequence of onchocerciasis is the almost complete depopulation of the rich fertile zones and people are driven to the barren plains and desert further east. The good land lies fallow through lack of the able-bodied. The few who remain are incurably afflicted and become unfit to work the land." He had certainly not exaggerated the true position. The zone we visited is bounded by the Senegal river in the north and by the Faleme in the west. The population was in the region of nine hundred thousand. According to the Military Governor at least well over fifty percent of the population were blind or going blind, thirty-four percent had other disabilities (mainly physical ones) and about five percent were mentally ill. These figures were included in a report he sent to me dated 5th July, 1975. (The obvious implications were that almost the whole population has some form of progressive disability!) The comments by the Military Governor of Kayes did not over-dramatise the situation.

My own report amply confirmed an horrific state of affairs which was being aggravated by the presence of trachoma (another fly-borne blinding disease) and of course the ever present lack of good diets. In my report to the Government of Mali and to the UK government, I noted –

That at Niodougou a village which twenty years ago had an active population of well over four hundred had now less than sixty inhabitants. All of them appeared to be infected by the simulium fly and most of them were blind or in a progressive stage of blindness.

That my visits to the more remote regions of Kayes where roads are non-existent have made it clear that villages are being wiped out by river blindness alone, and...

That a depth of human misery and suffering is evident which may seem incredible to the outside world.

But it was not all a depressing picture for there are many other more cheerful faces to Africa. Some are incredibly brave – like the blind young men from East Africa who climbed the nineteen thousand foot Kilimanjaro "to prove", as one youngster remarked, "that blindness like mountains can be conquered." There are the courageous men and women who staff the RCSB mobile eye clinics and 'eye camps' in both Africa and Asia and each year save and restore sight to hundreds of thousands of people. All this was originally conceived and organised from the offices of the Royal Commonwealth Society for the Blind in England. Certainly this organisation has spear-headed the attack against the scourge of blindness on many different fronts. These are the people, volunteers, doctors, nurses and teachers, who year after year are fighting a war which is worth fighting.

Amidst all this one is inclined to forget that the handicapped were earmarked by the Nazis for elimination. This was the edict which emerged from a secret conference held at Wannsee, a village near Berlin, on 20th January, 1942 at which fifteen high ranking Nazi leaders were present. The last member of that macabre gathering, General Gerard Klopper died in February 1987. It was an outrageous state of affairs which culminated in a directive being issued marked *of the greatest secrecy,* setting out for selected SS commanders and Gestapo officers the categories which were an encumbrance to the state and which must be exterminated forthwith. (Some well placed Allied intelligence sources could not accept that the reports they were receiving from their agents in the Reich were genuine.) Within a short space of time the truth began to filter out. Jews, gypsies, Poles and the severely handicapped were driven down the slippery concrete slopes to the gas chambers first at Dachau and Treblinka and then the whole range of elimination camps which had been hurriedly built to provide the 'ultimate solution.' As the war in 1944 reached its climax the momentum of these incredible crimes increased and the world was to number those who had perished at the whim of a handful of psychopaths not in thousands, or hundreds of thousands, but in millions. Some of the wraiths of humanity still lodged in death camps were fortunate: "the gas chambers had not managed to swallow them all because the Allied advance had overtaken the 'killing schedules.'"[3] Society has in many ways tried to make amends for these outrageous events, but my colleagues in the war against the scourge of blindness and handicaps in developing countries came from both sides of the warring divides. We worked together in the desert lands, in the bush country and amidst the squalor and misery left by famine, tidal waves and epidemic in the Bay of Bengal. Just as the revelations of Nazi mass murder in the extermination camps was a justification for a frightful war, (though it was late in the day before the horrific truth dawned on most of us) the war against the scourge of blindness and disability in developing countries is an equally vital component if civilised society is to remain intact. River blindness will be conquered. The decimation of ghost villages in Mali in the Kayes area will be halted and already the name, the Valley of the Blind, in northern Zambia is now, at the end of the 1990s, largely a misnomer, thanks to the sterling work of medical teams and mobile clinics. The deadly scourges which swept the valley are disappearing.

Yet, sometimes under the guise of scientific research or administrative expediency, we are still discovering that there are many in the Europe of today who consider the weak and impaired expendable because they are an economic burden on society! Some of us have gone this way before.

We have seen the gas chambers. We have seen the corpses of men, women and children stacked in neat rows like piles of cord wood. The reason that they lay rotting before us was because the incinerators were completely full and unable to cope with the deluge of bodies. The only 'crime' of these ghostly wraiths was that they were the rejects of the Reich: beggars, Jews, children from orphanages, the patients from entire institutions and hospitals for the handicapped. This was the grotesque result of the Wannsee Directive.

---

[3]Quotation from a former SS Officer to the author.

Of course this was only a sample, for the Nazis threw their nets in the France I knew in 1944 widely and ruthlessly. It seems then that the dividing line between the Wannsee Directive and the *en avant garde* thinkers of the present day who consider 'benign neglect' as a legitimate tool in exterminating the weak and impaired is fragile indeed. In a decent society the handicapped are not expendable. Captain Josef Weisensee, a former adversary, was sentenced to death "for crimes against humanity". Nasora bin Suliman, the slave chief, had the blood of many hundreds of Africans on his hands. Are we sure that some of those in our society who allow the helpless to die through 'benign neglect' (or worse) are not in the same category as the task-masters who fed the gas chambers and slave caravans?

Geoffrey Salisbury
Roscairn, Enniskillen and Westport, Mayo

Chapter One

It was one of those heavy sombre September evenings which seem to herald the approach of autumn. There was a slight chill in the air. A yellow watery sun was sinking behind a distant avenue of tall poplar trees and a cluster of church spires was fading into the evening sky. This was the Paris of 1944 – a stark Paris, but one which was still tasting the flavour of 'liberation', a freedom still only a few weeks old.

We were in a spacious room on the third floor of Hotel Meurice which had been requisitioned by MI9 within hours of a large aggressive Gestapo unit vacating its splendour after an uninvited stay of four years! In spite of its unwelcome guests, this famous pre-war hotel had managed to retain much of its elegance and decor. I felt distinctly uncomfortable. Perhaps it was a fleeting recollection of the local Gestapo in rue Jeanne d'Arc or, more likely, the incongruous country-style clothes my helpers had generously provided for me when I had parachuted into France a few months earlier. I can still remember with some clarity the seasoned veteran of MI9 who sat at his desk opposite me shuffling a stack of papers which included my report, announcing in an authoritative voice that my debriefing until I arrived in London had concluded. He was a tall greying figure, a man of few words, but an individual with an incisive mind, an incredible memory for detail and one whose exploits (known only to a few) were legendary. His main claim to fame had been an escape from a formidable fortress in the heart of Bavaria during World War I, but this gentleman with the penetrating blue eyes was concentrating his thoughts this evening on other matters. He read through the notes he had made and then got up from his desk and strode over to the large window heavily framed in fading damask curtains. There was a prolonged silence as he gazed out at the Paris skyline and stood in a pensive mood, automatically filling a briar pipe with Rattray's Old

Gowrie tobacco. "Blended in Perth," said this senior officer when he saw me gazing at what was a rarity in a war-torn Europe. "You get a quarter pound tin for twelve shillings and three pence – post free," he added as an afterthought. He proceeded to send spirals of smoke rings up to the crenellated edges of the ceiling and then resumed his seat in front of me. "Your Maquis days are now over," he said in a quiet cultured voice. 'Tomorrow", he went on, "arrangements will be made for you to fly with your companions to Northolt from an airfield near Meaux, which has just been made serviceable. You will be met and escorted to our headquarters in Marylebone." He nodded and I assumed that the interview was over, but he indicated as I made towards the door that he had not yet finished. "This is the end of one chapter", he said, getting up from his desk, "but for youngsters like yourself it is only the beginning. Do you realise", he asked, "that those of you who have been through the mill of Resistance work will probably never quite succeed in ridding yourselves of the mental scars and wounds which may have been gathered?" Such thoughts had never crossed my mind. At the ripe old age of twenty-two I was, on reflection, quite selfishly oblivious to the legacies of hatred and love, of violence and tranquillity and of care and indifference. My immaturity, indeed the naivety of youth, had in the last few months never allowed me to pause and ponder on the insanity of man and his penchant for destruction. The tall distinguished colonel had been through it all before – indeed under a *nom de plume* he had written a well-received book about the art of evasion, escape and its aftermath. He hadn't finished with me yet: "I have found", he added in a thoughtful tone, "that there is not much difference between the wit, grit and courage needed to out-manoeuvre your enemy in war as there is to out-wit your enemy in peace."

Those were the musings of a man who had probably seen life at its best, as well as its worst. The substance of that brief, terse conversation which, for me, heralded the transition, albeit a slow one, from war to peace and its ultimate influence on my future plans was significant, perhaps a turning point. But who was my enemy in peace? Years later I came face to face with the answer.

*

It was morning and I was leaving France. The din of war had drifted eastwards and a mantle of calm had settled on the restless countryside which I had come to know so well. A soft rain was falling from a leaden sky and, on the distant horizon, a heavy blanket of motionless cloud was silhouetted against a fading yellow sun. It seemed to herald the approach of autumn and yet another winter of war. I felt a keen tinge of regret and perhaps a touch of sadness that I would soon be leaving behind a country of which I had grown fond. I would miss its expressive lilting language and the tantalising morsel of its culture which I had found time to absorb.

I had said farewell to companions who had steadfastly stood by me, indeed risked their lives so that I could now make this homeward journey. When I had reminded them of this just before leaving the Champagne area, they had merely shrugged their shoulders and with broad smiles remarked, *"C'est notre plaisir, c'est pour la patrie."* People of that calibre are unique. As I sheltered behind a partly ruined control tower from the continuous rain which was now sweeping across this airfield some twenty miles outside Paris, my thoughts turned once again to the actors who had come out of the mists and surrounded me. There was the quiet but brave Bouster family, Marcel and delightful Irene, in future years to become the god-parents of my handicapped son Anthony.

It was with Marcel that I had waited with considerable trepidation on a lonely trackway for a *parachuteage* which never materialised. *Parachuteages* had become sensitive operations in those days when it transpired that the German counter-intelligence service was monitoring these activities with some degree of success. I thought as well of the courageous Poupart family, always cool, invariably calm and rigidly resolute in the face of adversity. Inwardly, they suspected that their father would never return home. He knew too much. Outwardly, they refrained from recriminations and blame. They never once voiced their terrible worries and concerns about his future or their own and still managed to raise a smile and an assurance that, "one day everything will be all right". But of course it wasn't. There were many others whom I can remember with clarity. Daniel Mancier of Tramery and his beautiful young wife Christine. Paul Poittevin and ice-cool Jacqueline, charming and attractive, who seemed to regard the night trips of the men from her household, who were tangling with the Boches, as an almost boring routine. Next door lived her parents the Bouchés. There were, as well, the Truncheons of Chaumuzy who greeted German black marketeers with feigned charm but Madame, as all knew, saved her real affection for the two or three Allied parachutists who spent the 'weekends' being entertained in her hayloft. All these good people and many more are special to me. They make up the kind of friendships and attachments which are meant to endure the ravages of time. When, over the years, I have compared notes with other evaders the one common theme running through our experiences was not the inroads of the Milice and their disloyalty, or even the brutality and stealth of the Gestapo, but the close affinity one developed with those who helped one.

The existence and work of the Royal Air Force Escaping Society bears witness to this. Indeed, for those locked away in forest strongholds or masquerading in French towns or villages, it was the type of life which many of us embraced almost naturally. As one French veteran remarked to me just before I left Rheims: "There were no half-way houses in our life, no, not even safe houses. You either married the life and accepted the damp, cold and discomfort of the forest or you hated every minute of it and yearned for a soft bed and a solid roof over your head." It was true. To many an Allied airman or Resistance worker on the run this reflected the situation.

It had been, for me at least, a mode of life which my country up-bringing had assisted me to assimilate. It may have suited my temperament for I had always harboured a remote nostalgia for an unconventional way of life. In any case, the training given aircrew at Advanced Flying and Operational Training Units was an excellent preparation for life in the misty world of Resistance movements. This fact has rarely been emphasised in discussing escape and evasion tactics but Hitler, in his directives to the SS and Gestapo, had evidently got the message. In essence, the type of life I was leaving behind was a free ranging one or, as an MI9 Officer remarked rather jocularly, "a lifestyle of legalised brigandry". Of course he was not serious, but I think it stressed an important point that if you were keen to survive and carry on the battle, your own individuality and initiative counted as much as anything else. I found that there was an art in living rough and enjoying it.

It was on 10th September that we took off from a badly bombed airfield. I remember the date well because it was the time when the British started to make a concerted effort to capture the Channel ports which had been by-passed in the rush forward into Belgium. We were flying in an American Air Force Dakota. These machines were noisy and rattled, but were generally reliable. Certainly they were functional and utilitarian. A few months earlier the plane we were flying in had been used to drop paratroopers on the Cherbourg peninsula, just behind Omaha beach, one of the five D-Day landing points. The aircraft seating was primitive – just aluminium slatted seats along each side of the fuselage. That evening my companions included Arthur Jones (my air crew colleague who was shot down with me) and three or four other people dressed in creased civilian clothes (they were former evaders or Maquisards) and a few walking wounded – a total of about a dozen formed this odd passenger list. The four crew members had their parachutes stowed away but the passengers had to take their chances. We were lucky to get a lift home. Our route took us to the north of Le Havre and it was clear that the city was still in German hands. Hitler in almost customary fashion had given his final orders to the German Commander that the port was not to be surrendered on any account and that the battle would continue until the last man had died. A massive air bombardment was in progress preparatory to an attack by General Crerar, the Canadian Commander. He had two British divisions at his disposal. Hitler was apparently prepared to sacrifice one division which he could ill afford to lose. The place was wreathed in a pall of smoke and dust. The battle was just starting and for ten minutes we had a grandstand view of the proceedings as we lumbered ten miles to the north of the place. It took just forty-eight hours to ensure the fall of Le Havre, up to twenty thousand prisoners were taken, but vital areas including the port installations were completely destroyed. The Allies needed the port badly and it was another four weeks before it could be brought back into partial service.

Our Dakota cruised on unconcerned. It was an entirely new experience to be flying around over France in broad daylight. We quite expected to be blasted out of the skies. But times had changed since our flying days a few months earlier. We learnt later that the Germans were in no position to tackle us. They had their own problems. Some of the older generation may recall that the Dakota or DC3 was once described as 'the workhorse of the skies'. I little thought as we cruised over the French coastline at a steady one hundred and forty knots, half expecting to be bounced by a stray

FW190 which might have slipped through the air defence curtain, that many years later I would be flying in exactly the same type of machine over equally dubious territory but this time in Africa and with an equally incongruous collection of passengers.

*

To digress for a moment, war-time Dakotas could be found years later flying in all sorts of climates and terrains in the most isolated parts of the world. One aviation authority confirmed that there were a few at work right through to the end of the Seventies, ferrying passengers and freight over some of the roughest routes in the world. I recall that years after this Paris to Northolt trip via Le Havre, I travelled from Addis Ababa to Jemma, an isolated bush station at the foot of a mountain range, in one of these utilitarian 'crates'. The passenger list was in some ways more interesting than that of my 1944 journey. The plane carried a cargo of over-ripe pineapples, dried fish and four goats (who fed happily on the fruit). An elderly Ethiopian peasant woman who sat next to me was nursing a kid goat. Opposite, on the long slatted bench seats which were on either side of the fuselage, was a friend of mine, Edgar Marland, a United Nations official. He sat next to Princess Seble, one of the late Haile Selassie's daughters and her lady attendant, Woizero Tayetch, a distinguished looking girl. (There was as well the Royal bodyguard under the command of Ato Kebede.) I had been invited to join this small party so that I could report to Haile Selassie on the suitability of rural sites we were due to inspect for use as clinics and schools for the handicapped. Our Princess companion was a professional in her own right and was leading the team. This lady was not afraid to walk miles through remote bush country even though at the time there was a security risk from bandits. She was not afraid to get her hands dirty either looking after a sick child in a village. Ethiopia may have been slow in coming out of two thousand years of feudal rule but, in thirty years of working amongst the handicapped in developing countries, I have rarely found such practical concern for the weak. This is a side of the House of the Lion of Judah which has been submerged by alien Marxist political attitudes, yet Ethiopia, during Haile Selassie's time, had some of the best training centres for the disabled in Africa as well as a string of clinics and homes for orphans and the severely handicapped. I was certainly impressed. At one stage Ethiopia appeared to be well ahead of most other African countries in this area of social and educational work. Such facts are now forgotten except by a few like those of us who were privileged to see some of the work which had been developed.

According to Dunn's work *An Experiment in Time* (which I read in my teens) the past, present, and future merge into one. The events of 1944, later the Ethiopian episode and finally a gathering in 1987 at my old squadron's base, Holme, in Yorkshire, suggest that there might be some validity in this hypothesis! It was in the slums of Addis Ababa that I saw my first Cheshire Home, a beacon light by any standards in its unpretentious loving service to a group of horrendously handicapped children. This was in 1964. Yet twenty years earlier its founder, Group Captain Cheshire VC,[1] had been busy 'marking' with pinpoint accuracy some of the most prickly targets in France and Germany. I can still recall his cool no-nonsense directions given to the approaching planes coming into the storm of fire as his own Mosquito circled leisurely thousands of feet below, silhouetted against a background of flares. It was an inspiration to most of us, just as the worldwide network of homes he and his fellow workers established for the severely handicapped are today an inspiration to parents, like my wife and myself, who have a badly impaired child. It was whilst in Ethiopia that I grasped the unswerving commitment and degree of care, which is now a password in a caring society, of the Cheshire Foundation. Here in Addis Ababa was a haven, a life-line for those who had been written off in the struggle for survival. Now after five decades the Cheshire Homes are a model of unobtrusive self-sacrifice. Whilst at the Foundation's home in Addis I remarked to the British nurse who ran the place with a handful of Ethiopian helpers, something to the effect that, "this was yet another side of the Leonard Cheshire story". She understood.

For a brief moment in 1987 we saw the Group Captain of 1944 still slim with a bearing of determination which age had not blunted, at a poignant ceremony at Holme in Yorkshire where No.76, my old Squadron, had been based.

Leonard Cheshire had been one of its commanding officers and knew many of the names inscribed on the granite memorial stone

---

[1]See Appendix I

which was being dedicated at the church on the hill just outside the airfield. Arthur Jones, with whom I flew on many missions until we were shot down, wrote and told me the details. Those present on that sunny September Sunday afternoon included Douglas Iverson, then a Wing Commander and a Squadron CO, and a host of survivors who had come out of the shadows to pay tribute to our comrades who failed to return, amongst them Pilot Officer Gramson, a Canadian pilot and companion who died, when our plane was a blazing inferno. (His parachute may not have opened.) Here then at Holme was not a mutual admiration society but a gathering of men who, after the trials and tribulations of war, had set out to make amends for the follies of the past. Perhaps Dunn was right; maybe time does merge into one dimension!

*

But my thoughts on my trip from Paris on that sombre evening in 1944 when I had first been introduced to the noisy but solid Dakota with its odd assortment of passengers, were concerned with a multitude of other personal problems. I had tried to contact my parents by telegram through the good offices of the Army both in Rheims and Paris, but I was aware that it was probable no message would have got through. Like Arthur, I was penniless and possessed only the clothes which I was wearing but the RAF reception committee in London was well organised, so that was the least of my worries. Quite honestly, most of the chaps in the plane on that September evening were not looking too far ahead. It was a lesson that those of us who had spent a few months with the Maquis had learnt the hard way. The point which concentrated most of our thoughts was a safe arrival. As Beachy Head, gaunt and massive even from eight thousand feet, fingered its way out into the steel blue restless Channel it looked as though we were finally going to make it home! On a number of occasions this unique peninsula had been our final sight of the home country when we were leaving on one of those raids deep into France. Even on a dark night it looked magnificently impressive, laced with a faint white string of breaking seas half circling its protruding mass. We crossed the coast line and there was, visibly, an air of relief – a few shook hands, lads whose recent adventures may have made another English landfall doubtful!

The people in Northolt clearly had no time for red tape and paper work. Such things as customs formalities did not appear to exist; a war could be a marvellous purgative for those who had built walls of paper work around themselves as some form of protection. Transport was waiting for the handful of RAF evaders on the plane and we sped off into a drab but friendly London, where gaping gaps in the city told their own story. Spasmodic V1 attacks were still taking their toll and the quite new V2 weapon caused quite a few raised eyebrows amongst even seasoned young warriors. It was clear that the war was far from over. Half the city seemed to be in uniform. Our destination was the Marylebone Hotel. No, we were not being exposed to a luxury life. MI9 was, at that point in 1944, a growth industry and had taken over the hotel so that the 'clients' they were interviewing could all be conveniently lodged under one roof for as long as they were needed. It was a highly efficient place as one might expect.

But it was back to the realities of life with a bang. There would be no more flying for the time being; that was completely out. The official line was that aircrew who had been marauding behind enemy lines engaged in clandestine activities would be 'at risk' if they were captured. In any case one could not be officially considered fit until a specified period had been spent away from the scene of operational activity. It was disappointing both for Arthur and myself. Flying and Resistance work had at least one thing in common – they got into your blood.

The succeeding months were painfully frustrating. To begin with I arrived back on the doorstep of my parents' home to be told by our neighbours – kindly Mr and Mrs Crimmins – that my parents had gone to Shropshire to stay with one of my sisters but that they were expected back either that day or tomorrow. Sure enough they arrived back a couple of hours later and got the shock of their lives. The telegrams from France and the one I had sent from London had not reached them and so when they saw me standing in the doorway they thought they had seen an apparition. My parents had in fact given up hope and assumed that I was dead. My mother was clearly shocked, but give her due credit, outwardly she showed a great degree of composure, of the stiff upper lip variety, with which that side of the family is well endowed. My father, bless him, seemed to be well-drilled for such traumatic occasions as well and found time that evening, not to go to the pub to celebrate – he was TT and in any case considered pubs non U – but mounted his bicycle and cycled off for half an hour of meditation and prayer in our little parish church on the sand dunes. I learnt that evening as well that our Vicar, a saintly man, had lost his son only a few months earlier attacking shipping off Norway. For this devoted Christian father there was to be no reunion, at least not in this world. The beautifully carved doors, now hung in the entrance porch of this old church, were erected as a memorial to this young man who, with the crew of his Beaufighter, lies somewhere under the cold waters of a Norwegian fjord.

I found on that six week spell of leave an almost terrifying psychological gap between myself and my parents. They were kind, good hearted and well-meaning but we were really on two different wavelengths. They just wanted the war to end and for me to settle down in a pleasant backwater and to schoolmaster away peacefully for the reward of security and dignity! I could think of nothing worse. It seemed a dreadful prospect to be faced with. I am quite sure that this was the feeling of thousands upon thousands of men and women who had been jerked out of the office, factory floor or professional back room and given a chance to show a side of their makeup which they had never suspected existed. What a challenge, what opportunities and now, perhaps within a few months, it would be back to – 'as you were'!

I settled down with some trepidation to a lengthy leave in Burnham-on-Sea. On looking back I realise how much I was out of my depth in this gentle backwater. I met an elderly retired clergyman who was certainly no fool. He was a close friend of my father in this well-mannered and largely self-centred society. He had retired after a lifetime of teaching classics at Repton and, I rather suspect, he too was finding the change artificial and galling. One morning he came round and asked me if I would like to join him in a round of golf. During the course of a dull game he gently explained that though both of us were engaged in widely differing spheres of activities our problems were largely the same. I had termed it the 'generation gap' (a factor which seems to be always present in a petulant society), but he considered it both a generation and a 'credibility gap'. He was a great conversationalist and between the lines I could read, that just as I missed the vibrant life I had left, his problems of adjusting from the humming beat of a large residential school, went back not four but forty years. His company made some amends for the isolation I now found myself in.

Most of the local younger crowd were away slogging it out in Burma or on the western front. A week or so ago I could have been shot into the next world, but now my kindly father and mother, who did not wish to think about such things, expected me to make polite conversation with their peers, balancing a cup of luke-warm tea in one hand and watching the old ladies knit balaclavas for the young men "up front"! I just wanted to get back with the flying fraternity and be my natural self. One pleasant lady presented me with a thanksgiving prayer which I still have tucked away safely amongst my other treasures. And yet another retired gentleman handed me what was probably the last wartime guide issued on Burnham-on-Sea – something I did not need at the time but which I kept because I respected his thoughtfulness. Today it makes interesting reading concerning a Somerset backwater in wartime. A round of golf on the famous Burnham and Berrow course cost 3/-. You could stay for a whole week, everything included, at the Richmond Hotel for £4 and most of the smaller hotels were cheaper. The old Somerset and Dorset railway (the slow and dirty was its local tag) would take you across the Somerset marshes via Glastonbury to a point on the English Channel coast for less than 6/-. The guide spoke about the miles of golden sands extending northwards for six miles. In those days they were studded with large concrete posts, originally intended to stop Nazi gliders making a landing in 1940. Fortunately in September 1944 they did not manage to stop a skilled pilot of a badly damaged American Flying Fortress making an almost trouble-free landing between the Lower Lighthouse and the old St Margaret's school, which bordered the beach. Burnham, so the guide book said, apart from being healthy was clean, the healthiest place in Britain! I wonder if that was true? The sewage as in most other seaside resorts at that time was pumped raw along a pipeline into the sea at low tide. It depended on the ebb and flow tide to disperse the daily load. But, the prevailing westerly winds were not usually very helpful so the high tide on the golden sands was a paradise for those gluttons of the high seas – the gulls.

Burnham-on-Sea, compared with many other places in wartime Britain, was a great place to unwind in. Whether one wished to relax or not there was, it seemed, no other alternative which was just as well. Consciously, most of the men who had been up in the front of things, wanted to get back to the camaraderie they had left behind but subconsciously there was occasionally a yearning to break away to some quiet spot where time and tolerance would assuage the tempestuous and sometimes nightmarish scenes which floated to the surface. I was lucky and had considerate parents but they could not really understand the unsettling life that I and others like me had been following. For my part I found it difficult to accept the quiet life they loved so dearly – though today I have embraced exactly the same pattern of tranquillity and seclusion! Youth usually rebels against serious parents and I was no exception. At least I tried to do it in a way which would cause the least anguish to them. My aunt, who had nursed on the western front during the first war, saw things differently. She was a brave broad-minded lady with whom I established something of a rapport. She would have been disappointed if in future years I had taken the easy way out. It was a restless tussle. The war had only a few months to run and youth must, she said, still go ahead and make its mistakes! And that is exactly what I did over the next few years, once the fighting was out of the way.

Chapter Two

Although the war in Europe still had six or seven months to run there were bloody days ahead and some unpleasant shocks as well. The Bastogne breakout at Christmas was one. Earlier another was the fighting around the Aachen gap as General Bradley got ready to start an offensive in November aimed at crossing the river Roer. He hoped he would take his men through to Cologne and Bonn. As for the Pacific war zone, it looked as though this had years to run. The Japanese were hardy fanatical fighters and at times incredibly cruel. They appeared in those days at any rate to be an almost dehumanised race – treating such a foe at the end of hostilities with magnanimity was courageous. Time, trade and tolerance seem to have done the right things and refreshed the minds of most of us and certainly the younger generations who never knew these people as an enemy. But for some of us the deep rooted prejudices remain. Certainly they are brilliant, but what an enigmatic race!

Sometime in October the telegram I had been waiting for arrived. It read, "Report forthwith to RAF Bentley Priory, Stanmore, for further instructions." I was quietly delighted but I was in for a shock. In those days I did not know my way around the RAF as well as I should have done. Perhaps this was due to my absence abroad, firstly in Canada and more recently in France. Added to this was the fact that for security reasons RAF Bentley Priory was a place one did not talk about too much and, if one did, it was usually in whispers. It was Fighter Command Headquarters from where the Battle of Britain had been waged. This was the place where the Commander in Chief, Lord Dowding, conducted with impeccable skill and *sang froid*, the whole critical battle. His astute judgement won the day as much as the planes and men flying them. When I arrived at its gates in October 1944, Bentley Priory, to those who knew the whole story, was already part of history and legend. It was a salutary experience. Bentley Priory was still as much as ever in the front line, but in a different way. Whilst still the lynch pin in the aerial defence system, its efforts were concentrated on destroying as many flying bombs as possible. Secondly, it was organising strikes right across western Europe in support of the advancing Allied Army; and thirdly directing its efforts at the latest menace – the V2 secret weapon which was capable of being launched from the most innocent looking of places, a park or school yard.

At Command Headquarters a mass of administrative detail covering everything from equipment and postings to the requisitioning of land for airfields, was dealt with. The age of computers had not yet arrived for administrators but the first batch of them were making their presence felt in the air operations which were being mounted from the Kent coast through to the skies over Berlin. The Command post at Bentley Priory was the overall co-ordinator of every aspect of the life of Fighter Command and that stretched a mighty distance from the north of Scotland over to the Second Tactical Air Force who were living rough in France and Belgium. In other words it was providing the sharp prodding end for defence and offence. It was an amazingly diverse organisation with a most efficient administrative system which operated to the four corners of free Europe with an absolute minimum of fuss or 'bull'. It was something of an eye-opener to see how the brains of the service managed to tick and remain human and approachable. The high powered had time to talk about and to explain and to understand the problems the teleprinter clerk may have been encountering or some other human detail which dogged a signals unit. Officially I was now on 'operational stand down' and found myself attached with a handful of other flying fraternity, some from Transport Command, others from fighter squadrons, to fit in and make ourselves useful. I was given a comfy niche in the map section of the navigation wing dealing with all types of maps from those used by the TAF (Tactical Air Force) to the latest radar creations which under the right conditions would give you a correct position over Europe to within a few yards or so. The daily 'milk run' of Mosquitos going out to Berlin would be controlled from a computer unit down the road at Command HQ which, when the weather was bad, would even control the bombing run with considerable accuracy. (Out of three hundred and twenty raids on Berlin only twelve Mosquitos were lost.)

Bentley Priory was unique in a number of ways. It had just one small airstrip for communication flights. It was located in front of the main house. There were more women than men on the Station, at least that was the happy state of affairs which was said to exist, and its central feature, the Mansion, lay in magnificent woodland and still does, just off the Stanmore-Watford road near Bushey Heath. Even with the sprawling mass of Nissen huts and network of roads the estate was still large enough to retain some of the idyllic setting which, for over two centuries had grown up around it, even the shrubs and wildlife, birds and squirrels had adapted themselves marvellously to the brash intrusion upon their privacy.

The Mansion itself was said to have been the home of Lord Nelson and Lady Hamilton. It is of early Georgian design and its large south facing windows face on to lawn and rose gardens. In 1944 the airstrip was almost at the edge of these gardens running in an east-west direction. The rooms of Bentley Priory are well proportioned and spacious. In my day they were filled almost to bursting point with busy staff, mainly WAAF keeping the administrative life of the Command intact. Most of the sensitive work was tucked away from ordinary view. Scattered throughout the grounds was a network of paths and roads leading to well-spaced prefabricated Nissen huts where other elements of the life of the Command were taken care of. The reason for the careful separation of the administrative offices was to foil any massive air attack which might have been launched.

The 'holy of holies', the main operational Command Headquarters with its teleprinters, codes and ciphering department, intelligence unit and countless other essential components were deep underground. They surrounded a unique operations theatre from which the build-up of air battles and the actual progress of the fighting was monitored and controlled, minute by minute. The staff working in this huge subterranean complex were often on duty rosters which meant that they saw little daylight. In winter this situation may have gone on for weeks at a time. Located to one side well away from the operations room was a small gym and a number of ultraviolet ray machines which were well patronised when there was a break in activities.

The Priory was a great place for sport. There was rugger. During my stay, young red-haired Geddes the Scottish international, who was having a rest from flying Spitfires, did a fair amount of coaching. We must have been pretty hopeless material. Aldenham School, which was a few miles into Hertfordshire, gave us a sound thrashing. The hockey team led by a middle-aged Signals Officer was not much better, but our Sports Day was a huge success with the Commander in Chief, Air Vice Marshall Robb taking time off to hand out the medals. (The recent former C.-in-C. Leigh-Mallory had just been lost flying out to the Middle East.)

Bentley Priory presented a busy cosmopolitan atmosphere. There were Czechs, Poles and Free French pilots en masse, a few Belgians and a handful of Norwegians. In addition there was a heavy weighting of Americans, largely because Fighter Command was closely tied in with SHAEF (Staff Headquarters Allied Expeditionary Force.) If you wanted to meet some of Britain's top fighter pilots they were all round you, usually impatiently pleading or conniving to get back to operational duties, away from the 'flying a desk' type of situation. The grounded flyers like myself were the odd men out. Everyone was very pleasant but as the Wing Commander said to me when I went up to ask for a posting back to flying duties, "Salisbury, you have had your crack at operations, don't be selfish, just stand back and let the other people in the queue have a go!" And that is exactly what happened. There was no real work to keep one on the straight and level, but there were plenty of distractions. It was the old story of getting to know the ropes.

It was possible to get a little bit of flying experience through Geoff Elphick, the Aircraft Controller at one of the airstrips just outside the base. The communications pilot was a Czech Flight Lieutenant who had a most complicated surname - both to spell and pronounce. For convenience, and because he must have been over fifty, he was known to all and sundry as 'Daddy'. He was a brilliant pilot but because of his age and after three or four years of concentrated fighting both on the ground and in the air, he was now flying VIP's around in Austers, a dainty little machine which was to become something of a docile pet. 'Daddy' had seen life. His face was heavily wrinkled. He was small and stocky with blue eyes, his thoughts always seemed to be on distant horizons. He had been obliged to leave his wife and children behind when he had been forced to flee his native country. Their home was near Prague. There were plenty of men around Bentley Priory like 'Daddy' who had been obliged to leave their native land and continue to fight from British shores. There was a nineteen year old

Norwegian who had escaped in a leaking fishing boat and had just been picked up in the nick of time.

The French contingent from time to time included men like Pierre Clostermann, the author of a number of books on wartime flying. Jacques Remlinger, another veteran, was now based at Bentley Priory and from time to time Max Guedj, the Free French ace, came to Headquarters. He was shot down a few months before the war ended on a 'ship busting' attack off Norway. He had left his father, who had been arrested by the French Milice, in a concentration camp and his wife and small daughter were living in North Africa.

I had a fairly close insight into the hopes and fears of some of our Allied comrades. They had done so much to carry on their own private war against the Nazis only to find that the evil of Hitler was, for a number of our friends, to be replaced if not surpassed by the brutality of Stalin. Max Guedj was one who in his early thirties, a lawyer in peace time, had already done far more than his share in a sector of aerial warfare, 'ship busting', where the losses were sometimes as high as seventy percent. Then was one horrific day in the 'ship strike' records when twenty aircraft of Fighter Command (eight Mosquitos and twelve Beaufighters) attacked two destroyers in the Channel off Pointe de Graves. They sank them but only three Beaufighters managed to get back to base. You needed steel nerves on those kinds of jobs. The 'flak came up at you like a curtain of fire' said one who got back (that was how he described it when months afterwards we were talking in the mess.) 'Ship busting' work never came my way, nor was I to be involved in low level operations. We thought in Bomber Command the odds were stacked against us, but if you looked around you could always find someone worse off. To sweeten the bitterness or as some may say to add spice to the flying talk, we seemed to be always absorbed in, the WAAF exerted a considerable influence especially in off-duty hours when we were gathered together in the mess. Talking 'shop' was considered unsociable and these girls were not backward in reminding us about our lack of manners.

I ventured out on the social merry-go-round from time to time. We were usually pretty hard-up but I went out with an attractive WAAF, a brunette, who hailed from my own part of the West Country. For some reason which I could never explain to my own satisfaction, we went to see *Die Fledermaus*, which was on in one of the West End theatres; I didn't like opera and neither did she. It was a disastrous evening. The theatre was almost empty because of the V1 and V2 bombs which from time to time still fell spasmodically on London. In future we confined ourselves to less demanding entertainment like the Friday night dances which were a feature of Bentley life. These boisterous affairs probably helped to anaesthetise some of us from the traumatic events which were still unfolding not far away – the V bombs which wreaked frightful damage on London and the irony of some of our pilot friends who, after a six month rest from ops went back to their squadrons to be killed a few days before the end of hostilities.

Those seemed to be the days when sexual deviants and homosexuals did not monopolise much public sympathy for evidently there were more important social and survival manifestations to concentrate one's thoughts on. Maybe some of us were existing in a more restricted and confined environment! Up to now the girlfriend situation had not played a significant part in my young life but my Bentley Priory WAAF was one with whom I remained in close contact after the war. I was then teaching at the Cathedral School in Wells but an Army husband turned up from somewhere in the Middle East and so this strange affair, for the good of all concerned, ended abruptly. There were quite enough social and marital problems without adding to the already enormous complicated catalogue, was the sane advice of my friend.

A few weeks before my spell at Fighter Command Headquarters was due to expire, it was clear that the war in Europe was drawing to a close, so I saw the Station Commanding Officer and again requested a posting back to flying duties with a Bomber Squadron in the Far East. I suspect that he thought I was 'flak happy', but eventually agreed that he would put in a strong recommendation to help me on my way. VE Day came and Fighter Command HQ at Bentley Priory celebrated the occasion in the style one would expect from a body which had borne the brunt of the fighting from 1940 right through to the last day of the war.

One thing about the RAF was that it was always mindful of the debt it owed to occupied Europe. Once hostilities ceased the word went out that flying personnel who had been involved in escape and other activities with the Resistance movements, should return to their former stamping grounds and personally thank the people who had risked their lives for them. I think the CO was glad to get me out of the way for a couple of weeks. He summoned me to his office and after outlining the purpose of the exercise said, "Sergeant Halter has made out travel warrants for you. Go to the Orderly Room and pick them up with any subsistence allowances the accounts people are giving you."

It was around June 1945 and travel in France was something of a nightmare. On looking back, it was not a very successful trip as the people I had to contact lived miles away from communication points and apart from a brief stay in Rheims when I met the Poupart family and heard final confirmation of the sad news about their father, I only managed to contact a few ex-Maquisards. It was not the occasion for reunion celebrations. There had been too many grievous losses in the villages and amongst relatives who had been deported and then executed. I saw Père Grenier – that great old survivor, but people were now getting back to the hard facts of life, setting about earning a livelihood and beating the black market which was getting out of hand. It was amazing how quickly life was getting back to normal, but cars were still few and far between and people's minds were directed more to the state of the men and women, in most cases pathetic wrecks who had survived the execution squads, the gas chambers and the diseases which swept through the concentration camps and eventually carried away countless numbers of former inmates and medical helpers. At that time I picked up one or two stories from one of the decimated creatures who returned only to die a few months later from his experiences. He spoke of the stench of death, the piles of corpses, the continuous ribbon of grey smoke from the huge crematorium. "We lived", he said, "in the midst of death" – an expression I had heard many times before. "To be shot", he exclaimed, "was something I would have welcomed rather than face the claustrophobia of gassing in that concrete hall of death."

On my return journey I passed through Paris where I tried to trace the grave of the one man who had died on that disastrous night when we were shot out of the sky. The authorities in Rheims had told me that Pilot Officer Gramson's body had first been laid to rest in a village near Sarcy and then reburied with other Commonwealth flyers in the military cemetery in Clichy, a suburb of Paris. Unfortunately the information I had been given was wrong.

It was whilst I was in Paris that the trial of a strange character – a Dr Marcel Henri Petiot – was taking place. It was exciting much interest locally as this sinister character was said by the police to have murdered at least two dozen people but he himself claimed the total to be sixty-three, alleging that they were all traitors! Dr Petiot was said to have systematically murdered his victims, dismembered them, half burnt some of them in an old stove in his house at 21 Rue Lesueur, a large rambling place which overlooks the British Embassy back gardens and garages, and dumped the remains in a well topped up with lime.

It was a long and complicated story. As I had a few hours to wait for the next train out of Paris I went to the Palais de Justice where the trial was being held and one of the gendarmes on duty recognising an RAF uniform propelled me through the large milling crowd to a place in the courtroom. This was quite an achievement as there were crowds baying for the wretch's blood. Dr Petiot was a swarthy, lank, dark-haired individual, wearing a black beard, tall, slightly hunched at the shoulders with flashing piercing brown eyes. He was fighting for his life – an animal at bay – and everyone seemed against him except, one presumes, his defence lawyers whom he dismissed later, but he seemed to be handling affairs with acumen. His statements were hissed, booed and jeered at by the partisan spectators who were packed like sardines into the public gallery. There was laughter and ridicule as Petiot screamed at his tormentors. (These fantastic scenes and furious arguments with the public gallery continued throughout the trial.) Petiot at times lapsed into silence and then with his mad hypnotic eyes apparently tried to hypnotise the jury. It was to no avail. After a sixteen day trial he was condemned and subsequently executed.

What was the truth about this weird case? There were two versions; either he was a Resistance hero (he worked under the code name of Captain Valery), or a demented Gestapo collaborator. Petiot said on the day I was present, "I was doing my duty by suppressing undesirables who collaborated with the enemy." Significantly, the police claimed that at least fifteen of his victims were Jews and others were people who 'knew too much!' It seems that the Gestapo were aware of some of his activities but they decided to remain quiet as he was doing some of their work for them. The prosecution alleged that he was offering a bogus escape route to Spain for Jews and other fugitives. Victims were told to report to his consulting room with all their personal possessions and money. Subsequently they disappeared. One or two survived and that morning gave evidence at the trial.

Petiot had a chequered history which demonstrated criminal leanings. He was discharged from the army for selling drugs, but was also given a small pension and was treated for psycho-neurosis. His crimes started coming to light when it was discovered by new tenants of 21 Rue Lesueur that it was a huge charnel house. On reflection Petiot was a most abnormal individual. He looked the part. A sinister, mad psychopath; another that wartime France had pushed over the brink. It was a sad unedifying business. At least fifty-four sets of unclaimed clothing were found in the house so his claim of murdering sixty-three people may have been correct. I left the Palais de Justice that evening wishing I had never seen or heard of Dr Petiot. The evidence that day had been gruesome in the extreme.[1]

I arrived back at Bentley Priory in July to find that I was on standby for flying duties in the Far East. I would be getting kitted out and fixed up with all the various inoculations within six weeks. It was back to a Bomber Squadron. Although I was pleased about the news, the idea of flying against a fanatical enemy was a little disquieting, but it was what I had asked for and would be more useful than sitting behind a desk at Bentley Priory chatting to the WAAF. But I need not have been too concerned. The war against Japan finished with that massive bang which heralded in the nuclear age.

On reflection, The Bomb must have saved thousands of American and British lives. Tackling Japan through the conventional ways of war would have been a bloody business for the Army. The Air forces would have been engaged in equally vicious actions where the losses would have been just as bad as those experienced over occupied Europe and The Reich. So, when the emotive subject of the rights and wrongs of the use of the Atomic Bomb in 1945 are discussed, some of the old timers like myself usually keep a respectful silence. Most of us agree that it was appalling that a civilian population should have been made to suffer such an horrendous experience. The question facing the Americans who had borne the greatest brunt of the fighting in the Far East was an unenviable one – who was to be sacrificed? Was it the Japanese civilians or the flower of the Allied

---

[1]See Appendix II

forces? It would be churlish if we failed to acknowledge that many young men fighting against a desperate, cruel and fanatical enemy owe an extended lease of life to that momentous decision. This line of thought can be taken a stage further. The hundreds of thousands of Allied lives which were saved meant that they were enabled to father a new generation many of whom are now ardent exponents of ban the bomb propaganda. It can be argued with some cogency that a considerable number of these people – offspring of the men who would have probably died in an extended Far East war, owe their existence to the bomb! It is an odd philosophical position. Like many other people I am against this type of weapon but some of those who are loudly proclaiming the odds might sit down quietly and reflect that they or thousands of people like them are in this world because of Hiroshima and Nagasaki.

The Hiroshima and Nagasaki bombings, apart from the utter chaos they inflicted, introduced a new dimension into life at Bentley Priory. The war was over and there would be no more opportunities to fly or to fight. Everyone was thinking in terms of demobilisation and getting back to the sort of life they had known pre-war. Service life was not disintegrating but it was made pretty clear that men in the flying category had very little future. There were too many around. The bottom had almost dropped out of the world for many of us youngsters who took a jaundiced view of quietly settling back into the home town and following the quiet routine of earning one's living in the nine-to-five rut.

A few of us were brooding on this prospect and on some of the events of the last few weeks. One of our late Spitfire pilot friends was, one of the topics of discussion. He had gone back to ops and within a few weeks prior to the end of the war, had been killed, dive bombing a V2 site, a well hidden launching platform in a Dutch parkland. There was a long silence. A young WAAF sergeant came up to me and drew me aside. "You may be on your way," she said, "the orderly room have a message for you." I popped down to see Sergeant Halter who gave me a slip of paper. It was an address complete with room number in the Air Ministry.

"Squadron Leaders Toft and Weighgill wish to interview you tomorrow," said Sergeant Halter with a worried look. The two names were synonymous in those days with the international rugby scene and I believe even today in English RFU circles they carry considerable legendary weight. When I met this pair they were a few years older than me but seemed in the odd perspectives of the time to be vintage pilots. The stiff and formal interview I had expected did not materialise. After a brief discussion on Bentley Priory and my operational experience, Squadron Leader Weighgill came to the point. There were vacancies for chaps with operational flying experience at one or two University Air Squadrons. Would I be interested in a change? I had already made up my mind that there was no future in staying in the RAF but this offered a glimmer of hope until my demobilisation papers came through. Within a fortnight instructions arrived for me to proceed to Bristol as an instructor at the University Squadron.

In those days a provincial university like Bristol was a pleasant enough place to find oneself in. The UAS (University Air Squadron) Headquarters at that time was lodged in a large house in Tyndalls Avenue just behind the University and the Royal Fort. We were a very small contingent, exactly five people. The CO was Flight Lieutenant West who had been having a very busy time flying Mustangs on photo reconnaissance missions over Europe until the war ended. The adjutant was Flight Lieutenant Jennings, an interesting middle-aged chap who had one perpetual bind that because of his age he had never been allowed to go on ops, but his wealth of flying experience more than made up for that oversight. In pre-war days he had been with Imperial Airways on the London-Paris run flying Hannibals. He then joined RAF Transport Command and was busy flying Wellingtons out to the Middle East, which was something of a hazardous exercise in those days. He was a great pilot and flying was his life. We used to fly from Filton which is now part of Bristol. When the airfield was reasonably free Jennings would demonstrate his favourite acrobatic stunt: the "falling leaf". I was with him on one of these demonstrations when, at a vital part of the manoeuvre, the engine of the Tiger Moth spluttered and cut out a few hundred feet above the airfield. We were well below the three thousand feet usually permissible for aerobatics, but as we were coming into land I suppose we could claim that we were excluded from this regulation. Anyway, the engine gingered up a little and we scraped over a housing estate and glided into a quiet landing.

We all made mistakes. A few weeks earlier we had flown in an Air Speed Oxford bound, I think for Fazakerley or an RAF airfield somewhere in south Lancashire. The weather suddenly closed in with one of those nasty industrial-type fogs and instead of arriving at our correct destination, we landed in error at an American airbase, Burtonwood! I still feel embarrassed about my appalling bit of map reading.

The visit had its compensations. The USAF had half a dozen Luftwaffe planes on the tarmac which had been captured intact. They were in mint condition. It was fascinating to get a close up of some of the planes of our former adversary and to crawl into the cockpits and fuselages and admire the methodical layout of the instruments. There was a JU 88 night fighter, a sinister-looking machine, coated in black with a variety of antennae protruding out of the nose and tail. The ME 110 looked equally formidable but the Heinkel III, a twin-engined bomber, in many ways a good-looking machine, seemed already destined for the war museum. It was an interesting eye-opener and we flew back to our base at Filton with plenty to think about.

The end of hostilities had knocked out the enthusiasm for further flying training and most units including the University Air Squadron were caught up in the same malaise. One could not really expect students who were swotting for finals to throw themselves into a training which may lead to nowhere. This was the most knotty point for us all. None of us, young veterans or career men knew whether we were wanted or not. The signs did not look good as the new Government was making swinging cuts in manpower. Reluctantly it seemed a case of getting out whilst the signs in the outside world were still favourable. It was time to abandon ship.

Chapter Three

It was March, 1946. I was back as a civilian in a numbingly cold and bewildered Britain. The social consequences in the aftermath of six years of war were coming home to roost! In many cases the enforced periods of separation in one of the services had wreaked havoc on many family lives. There were misunderstandings, marital traumas, there were personality changes as well, both in those who had been trained to kill and those who had stayed behind immune from tragedies unfolding in distant lands. It seemed to many of us that the emotional debris left over from the first world war, and now the most recent conflict, had split the social fabric of the country at its seams. There was a deluge of marriage breakdowns, a frightening increase in vicious crime, and teenage delinquency appeared to increase at an appalling rate. All these manifestations rattled the staid strait-laced world which many of us had been reared in. The simple notions which had been inculcated into us of right and wrong, of keeping one's word, and of integrity in our dealings seemed almost alien in a world which was becoming increasingly greedy and grabbing. On looking back many of these attitudes seemed understandable for we were living in a world which seemed increasingly insecure and bent on self-destruction.

It was a new era and indeed a perplexing one for both the young and the old. I had my own problems. The time had come to make far reaching decisions – whether to embark on a teaching career or to accept a place which had been offered to me by the Dean in the medical school at Bristol. (I had met him during my stint as instructor at the Bristol University Air Squadron). After some hard thinking conditioned by a number of factors which included finance and vocation, I opted out of this career possibility. On looking back I consider it a lucky escape but it brought home to me an interesting point; in those days most applicants for places in University medical schools were personally interviewed by the Dean and a small examining board. This system it seems has now largely been dropped but at least it had the merit of eliminating the odd misfit and weirdie whose presence can sometimes demean the profession.

My flying career with the RAF concluded with an extravaganza of stimulating aerobatics executed with precision by Flight Lieutenant Jennings in the squadron Tiger Moth. I think he included about everything in the aerobatics book except a tailspin. That afternoon we made a fast low level sortie to the Dorset coast line in a new Air Speed Oxford and on our return rather irreverently did a shoot up of Glastonbury Tor followed by a steep turn around the old tower. I suppose these days our behaviour would have been looked on as abnormal but after the pressures of the past few years as Jennings said, "we were entitled to let off a little steam". A glass of champagne (left over from Maquis days) toasted my departure from Headquarters and sadly I was out of the RAF but still on the reserve list.

Maybe after that kind of send-off I should have been delighted to slip quietly and suitably subdued into the frosty world of teaching. Within the space of three years as a supply teacher I seemed to have covered the whole spectrum of educational establishments, prep and public school, primary and modern ones but eventually I found a niche in a school for handicapped children.

There were a number of reasons for these diverse changes. I had a dread of taking root in an establishment and staying on in security until a frail hand grasped its reward: a meagre pension. There were some quiet little safe havens where I could comfortably have stayed but, thank goodness, I read the warning signs and packed my bags just in time.

What I saw of the teaching world in those days was not always encouraging. Everyone seemed exhausted, almost jaded. Retired men and women had been holding the fort whilst the younger brethren were away on active service. Some old timer teachers could not get out fast enough whilst others, those who may have been exempted from military service on grounds of health or conscience, resented the new men and women coming in after they had been battling with evacuee problems, shortages of equipment, rationing and a lot of other irritating matters. Now, a group of bumptious young people were joining a staff which had not changed for years. Their ideas and attitudes were often quite alien and the old brigade found it difficult to get on the same wavelength as these new-comers and their brazen line-shooting. So, there were adjustment problems for us all, the old and the new.

Outside the sheltered precincts of the school it was even worse. How could you expect a recently returned shop assistant or bank clerk who may, a few months previously, have narrowly missed being carved up by the Japs, to resume where they had left off in 1940 and treat people with the same deference, people who had stayed securely at home. It was just not on – too much had happened. Keeping such things in mind and the host of personal and social crises, it was remarkable how so many people settled down so quietly and quickly.

I was lucky. My transition to civvy life was cushioned by having a few companions who had had their own shattering experiences, not that they talked about them much but we spoke the same service type language, and had the same attitudes. But there were some strange oddities and misfits around as well which, in its own way, made my entrée into the teaching profession something of an induction to be remembered. I first did temporary duty in a fairly large boarding school in southern England for a three week period.

The school is now defunct which is perhaps just as well. The Matron fell for the Head boy – I calculated that the age difference was around twenty-eight years – unfortunately somebody had tripped over them in the coal cellar on the last day of the Easter term and that was the end of that bizarre romance. In my innocence I had asked the Assistant Matron, the person who had spoilt this curious relationship, "Why choose the coal cellar?"

"Well," she snapped in her best bitchy tone, "if you had known Miss X, I expect you would have chosen it as well." During my spell at the same school, the Head, obviously an alert individual, saw off a swarthy, plump and dumpy bachelor priest who, as he put it, must be having 'body chemistry trouble'. The story went that this unwholesome little man had been making passes at small boys, seating them in the dark in a corner of his study 'for frank discussions'. He left in a hurry. The poor old music teacher, so I was told sometime after I had left, was not so lucky. He got three years.

I had made a bad start but fortune shone on me and I picked up a post for a term at King's College, Taunton. It was conveniently near my home. If you were sold on the public school system there was, I suppose, a fair amount of snob value in such an appointment; at least I suspect that is how my family saw it as they were rapidly coming to the conclusion that what with the RAF and the Maquis, I was spiritually ruined and now almost unemployable, possibly a psychiatric case, though in those days most of us looked on psychiatry as a dubious field. At any rate King's gave me the opportunity to look around and enjoy Somerset country life, cricket at the County ground and a trip out to the Quantock Hills. The school was well run. The teachers, conscientious men of the world were still old-fashioned enough to believe in character formation training, sports, and mental as well as physical gymnastics. There were some interesting people on that staff who had plenty to offer. There was an ex-missionary from China, an elderly man who seemed to bring with him something of the calm and inner peace of the East. I think he had taught at the school throughout most of the war and was well respected by the boys. One of the French teachers was a young man called Massot from Paris who found public school life hard to understand and, as King's had a definite Christian bias, he may have found this difficult to accept as well.

The Headmaster was one Mr Unmack. Academically he was brilliant, certainly shy and I suspect not a great leader of men which was a pity. He rarely spoke with junior staff but remained aloof and detached. I suppose it was part of the act in those days. He reprimanded us through frosty little notes which we found marked "confidential" on the staff letter-rack. It was a system of communication which the younger generation found difficult to understand. Those who had offended would have been delighted if he had come off his pedestal and had torn a mighty strip off us. One of the rituals each term was a Sunday lunch with the Headmaster. Poor old Unmack must have loathed this social occasion as much as the two or three staff he invited each Sunday. Conversation was stilted but he did his best. To try to run a school with King's traditions and standards in the 1940s was not an easy task. King's was academically orientated – I think now that the war was over, financial problems were beginning to loom as well. Fees were around £300 a year which were modest.

One could not work in residential schools those days without catching the whiff of student worries on the home front, debt and broken homes were some of the casualties of the war and something most of us were not used to, but, it was to be only another decade or so, before the flood gates finally burst open and society was presented with a social upheaval which has to this day penetrated almost every crevice of community life. One or two of the older teachers were perceptive to these changes and tried, when a youngster returned from a school holiday showing the gruelling signs that marital upheavals had shaken his little world, to make amends. It was difficult. What could one do? As poor Beckett, the Head of the junior school, once said, "You just feel so utterly useless and inadequate." But in those days the broken home situation was only a mere trickle and I suppose the pastoral side was able to meet, partially at least, such challenges. Boarding school life in those days was tough but considering the era which held sway just before the war, King's was one of those schools which was in its own strange way caring but remote. I could have stayed longer at King's: one had to work hard, long hours teaching and long hours in residential duties, but the holidays were long as well!

I signed up when the term at King's was finished for a year at Wells Cathedral Grammar School. What brought me to that medieval gem is something which has always puzzled me. One of my WAAF friends from Fighter Command days lived there, that may have been one reason, but probably the truth was that, if I did not get myself fixed up with a post soon, my parents would have almost disinherited me, as it was a case in those snobbish times of 'what would the neighbours think.' When I landed an assignment at the Cathedral School, all was forgiven. My father, a champion of the ecclesiastical fraternity, was delighted and my mother, who came from a family with long snob pedigrees, was delighted that she would have something to talk about at the WI or the next coffee morning.

The Headmaster of the Cathedral School in those days was one Canon Ritchie, whose main claim to fame seems to have been that for one brief period he compiled *The Times* crossword puzzles, and so the main discussion at the breakfast table every morning was the correspondence he received from those who had pitted their wits against him. He was a paternalistic figure, tall, greying at the temples, supported by a cheerful wife with something of the school mistress about her, but she was apparently a trained nurse which, in those days, may have been considered even more formidable.

It was essentially a happy, family type of school, reflecting I imagine the character of the man at the top. I was surprised at this

58

free and easy atmosphere, nothing seemed to be taken too seriously, neither study nor sport, the system ticked over smoothly and no one appeared to be too worried about allegedly outlandish pieces of legislation like the 1944 Education Act, or the new approaches and methods in education which were starting to thrive like mushrooms after a shower of rain on a summer's day.

At King's College, Taunton, there was a Common Entrance examination to pass before a boy could be admitted but provided one could pay the fees which were very modest, almost all comers were welcomed at Wells and as for those who joined as choristers and sang in the cathedral, they received their education on the house. Sometimes when parents were having a bad time financially, the kindly Ritchie, unknown to most, quietly forgot about monetary matters. It was a small school, somewhere around a hundred and fifty day boys with a large complement of boarders. Most of the students were drawn from the farming community, some were from the famous cider orchards and were to make their names with brand products like Baby Cham from Showerings and Coates cider, some were nephews of well-known stage personalities of the time like the Waters sisters. There was a reasonable corps of clergymen's sons, a few had failed their eleven plus and came to the Cathedral School, I suppose, as a last resort, but a substantial number were the sons not of the well-to-do but of modest shop keepers, plumbers and tradesmen. It was an interesting and democratic mix. Those were the days, I should emphasise, immediately after the upheavals of the war. All that malaise was within a few years soon shaken off and the school, a few years ago, became co-educational and is now considered one of the most efficient in the country. It has high academic standards and exciting all round development. Admission standards are high.

Canon Ritchie was steeped in the history of Wells. He claimed that the Cathedral School was the second oldest school in the country. (The oldest he admitted reluctantly was Canterbury.) No-one on the staff dared to question these claims; he was a man who understood the ways of the world more than most of us and when a young 'left winger' straight from the Cambridge stable, put forward his views on the privileged position of schools like Wells, Ritchie quietly asked him what he was doing gracing such a system. Ritchie was tolerant enough. His main theme as he explained to this naive young man was, "It is easy to destroy the works and principles of nine hundred years, but it will not be so easy to build new values and attitudes to replace them."

On reflection I enjoyed my stay in Wells. I was grateful for this respite. It gave me a chance to think things through and to relax in the balmy atmosphere of a unique setting. It would have been so easy to slip into the rhythm of that medieval backwater. I watched some of my colleagues do it and I believe they were there until pension time called them out to graze! Among this contented throng were people like Alan Tarbert, who was in charge of the junior school. He loved Wells and the countryside around. He was a large, tubby, genial man, who in those days marched his troop of boys around the countryside in crocodile style like an invading army. They loved him. Then there was Colchester, in his mid-thirties, tall, bespectacled and aesthetic, intellectually a giant of a man who was torn between the wilds of East Africa, where he had spent most of his wartime service, and the tranquillity of Wells. Most of the younger chaps fresh from the services found the atmosphere of life in a cathedral city relaxing but restrictive. In those days teaching was just one aspect of the work. Residential duties were set for every other evening and alternate weekends. This meant that free time was limited. It was not infrequent in those days that the Duty Master could sometimes be found in the Fountain Inn near the cathedral, almost adjoining one of the school houses.

You could not fail to be impressed by the magnificent Cathedral resting like a jewel at the foot of the Mendip Hills. It was this heritage which, like Rheims Cathedral, had stood immovable through the centuries. Aloof from the insults of Cromwellian England and the hordes who stabled their horses within this treasure house of the past during the Monmouth Uprising. Who could fail to be impressed by the Bishop's moated palace and the swans gracefully gliding past the drawbridge, or the uniqueness of Vicar's Close, possibly one of the oldest and best preserved pieces of urban medieval planning which can be found in Europe? I can well remember the spacious Cathedral green on a summers evening and the echoes of the organ pealing across the still air as Mr Pouncey, the Cathedral organist, or young Peterson, his assistant, concluded another day of musical richness. The tourists had started to come. They were impressed as well. The Copper Kettle where Alan Tarbert enjoyed afternoon tea once school was over, with its rich pastries plastered in Somerset cream, and its old-world atmosphere was a popular venue for visitors. It was a few yards away from the Old Gate House by the green.

In the midst of the tourists' coming and going, and a community basking in the glories of the past and making a fortune out of it all, we managed to do some teaching. Douglas Clapp, a 'self-failed' theological student with a good Oxford degree taught Latin and French, young Keenan, an ex-Marine from the Isle of Man, attached to the Junior Department, seemed caught up in the Wells atmosphere, but managed to escape just in time. In addition there was a whole bevy of attractive lasses doing the child care and nursing stints. It was all a bit unsettling and as one cynical master, who was on the point of retiring remarked, "Anyone who appoints good looking females to the staff amongst this set of virile sex starved men, is asking for trouble. Ritchie must have been sorting out his *Times* crossword problems!" It was not quite as bad as that and as Doug Clapp said later:

"Give the poor man credit – at least he is in tune with the younger generation and prepared to give us a chance which is more than you can say about some of his peers."

In the winter we took the boys tobogganing on the Mendip slopes which sweep down almost to the edge of the city. In that blazing hot summer of 1947 Doug and I went swimming up in Priddy Pool, supposedly hundreds of feet deep and reputedly an old Roman lead working, so the ancients in the district told us. The facts about its depth we never proved except that there was sufficient water to drown in. Doug slid off the bank in great style expecting to be in shallow water but Priddy pool was supposed to be bottomless – bottomless even within a few feet of the side. Doug was obviously no great swimmer (I really don't think he could swim if the truth were known) and soon he was floundering and bellowing, so in a semi-naked state – I hadn't finished changing – I gave him a helping hand and we both landed safely on the steep embankment. It was close enough for us to call it a day.

My teaching was equally prone to hazardous pitfalls. Former students to this day will recall my carelessness in handling sodium in the lab. A large chunk of the metal, instead of a speck, fell into the water and a flame of hydrogen shot up to the ceiling. The boys loved it and Science became a popular subject! I taught Geography as well up to School Certificate level, with a modest degree of success. I was an appalling Rugger referee although I was now taking the game up quite seriously again and over the next two years played for a variety of clubs, including Winchester and my home side Burnham-on-Sea, when we went through the whole season almost unbeaten. From time to time I saw my ex-WAAF friend from Fighter Command days but as Wells was a perilous place for gossip, we came to some sort of vague agreement that we would call it a day. She was a nice girl, but probably didn't have much time for poverty-stricken schoolmasters, who were sheltering from the world in an artificial haven.

I suspect that this was a truism which came home to roost as my first year at Wells drew to a staid and dignified close. It had been a happy, almost carefree year and should I have wished to stay on there was the promise of years of security, comfort and intellectual company ahead. The pay was modest, the hours long, but I had delightful living quarters, no worries about where the next meal was coming from and even one's laundry was taken care of. Yet, though it suited some who had travelled much more widely and adventurously than I, it did not really seem right. I don't mean 'right' in a social, political or moralistic sense, but rather in the degree to which it suited my personality and character. I had had a rest, a change, yet I still hankered after vague challenges and nebulous fields to conquer. I was still wonderfully free, with no wife or family ties to consider, but the thought of settling down at the age of twenty-four or five and becoming another 'Good Bye Mr Chips' character seemed appalling.

So I left Wells Cathedral School with regret. The fault lay with me not with the school. Like a lot of other men and women at that period of time some of us were suffering from our various sins in 'adjustment' problems which made themselves manifest in numerous ways. I came to the conclusion that it was up to ones self to resolve these problems. Poor old Unmack at King's, Taunton, seemed hardly of this world, whilst Canon Ritchie, a man certainly of this world understood well enough. "Let the boys", he was referring to three or four of his ex-service staff, "have a good time and work it all out of their systems," was what he told one of the more mature matrons, who had complained about 'unseemly conduct.' That was surely a reasonable and fair approach from a gentleman who could quite easily have kept us in our place.

I have often wondered what kind of individual I would have turned out to be if I had stayed on in that little bit of paradise. The older hands were not the frustrated, bitter characters I would have expected.

Time had mellowed them, they loved the Cathedral and the way of life which surrounded it. Alan Tarbert, that delightful genteel Head of the junior Department once told me, "If you can find a little bit of peace in this world, a quiet haven, hold on to it." He did exactly that and he seemed a happy man.

After leaving Wells I joined the rough and tumble of first the primary and then the secondary modern school (now termed comprehensive) at Burnham-on-Sea. It was another useful experience which lasted nearly six months whilst I was waiting to get into Special Education. The 'modern' school was in my home town, small and cosy. The five male staff all played for the local rugger team and we had a remarkably good season. 'Chalky' White was the Headmaster, a young thirty, who just missed getting into the Olympic squad as a sprinter at the tail end of the forties. It was co-ed. Those schools could be great fun. I must have been growing up as I was about to settle into a career which would take me pretty well all over the world.

The one advantage of filling in as a temporary at a fairly varied selection of schools was that it gave me the chance to survey and gauge the educational scene in England with a fair degree of accuracy. These were two inevitable conclusions: that people who had stayed at home during the war were at an advantage when the promotion stakes were at hand and, secondly, those who had specialist qualifications in the current fashionable fads in education were likely to have an easier passage. I managed to identify the one growth area which might give a teacher a reasonable amount of flexibility and job satisfaction. It was in the up and coming special services field, dealing with handicapped children; for years it had been the 'Cinderella' of the service and was still largely coated with the do-gooder image and a poverty-stricken 'voluntary organisations' face with roots going back to the days of Shaftesbury and beyond. I must be honest, my motives were not as altruistic as they should have been, but at least when I joined the Special Education Service I felt it was one way of getting out of the rut and, as time went by, the altruism which I may have lacked in the early days became, I like to think, grafted onto my work, and at the end of the day, was that much more genuine and solid than if it had sprung from spurious emotional reactions.

My first post in this new field was in Hampshire at the Lord Mayor Treloar School where I was given a good grounding in physical handicaps – anything from polio (which was rife in those days) to conditions such as *ossium fragilitas*.[1] There were orthopaedic cases galore, plus a variety of ages and intellects; indeed, general experience which years later I found tremendously helpful, when I was working on assignments with United Nations, the Commonwealth Secretariat and other international bodies. It was at Treloar's that I met my wife Cathleen, who was a Nursing Sister, but, as I was penniless and could just about manage an evening out on Saturday night in Winchester, after a rugby match, there was no chance of getting married until I was financially a sounder proposition.

I followed up the stint in Hampshire with a long session in the Royal School for the Blind in Bristol, and eventually qualified in Special Education with a couple of useful diplomas and later became Head of the Bristol School. At least it was a sign of the times that I had made it but I think it was one of the most frustrating periods of my life and drove me overseas to Africa and beyond. The school traced its origins back to 1793. The Liverpool School for the Blind was two years older and for good measure had been founded by an ex-slave ship's Captain, William Rushton, whose conscience must have caught up with him, for after getting smallpox (the unkind ones said VD) on the West African coast and partially losing his sight, he decided it was time to reform.

These schools like Liverpool and Bristol still clung to tradition with a vengeance. The staff at some of these schools seemed to be installed for life. Boarding school life seemed infinitely worse than anything I had experienced elsewhere. The staff were kindly enough but they seemed so staid and inward-looking that change and new ideas seemed an anathema to many of them. We seemed to be living in a tight closely knit society, detached from the ways of the world which threatened those who were blind. This was, of course, the well-meaning state of affairs which had percolated down from early nineteenth century social thinking, based on the belief that the kindest thing to do for the blind was apparently to shelter them from the trials and tribulations of life, so they lived in Asylums for the Blind. (The Royal Bristol School was originally called the Asylum for the Blind.) According to some of the more elderly who had been students at these places, discipline was exceedingly hard, the diet basic, and the whole

---

[1] A condition in which the bones are exceptionally fragile and hence very easily fracture.

routine of life regimented and starchy to an almost unbearable degree. I was told that in the Bristol School even up to a few years before the war, meals were generally taken in silence, but that the teacher on duty might possibly sit up on a pedestal and read suitable extracts from the newspaper! Prayers, and due thankfulness for the mercies bestowed on them, and suitable meekness were the legacies of a past era which survived in thought and partially in deed up to the time of my arrival.

Many people do not realise that until recently if a child was born blind or went blind in infancy, his parents were compelled by law to send him to a school for the blind. As such schools were few and far between it meant that at the tender age of five or six, he was taken away from his own home and lodged for the rest of his young life (except for holidays) in a boarding school which may have been ideal during the social turmoil of nineteenth century England, but was often a terrible indictment on modern society. It was bad enough for a youngster to be blind, and in some cases to have additional disabilities to cope with, but to be torn away from his family at an impressionable age seems unfair and insensitive. He would join a crowded dining-hall with a hundred and thirty other youngsters from five up to the age of twenty. Meaningless extracts from the paper would be read to him and then there would be the usual spate of graces and pious thanks. Clothing and uniform would be stiff and starchy, freedom of thought and activity strictly limited. He would sleep in a barn of a dormitory. The general routine was, it seemed, calculated to crush rather than to cultivate independent and well integrated young people into society. It is I realise fashionable to denigrate the past, the way things were done and the attitudes which prevailed. They were all part of the long and awesome growing-up pains. Some good things do come out of war. One of them is that the public conscience catches up with the staleness and wrongs of the past and, as far as handicapped individuals are concerned, and especially the blind, men like Arthur Pearson, who worked wonders after the first war, and more recently Sir John Wilson and his campaigns against blindness in Third World countries, bear out that politicians and the establishment have never led in this field; at the end of the day it is the public. War can stimulate action in social fields which have been neglected.

But one must be fair and see things in perspective. By the standards of the times, particularly in the nineteenth century when child neglect was rife, the 'asylums' for the blind which were established first in Bristol and later in Edinburgh and other large cities, stood out like beacon lights in a black sea. They were havens from the frightful social conditions of the times and though their rules were strict and repressive, at least they provided some tangible evidence of concern in a society which had precious little time for either the disabled or the underdog. Their starkness, their discipline and even in some cases their quaint thinking, that for example the blindness these youngsters were enduring was the 'righteous wrath of an angry God', cannot detract from the fact that these schools provided shelter and, almost unbelievably, were way ahead of both political thinking and that of the establishment as well. It is easy to scoff but these voluntary institutions which grew up with the blessing of local philanthropists, (frequently with Quaker origins) were the pioneers and laid the foundations of the future, many years before education was made compulsory.

But sadly, the long established attitudes of the past are hard to change particularly when the society one is trying to influence has been encouraged to think that they themselves need protection and permanent shelter. The school for the blind in Bristol had tried half-heartedly from time to time to shake off this depressing image and some of the foibles which clung to it like a leech. I recall that the corridors of the school (which were long and numerous) were tiled up to shoulder level with white porcelain tiles, the kind one sees in a public lavatory. The reason for this odd mode of interior decor was to avoid the grubby little fingermarks of blind children on the walls, at least they could be easily wiped off! Hygienically this made some sense but socially in preparing young people for the outside world only a few teachers mainly of the younger generation considered it retrogressive, which it was. The children's playroom in Bristol was large and barren; wooden bench seats and not a single toy. The wireless room, which was allocated for the older children (the juniors had no radio room) was equally plain, but entirely windowless, a room less than 10' by 7', utterly unhealthy. It all appeared frugal and utilitarian, reminiscent of conditions I saw in some old mental hospitals. Reform was not easy in this bastion of the past. Nearly half the teachers were visually handicapped and getting on in years and, with only one or two exceptions, they were usually vehemently opposed to the slightest degree of change. Some of the more elderly, sighted teachers, who apparently knew no better, were equally reluctant to accept new ideas and a new, approach, but for different reasons. It seemed a dreadful state of affairs to the two or three younger staff members who sought to inject a degree of normality into an antiquated system on to which mature people were clinging.

The buildings were bleak and cold but, when the central heating worked properly, the heat could be almost intolerable and, as the elderly staff seemed to resent fresh air, the windows were rarely opened. The result was that the children grew up rather like indoor plants with an unhealthy pallor. But beneath all this there was a warmth of camaraderie and fellowship which broke the frosty crust which seemed outwardly to adorn the place. If you wanted to get away from the world and did not qualify for a monastic setting this might have been the next best place!

Youngsters in those days were set indomitable tasks. I always thought that learning to read and write Braille was a frightful, but necessary imposition on young lives. It made nearly the same demands intellectually as those for studying Latin or Greek. But what was the alternative? No one after a hundred and fifty years has come up with a better system. Consider for a moment the intricacies of this medium for a child of average intelligence and maybe an indifferent sense of touch. They are tremendous, but Braille is still a main gateway to learning and to reading for the visually disabled. Consider again for a moment learning Braille music or studying GCE Maths to O and A levels. These are the mental gymnastics which for years visually handicapped boys and girls have taken in their stride. Look at it in practical terms. A maths textbook is in Braille and literally covered with complicated contractions, abbreviations and symbols which have to be transcribed by a student on a Braille writing machine and allied apparatus. He is expected to come up with the right answer and, at the end of the day, generally does. What a fantastic academic exercise. Yet, most of us take it all for granted!

During my spell as Headmaster we continued building on the changes which the previous incumbent had started to initiate, albeit somewhat reluctantly. The lavatory tiles started to come off the corridor walls thanks to the insistence of the Department of Education; playrooms and even classrooms were given cheerful coats of paint. The one great accomplishment of my predecessor, who seemed to like large impersonal institutions, was the building of a heated outdoor swimming pool. It was a blessing. Over the years this gave immense pleasure to hundreds of visually handicapped young people, many of whom became expert swimmers. It was a great advance in educational development at the time. The school started to take on a more outward-looking image. There were outdoor pursuits, camping, inter-school sports days and, most revolutionary of all, we started to link up with ordinary schools in a form of educational integration with suitable children attending schools in the neighbourhood. Most of our young people enjoyed games and activities in the gym. We had a large playing field and playgrounds and played a form of football and cricket with 'bell balls'. It was all quite exhausting!

There were two peak periods of the school year; the Swimming Gala when the school usually thrashed the staff in the relay events, and the Christmas play and pantomime which was generally of an amazingly high standard. Looking at the overall picture and considering attitudes and the times, some of the children especially where there were question marks over home conditions, they seemed to settle happily enough, but for the sensitive child from the depths of rural England, I suspect it was an unnatural existence. Some loved the place dearly whilst others hated it. These ambivalent viewpoints made somebody like myself wonder if the changes we were implementing were always sound; was it a case of change for the sake of change? I think not. Looking at the overall picture, the school had in the Thirties broken out (for a brief period) of its straitjacket-type of routine and the quality of life of the children had improved enormously, but the momentum did not continue. The war may have been one reason. There were others. I found I had inherited a staff who were experienced conscientious people, but whose average age was probably over fifty. With one or two exceptions this staff of sixteen was approaching pension age and so a few of the more vibrant young teachers with progressive ideas had little support from the 'almost pensionable' brigade on the grounds that 'we have done our stuff' etc. It was a great pity that a school with immense possibilities should be held back now that the field of special education was opening up with enormous opportunities. But, as one representative of the Department of Education, who had the place sized up, said to me over a sherry at the Commonwealth dining room in Queen's Road, "It is rather like pissing against the wind." I was delighted to find that a Government Department official could use such expressive language.

A few months before my arrival at Bristol a small but significant incident occurred which indicated something of the uphill road which lay ahead for anyone who wanted to change traditional moulds and attitudes. The story occurred a few months before my arrival. On Sundays the teaching staff dined with the Head Matron in the staff room. The Matron, of Irish vintage, was apparently of the old institutional type, with direct antecedents going back to the Dickens era in the style of her dress, complicated headgear and dowdy straight navy blue uniform almost touching her ankles. She presided at the top of the table. The older staff were well-conditioned to her firm but kindly rule but the latest recruit to the staff – an ex-naval officer – apparently found it too much. Lunch was long finished and the conversation had become superbly dull and inane. It was the custom for everyone to await the Matron's pleasure to retire, even though intrinsically her position in terms of professional qualifications and abilities was surpassed by most of those present. It was an absurd situation which could not last much longer. It didn't. At one Sunday lunch our Naval friend eased himself up from his chair and without waiting for the formal grace to be mumbled, nodded to the top of the table, with a mutter excused himself and strode over to the door. There was a horrified silence as years of etiquette went overboard. The Matron, who was fast approaching sixty, looked grim and drawn as she adjusted her thick-rimmed glasses to make sure her eyes had not deceived her. In a quavering but strident tone denoting both her prestige and displeasure she called out to the erring young man, "And where, Mr Jones, may you be going?" Jones paused at the half open door and with a lecherous leering smile replied,

"To bed. Coming?" Things were never quite the same again and the Royal School for the Blind, with all its old fashioned formalities, started at last to move into the twentieth century, late though it may have been.

Our navy man left and eventually I took his place. This involved three years of frustrating existence which eventually culminated in marriage and then over to Africa. In those days schools of this type were not places for young people who had imagination or were of the 'get up and go' type, but later better days dawned. After I had served a reasonable time to make amends for the numerous teaching posts I had held before moving to Bristol, a rescue operation was started by John Wilson, former Director of the Royal Commonwealth Society for the Blind. I had shown John around the school some months earlier with his wife Jean and I suspect he took pity on me. Quite out of the blue, he invited me to his London office to discuss the possibility of an assignment in central Africa.

It appears that following the aftermath of the war the more perceptive had realised that things would never be quite the same again in the colonies. There were war-blinded Africans from the Middle and Far East war zones to look after and in addition colonial administrators who were now laying the foundations of medical, educational and social development realised that in some areas the extent of blindness prevalent was absolutely horrific. Why? And what could be done about it? These were the questions which a British Government Commission set out to answer in 1948. They came back with some of the answers and recommendations in a fascinating White paper.

Sir John Wilson, who is totally blind (he lost his sight in a chemistry lab accident at school and then went through to Oxford and took degrees in law and social science) was a member of that Commission. He was finally asked to implement the blueprint which the Commission had drawn up. He entered into a lifetime commitment which has had absolutely massive results. His starting point in 1951 was a dingy office – 51 Victoria Street – almost within hailing distance of the Colonial Office. Funds were limited but he gathered around him a winning team. There were people like Freddie Rodger, an Ophthalmologist, who served as medical officer with the Wingate paratroops in Burma; Geoffrey Crisp, a twenty-six year old entomologist, who later lost his life in West Africa researching the simulium fly and its link with river blindness; Alex Mackay, an Indian Army veteran; on the fringe Sir Clutha Mackenzie, the New Zealander of St Dunstans fame and in the centre of West Africa Ronnie Babanau, another hardy war blinded veteran. Complementing this rugged band were women like Grace Ingham-Wright followed later by small groups of nurses and doctors who, without the escorts sometimes considered necessary, penetrated into some of the remotest regions. From time to time it was my good fortune to join up with these teams in a largely free ranging capacity. These were the teams which spread their wings, quietly but unobtrusively across Africa,

Asia, the Pacific Islands and the Caribbean. All this work gave an entirely new look to blind welfare and the prevention of blindness. The aftermath of these activities starting in the post-war era made themselves manifest in numerous international projects such as IMPACT, a world wide organisation committed to all forms of work with handicapped children and adults including, most important of all, the prevention of handicapping diseases. Looking back to those formative days we were clearly back to the pioneering era where, by general consent, you relied on yourself and failure was a word excluded from our vocabulary but, I might add, not always from our minds!

But the young men and women who cheerfully blazed the trail from RCSB's London headquarters into distant places whilst representing an essential element in the overall plan were, in retrospect only one part of the equation. Without realistic planning by John Wilson, who had already experienced the trials, tribulations, and perils of bush and jungle life, the flair and initiative of the teams he had collected around him would have been futile. It is significant that the tactics and general mode of attack spelt out by John Wilson in 1949 when he formed the fledgling Royal Commonwealth Society for the Blind with the blessing of the Colonial Office, are as relevant as ever. A glance through the RCSB archives reveals a consistency of purpose and action where frugal resources might have induced lesser leaders to shy away from some of the quite dreadful problems which researchers started to land on the doorstep of John Wilson's headquarters. Somehow, the meagre funds were spread thinly but most effectively over areas largely untouched by medical and educational niceties - in other words the maximum of benefit was secured in those days with the minimum of funds. It was a state of affairs accepted and understood by the overseas teams. These pioneers – for that is exactly what they were – often followed a spartan existence. There were no cosy inducements, no built-in subsidy benefits, certainly no air conditioning or fridges. Such a state of affairs was accepted with understanding and equanimity. The funds in those days, could never be sufficient. The object of each man and woman was to secure a foothold and then to enlarge the bridge head. This is exactly what they did and it was from these humble beginnings that the work spread to international levels of collaboration.

John Wilson based this overall attack on the scourge of blindness in remote areas on three practical principles. It is significant that these key elements which were successful almost fifty years ago are still the basis for work in many remote regions today and still hold good. The plan he enunciated contained three simple but vital components. Firstly, a detailed survey to ascertain the extent of the problem in a given area, the causes of blindness and other disabling conditions, followed by an action plan to reduce the prevalence of avoidable handicapping disease.

Secondly, for those who were irrevocably blind or whose eyesight was severely impaired, the procedure was to establish schools, classes, day centres and educational facilities particularly for blind children living in undeveloped rural areas. The aim of this was to enable handicapped children to remain within the mainstream of educational advances inside the country concerned.

Thirdly, the object was (and still is) to adapt the techniques of rehabilitation to the realities of life in rural and tribal settings.

John Wilson's comments when I discussed these points with him recently were interesting. "These objectives", he said, "may now seem pedestrian but, at the time, they were revolutionary and we were by no means certain that we could achieve them. The founding of the bush schools at Bwana Mkubwa and later work on open education in Tanzania and Nigeria gave reality to the second objective and is now the basis of the whole programme in Africa and Asia. It was mainly Ronnie Babanau and Grace Ingham-Wright who led the way with local organisations in establishing a new way of life and employment for the blind. Now, as the various countries became more politically independent they built on the foundations which RCSB had laid."

Meanwhile, in the overall context, the first element of the strategy to reduce the prevalence of avoidable blindness, has since become the main priority of the Royal Commonwealth Society for the Blind and this in turn has led to the formation of four major targets. They include the prevention and cure of onchocerciasis, trachoma, cataract and xerophthalmia. Significantly, all these main priorities have been incorporated into WHO's Global Programme for the Prevention of Blindness which RCSB initiated in 1971. It was then that RCSB had established with United Nations encouragement the International Agency for the Prevention of Blindness. Now, more recently, Impact, an Organisation funded and supported jointly by United

Nations, UNICEF and WHO has taken on the mantle of initiative with RCSB against avoidable disablement.

All this within the space of forty years pushed through by one man, Sir John Wilson. Little did those of us out in the field appreciate that the strategy he had formulated would still hold good four decades later and form the basis of a world wide attack on the scourge of disability in all its sometimes malevolent forms which would take us into the twenty first century.

Chapter Four

Our destination lay ahead of us down in the sweltering valley. From our vantage point on the edge of the rocky escarpment a vivid green mantle of jungle unfolded one thousand feet below. This was the Valley of the Blind. At least that is what people in Northern Rhodesia – now modern day Zambia, called it many years ago. The appalling incidence of blindness which was the scourge of this remote region has now been reduced to manageable proportions, indeed in some villages almost eliminated. Its sinister name, linked from time immemorial with the *impofu*, the Chibemba name for the blind, is now largely a misnomer but in the mid-Fifties it was accurate enough.

Today more recent maps describe this area which borders Zaire as the Luapula Valley after the wide Luapula river which emerges from the swamps of Lake Bangweulu and then meanders through bush-clad countryside swarming with game, tsetse fly and mosquitoes. It races over a series of rapids at Johnston Falls, famous at one time for the huge crocodiles which basked on the smooth rocks and haunted the deep pools. The river becomes wider and resumes a more leisurely pace as it passes well to the north of Chief Kasembe's village and pours into an almost unknown inland sea – Lake Mweru.

Here there are more marshes and reputedly an elephant graveyard where, in the early 1900s pioneers found masses of elephant tusks underneath the papyrus reeds and grasses. The swamps of Lake Bangweulu, the source of the river, are the subject of tribal stories of both fantasy and fact, of men in the interior with webbed feet and, almost incredible but true, of a giant python tackling an elephant and nearly winning the day. From the shores of Lake Mweru you can look across a twenty mile stretch of water and see Zaire. The lake is rectangular in shape and its eighty mile length runs in an easterly direction to where the Luapula river emerges again, but under a different name, the Congo, and starts its long exciting journey to the South Atlantic.

My wife Cathleen and I were now within thirty miles of Mbereshi, an old London Missionary Society station. This was to be our base for the next three months so that we could learn the local language – Chibemba – and I could carry out a survey on blindness in the area. The mission lay hundreds of miles from the throbbing copper belt, our nearest supply centre, and had been wisely built on a plateau away from the malarial lake and river waters.

But the worst part of our three thousand mile journey by road from the Cape to Lake Mweru still awaited us. This was the escarpment we had halted to survey and which we were now just about to tackle. Our timing had been bad. We had left Kawambwa, the last outpost, in the late afternoon along a sandy trackway interspersed with black *dambos* or patches of marsh in which we soon got stuck. A party of cheerful singing Bemba men hauled us out. The track a few miles further on, in the hazy light, appeared to drop almost perpendicularly to the valley floor hundreds of feet below and disappear into a tunnel of lush jungle. Night was falling with the usual suddenness one expects when located within ten degrees of the equator. The wet season had been late as well and even now we could see dark swirling banks of cloud building up over the distant lake.

On reflection we should have stayed in Kawambwa for the night where there was a 'rest house', but we were running days behind timetable. The one European storekeeper in Kawambwa, John Smythe, who seemed to trade mainly in crocodile skins, had given us final directions. "If you get stuck in a *dambo* stay put until morning", he advised, "unless somebody is at hand to help you. Take care going down the escarpment", he continued, "the rocks could play havoc with the suspension and pierce the petrol tank or crack the sump. Once you are in the valley, check that the wooden bridges across the streams are still intact and watch out for drifts of sand." The route was unmarked, he told us, except for a midway sign pointing to a path leading to a distant leper colony. Finally, he had added with an apology, "There will be no petrol around here for five or six weeks." We had just enough to reach Mbereshi. Johnny Smythe, who lived alone in his store, took all this kind of thing in his stride. We had much to learn.

*

Way back in London six weeks earlier I had been warned. John Wilson, the Director of the Royal Commonwealth Society for the Blind, was never a man to wrap things up in cotton wool. "If you still don't like what I've told you about the place you are going to," he had said, laying things on the table in his dingy Victoria Street office, "now is the time to pull out." John like any good leader told his men the score and exactly what they would be up against. He always made it sound a bit worse than it actually was but this was the traditional way of sorting out the wheat from the chaff. I think that with Ronnie Babanau and Geoffrey Crisp, who both went out to West Africa, we were the first of a steady stream of men and women – doctors, nurses, teachers and administrators who went out on RCSB assignments. Most of us were loners, whose job it was to lay the foundations of basic services for the blind. Except for a few like brave twenty-six year old Geoff Crisp, who died tragically in the tropics, we were largely seasoned survivors who tried always to complete our assignments as a matter of principle, however daunting the discomforts and problems may have been.

John Wilson was no stranger to travel in remote places and the hardships which may come one's way. He had an incisive mind and would reel off both the perils and the pleasures of life in the African bush in a manner which would either break the timid or inspire them to throw in their lot with a rugged streamlined organisation which operated across Africa and from Borneo to Guyana, in some of the most difficult country in the world.

The day I left on my first assignment he bid me a cheerful farewell. "I'll see you out at Bwana Mkubwa or in the Valley in a couple of years' time, don't upset the Bembas or Lundas," he added with a wry smile. "We'll tour the Luapula region together, but I expect you will manage to get us lost for a couple of days if your navigation has not improved since your RAF days," he added. (According to John Wilson's account in his book *Travelling Blind* something like that did, I regret to say, happen to us.)

Listening to part of the discussion that morning had been John Wilson's secretary, lively and attractive Edna Owen, who made sure that staff destined for overseas service were tuned up for the three year stint which lay ahead. "It's not really as bad as that," remarked sympathetic Edna to me. Edna had the knack of combining a high degree of optimism with a pragmatic sense of efficiency. She looked after just about everything, visas, arrangements for all the inoculations, shipping the RCSB car, one of the new 1952 Vauxhall Velox range, ideal for Europe, but a doubtful candidate for the African bush. Edna was an adept at cutting through paper work, making sure that the passage tickets which she had booked for us on the *Braemar Castle* provided outside cabins; something I had never thought of. Our route from Cape Town had been arranged to take us along the east coast to Durban up through Ladysmith to Jo'burg and then on to Bulawayo and across the bush to our new home: a complicated journey which meant that I would have met just about everyone south of Capricorn who knew anything about blindness, its causes and the services which might prove most suitable. John had the contacts and Edna did the rest.

It was the frosty chilly winter of 1952 and we had no regrets about our impending move. Britain that winter was dull and drab, dark and dowdy, the six years of war had almost knocked her reeling and people appeared to have changed with the malaise which seemed to hang over the big cities. Rationing was still in force. The cost of living was just about to take off. TV was still a novelty and was largely limited to the more well-to-do. London that winter was wrapped first in fog and then that yellow swirling smog and finally early in 1953 the floods along the east coast, Canvey island, and in the Thames estuary added to the dismal story with tragic loss of life. Although Africa had never really appealed to me in those early days, it appeared to be the one avenue of escape that I and lots of people of my generation appeared to seize on.

The *Braemar Castle*, seventeen thousand tons under Captain Mackenzie, slipped its moorings in King George V dock Tilbury and gently glided into the Thames with a passenger list of mostly young hopefuls seeking a new life and maybe adventure in southern Rhodesia and South Africa. It was Thursday 19th, February 1953, and in the long standing tradition of the Union Castle Line, departure time was observed to the minute. It was a bleak chilly afternoon with ice on the deck and a freezing fog setting in. It was a rather sad and depressing departure as though we were deserting for ever – as some probably were – an England which had not been able, after nearly half a dozen years, to shake off the malaise and exhaustion of war which had settled on the country. There was a final glimpse of the last outpost of our homeland the next day as one of the Channel islands loomed into view draped in a tablecloth of snow and then we were heading for the Bay, St Helena, the Cape and the Valley of the Blind.

St Helena, our first calling point, is one of those island jewels that is now well removed from the shipping lanes. In my day because of the mountainous terrain there was no airfield, something which I suspect preserved the character and charm of the island and its people. It was my good fortune to visit the island on many occasions. It lies one thousand, two hundred miles from the nearest point on the African continent, one thousand, eight hundred from South America and four thousand, six hundred from England. The climate is healthy and usually free from the illnesses one normally associates with the Tropics.

The island's chief claim to fame is that for six years it was Napoleon's prison. A personality of the times, Warren Hastings, who had frequently visited St Helena, declared that it was, "too beautiful to be a place for a state prison". One of the distant ancestors of the Solomon family who now run the island's only industry, flax growing, is reputed to have attempted to assist Napoleon in an escape bid by secretly sending him a rope ladder in a parcel of tea! This would have enabled him to have scrambled down the cliff to a waiting French ship. There is another tale handed down by the old folk on the island that Napoleon nearly escaped in an empty wine cask which was being loaded on an American whaler but was discovered at the last moment by one of the British garrison. Chat to the friendly islanders, and the folklore of St Helena unfolds with stories of mutiny, escapes and amazing incidents such as the time when a pre-World War I German gunboat landed its crew at a lonely cove and next came marching down the ravine into Jamestown, the capital, led by a massed band! They apparently boarded their ship and disappeared over the horizon! In those days St Helena was garrisoned with a detachment of 15 Marines! In the mid-Fifties and Sixties the island's economy depended largely on handicrafts sold to passengers from visiting ships, and the flax trade. Today many St Heleners work on Ascension Island which is the termination point for testing guided missiles and has NASA connections.

My main recollections of St Helena seem always to be those of having stepped back in time. The quaint waterfront scene with its rows of cannon of very early nineteenth century vintage which are for ever pointing seaward: this picture could not have changed since the day Napoleon stepped ashore. Neither could the only street of Jamestown, the capital, lined with white houses with well shaded verandahs, an avenue of trees and about half a dozen shops to serve the capital's population of seventeen hundred. The house just off the harbour at the bottom of the street is typical. It is the one where Napoleon spent his first night in exile on the island whilst waiting to move to the residence which had been provided for him at Longwood. The house borders right on to the street, a broad flight of eight steps leads up to the front door and five well-proportioned bedroom windows look down on to the thoroughfare. The climate treats buildings kindly. Even the landing facilities have not changed. Passengers still must land from a small boat which is difficult enough when a series of Atlantic rollers move in without warning and somebody mistimes their jump to the slippery quayside steps.

The sea front wall is well made and runs for about three hundred yards. The whole restless waterfront is in fact squeezed in between two masses of frowning rocks, on the east side Mundens Rock and on the right Ladder Hill, both over six hundred foot high. The narrow ravine on which the Jamestown houses cling runs from this natural gap at sea level for nearly a mile inland. Almost opposite the house where Napoleon stayed is the church of St James, over two hundred years old and a repository of island history. At the rear and clearly visible to ships moored offshore is Jacob's Ladder, a stone stairway consisting of 699 steps running in a straight line for nine hundred and twenty-three feet to the top of Ladder Hill, which at one time was fortified. Those who manage to clamber to the top get an excellent view of the town and harbour and as well from this pinnacle they are usually rewarded with a welcome cooling breeze after the humidity of the town.

It was here, almost a mile from the top of Ladder Hill, that a retired journalist from Fleet Street and his wife had found a sanctuary. Ron Robinson had worked for the *Daily Express* and then decided to get away from it all. Cathleen and I had tea with the Robinsons on their verandah one evening and gazed from a dizzy height across an azure sea which, as the tropical night descended rapidly, turned turquoise and then merged into an inky nothingness, but we were never allowed to forget the crashing breakers hundreds of feet below and that the sea encircled this puny land mass of forty-seven square miles in a massive restless ocean. Our friends had seen enough of city life and Ron, with a retentive memory and his ability to get at the facts that mattered, was already something of an amateur historian of the island's past. Not far away, he told us, there was Mount Halley where Edmund Halley, the astronomer, worked between 1676 and 1678. He told us, as well, the story of Commandant Smorenburg, a prisoner of the Boer War who made a brilliant escape from the island in 1900 only to be discovered in the baggage room of a ship when it called in at Ascension island. The telegraph cable between Ascension island and St Helena had come into operation earlier that month. When Smorenburg failed to appear for roll call his disappearance was linked with the ship and a mysterious packing case and the telegraph cable did the rest!

The Robinsons paid £8 a month rent for their pleasant house. Income tax was negligible at the time and the cost of living was reasonable.   The islanders were certainly not prosperous but the Solomon brothers with their three thousand acres of flax cultivation and industry was a welcome source of employment. These days many of the younger generation are obliged to emigrate. In the Fifties about twenty-five to thirty boats called in each year at the island. That number has dropped significantly and more recently Messrs Curnow of Cornwall have been running a service from Avonmouth to St Helena. On the several occasions when I called in at St Helena, many of the islanders came on board to buy items in the ship's shop. The Robinsons confirmed that the highlight each month was the visit of the Union Castle mailboat. Once the cargoes had been transhipped to lighters, the ship's purser organised a dance which the islanders always enjoyed immensely. Such were the days of less hurry, and support by a shipping line for the less well blessed who were living miles off the beaten track! The Robinsons were delighted to find that St Helena was free of snakes. If one wanted to shoot there were plenty of pheasants and partridges. Years ago they said there had been wild pigs on the island, but these had been killed off by dogs.

Napoleon's tomb lies at the head of the Sane Valley which is on the way to Longwood, a residence which had been set aside for the Emperor by the Governor, Sir Hudson Lowe. The Friends of St Helena, a French-based organisation, now look after both the house and tomb. Napoleon's body was returned to France on the frigate *La Belle Poule*. I saw an old print of Napoleon's funeral procession through Jamestown when, on 8th October, 1840 his corpse was put on board the ship. It shows that the town has changed little. Jacob's Ladder is in the background. The Church of St James is on the left and on the right the arched portcullised gateway leading to the drawbridge and moat. The Law Courts, Customs House and other administrative buildings are in the foreground.

The island had a small hospital but in the Fifties and Sixties particularly complex cases were often referred to Cape Town or Britain. Some years ago there was a serious road accident – a large passenger vehicle had plunged over a ravine. There were at least fifteen serious casualties and a number of fatalities, the one doctor on the island and the nursing staff coped with the emergency brilliantly. The social welfare and education service have over the years kept pace with the outside world. A number of the professional staff have been trained at Bristol University for special services duties, though the incidence of disabilities does not appear to be abnormally high considering the implications of a small and isolated community.

People in St Helena are normally healthy enough and most of them cheerfully look forward to living to a ripe old age, but the oldest inhabitant, who died a few years back, set high standards. He was reputedly over two hundred years old – the famous tortoise who lived in state up at Longwood! I recall one afternoon walking over the lawns of this residence and came across a delightful French matron kneeling down and, with almost an air of reverence, delivering a kiss on the creature's rough shell. He was huge, perhaps two foot across. She must have seen my incredulous expression. She smiled and beckoned me over to her side. "You are amazed?" she queried. I nodded. Gracefully she bent down and touched the ancient shell again. "No, I am not mad," she added with some haste and turning to me again said with a charming smile, "*Bravo, mon vieux, j'embrasse un copain du grand Napoleon*" (Bravo my friend, I kiss a friend of the great Napoleon.) She continued with final scathing words of admonishment, "Have you British no imagination?"

Such are some of the precious memories and glimpses many of us hold of an island which some must have hated and others loved, an island which mirrored history as though it were yesterday, where a simple way of life is still the norm and serious crimes are virtually unknown. All this amongst breathtaking scenery, a kind warm climate and deep blue South Atlantic rollers crashing on the rocky shores.

It was the infamous Cape rollers, a day out from Cape Town which heralded the end of the voyage for most passengers who were bound for south or central Africa. Table Mountain loomed large, the Cape holiday season was just about coming to a close. We were met on a crowded dockside by someone who was to become a dear friend, the slight but energetic figure of Miss Alou Gillies of the South African Council for the Blind. Much to my surprise she produced out of her handbag within seconds of our setting foot on Cape soil, a formidable lecture tour programme extending from the Cape down the east coast and through to Pretoria. There was no escape. There were three or four weeks of extra work ahead in a country about which we knew virtually nothing.

Today, politics dominate the African scene. When I first arrived in South Africa it was still a member of the British Commonwealth. The Queen approved the appointment of the Governor-General, the Union Jack was flown alongside the South African flag and 'God Save the Queen' and *'Die Stem van Suid Afrika'* were the dual national anthems. All that changed in 1957 and four years later South Africa became a Republic and subsequently left the Commonwealth[1]. The rights and wrongs of the issues which led to this state of affairs are alive as much as ever as I suppose other issues are alive in Ireland today, but less ostentatiously. Is it another case of entrenched positions, the inability to see the other person's point of view, or, more probably, a case of, "the sins of the fathers descending on the children?"

Pause for a moment and look at Africa as it was rather than as it is now. For people like myself who were due to spend the best part of the next thirty years on this continent, this was a necessary pre-requisite. We were the people who were to see the transition from colonial rule to independence in central and East Africa. We were the people who, whilst retaining our own culture, would cultivate a healthy respect for the cultures of those we lived amongst. Most of us were humble and tolerant enough to consider our own shortcomings before ridiculing a way of life which may have been sometimes richer, both spiritually and philosophically, than our own.

South Africa's history dates back to the early seventeenth century, yet the land where I would eventually be working, Northern Rhodesia,

---

[1] In 1995 South Africa rejoined the British Commonwealth

still retained the stamp of the pioneer. The early settlers, like *Chirapula* Stevenson, *Yangwe* Davison, Willie Lammond and a host of other unknowns came into the country in the late nineteenth or early twentieth century. These were the men, who in John Wilson's words, "had made something out of nothing". Certainly not their fortunes. They were poor. They were the men who were to be the mentors of people like myself. They had accumulated fifty years of experience. I and newcomers like me had none. It was my good fortune to meet the last of the real pioneers – to taste Africa as it really was, raw and rough.

South Africa was different. The pioneers who opened up the Cape in 1652 were the Dutch under Jan van Riebeeck. They were joined by the French Huguenots thirty years later and the British another one hundred and fifty years onward, well after the Napoleonic wars. A lot happened soon after van Riebeeck landed. Maize was sent out from Holland and was being grown successfully, four hundred slaves were imported from West Africa in 1658 and the first Cape wine was produced in the new Cape vineyards at Stellenbosch in 1659. Orange groves and apple orchards were introduced at about the same time and, significantly, a wagon-maker from Holland arrived – Roelof Zieuwerts. It was his skill and industry which was to revolutionise the ultimate exploration of the interior. During these early years, the Cape developed its own style of life – the architecture of the old Dutch farmsteads, typical Boer foods exclusive to the Cape: *biltong* (dried meat), *bobotie* (curried mince), *putu* (porridge), *braaivleis* (barbecue meat), indeed a mode of life exclusive to the tough Dutch settlers.

The Bantu, or the black people with whom I was going to spend the greater part of my working life, are primarily of mixed Hamitic and Negroid descent. Several centuries ago, about the time of van Riebeeck's arrival at the Cape, possibly even before that period, they had started to migrate southward from the heart of the African continent. They split up into three diverse streams, one of them called the Nguni group made their way to the Cape and to the eastern seaboard around what is now Natal. The Bantu, like the white settlers at the Cape, brought their traditional crafts and culture with them: carvings, pottery and beadwork. They are famous for their long folk memory stories, their fables, proverbs, riddles and war-like songs. The bushmen, those shy retiring hunters, who now haunt the Kalahari, some northern parts of South Africa and Caprivi, were pushed out by both the white settlers and the Bantu. Now they appear to be an almost dying race who still largely shun modern civilisation though they are succumbing to the ills and stresses it brings in its train when things alien to their way of life, like schools, are started.

On one of my last visits to Botswana we pushed out on a survey into the remote desert country and came across some of these delightful people with light yellow skins, flattened noses and an almost constant blink. They are surviving where you and I would quickly fade away. Their incredible instinct to find water, to live off lizards and other reptiles and to hunt with such skill are memories which will always stay with me. Their women folk are odd little people, usually with large fatty buttocks, sometimes referred to in the medical terminology as steatopygy. The bushmen are probably the ones who, if anyone, have a real claim to southern and central Africa. The bush wall paintings which they have left behind in areas where they lived centuries ago are found in caves from South Africa through to Botswana and Zimbabwe to within a few degrees of the equator. Tangible evidence of their presence in the land prior to the arrival of the Bantu or white settler.

The Cape with its rich variety of scenery, its wild coastline, has always attracted me and, after a spell in the real bush of Zambia or Tanzania, it was a great place to regain ones *savoir faire*, but on my first visit there was work to be done. The Athlone School for the Blind was for coloured children. It was situated in a small township ten miles outside Cape Town, a neat beautifully clean residential establishment which put many similar schools in my native England to shame. We visited the Worcester School, seventy miles from Cape Town to see the advanced work which was being done, even in the Fifties, for the visually disabled. By way of a change I addressed a multi-racial gathering at the delightful old Dutch Farm homestead of Captain and Mrs Keppel. Alou Gillies then packed us off down the east coast route to meet more equally interesting people. There was the Braille library at Grahamstown and by way of diversion near Humansdorp a delightfully secluded sandy cove called Jeffrey's Bay, famous for the unique variety of its sea shells. We swam on this wild coast line, that was until we reached Durban when an Afrikaans life guard called us to heel. Sharks and the heavy tow of the Indian Ocean rollers could, he said, prove our undoing.

Swimming was the one pastime that Cathleen and I had enjoyed on this stage of the trip. It was the only opportunity to get real exercise after a long run and the dust and corrugations of the coast roads. In those days there was little tarmacadam. The Cape-Durban route was one thousand, one hundred and sixty miles long and passed through some of the most magnificent scenery imaginable from the quaint wayside spots near the Cape like Riversdale, to the wildness of the Wilderness described by some as one of the most beautiful coast lines in Africa. We concluded each day's run with a lengthy swim in some remote wayside cove. We aimed at covering about two hundred miles each day which hardly gave one time to take in the diversity of unspoilt beauty which abounded, the rough track through the Tzitzikama forest and mountains, the lagoons and beaches around Kynasa and the sweeping grasslands of the Transkei which, I think, resemble the South Downs in England. They seemed unending and swept from the undulating coastline to the foothills of the Drakensburg. We passed through colourful native villages which dotted the landscape. There were herds feeding off lush grassland. In those days this huge area supported a population of one and a quarter million Africans. The European population was just over fifteen thousand.

If we had met our host in Durban earlier, one Piet van der Zyl, a retired Government administrator who did an immense amount of voluntary work with the African blind, I am sure we would have had second thoughts about bathing in remote places at the end of each day's run along the coast route. Piet was an authority on marine life, something he had studied as a hobby. I discovered this by chance. Before joining him for lunch I had read in the *Cape Times* that a skin diver had been attacked by a barracuda at Port Shepstone, a small resort just up the coast. He had sustained injuries to the head and neck which needed almost fifty stitches. I happened to mention this to Piet over lunch. That started him off. Within the hour I had learnt more about the hidden hazards of life on the African coast than I had bargained for. Piet's premise was that so long as one respected the sea and the creatures in it one could always enjoy one of the most beautiful coastlines in the world. Sharks, he considered, were the greatest danger. They were active from Table Bay northwards. The Cape, because of its colder seas, particularly on the west side, had sometimes been treated with contempt by the foolhardy, he said, but fatalities did occur. One of the most unpleasant was when an eighteen year old boy, who was swimming only a short distance off shore, was seized in front of a holiday crowd on the Clifton Beach. People do escape from the grip of these monsters, he continued, but usually their injuries are horrific and shock kills them. Sometimes, Piet went on, man-eaters come into the shallows. During our stay a girl was attacked in eighteen inches of water; she lost a leg and died. People have fought off attacks by hitting the brutes on the nose. (Similarly I found in later years cases of escapes from crocodiles by victims who had the presence of mind to go for the eyes of the reptiles.)

Durban, and its popular south beach, renowned for its magnificent surfing, usually has steel shark nets to protect swimmers and a spotter plane patrols the area, but annually there have been casualties in the area. The coastline tells many a story of tragedy by those who took a chance. "There are the usual old wives' tales", said Piet, "that sharks do not attack black skins or women. Absolute rubbish," he sniffed. "The sharks which cause the damage on this coast line," he went on, "are the grey ones, repulsive creatures, but there are the black and blue ones, often only six or seven foot long who are equally vicious." Sometimes, though very rarely, the whale-sharks from forty to fifty feet in length come cruising along the coastline. Piet had not finished. He rambled on about the black ray mantas. They are related to sharks. Their fins spread out like huge wings extending sometimes to a width of sixteen feet. Mantas are dangerous to skin divers and, like sharks, can attack in a ferocious manner. They wrap their victim in their wings, smother them and eventually consume them. I had to go to Barbados to meet a manta; it was a small one and had a choice of attacking either me or the islands' Chief Justice at that time, Sir William Douglas, with whom I was staying. (Fortunately it must have already dined.)

Piet briefly turned his thought to the sea snakes, of which there are at least thirty varieties. One rarely comes across them, he said, but they are often lethal and a person can die within the hour after being bitten. Again it was not on the South African coast that I met this species, but in the Gambia. I was walking along the shore of a river estuary when I saw a slow languid movement in a pool left by the receding tide. It was a reptile less than three foot long, a nasty yellow oily body colouration and an evil head. Normally sea snakes are swift moving and can attack but this one must have been exhausted by the fight against the tide. Piet reaffirmed that the chances of something untoward happening on a tropical beach were rare indeed. The only incident during my stay on the coast was when I swam into a shoal of Portuguese Man o' War which give a nasty sting. This produces a dark violet skin rash which can be annoying and quite painful. The incident happened near Port Elizabeth. I had visions of making a trip to hospital as the rash intensified, but an elderly African, on seeing the purple hue which was developing on my body, strode off into the sand dunes, plucked the leaves from a small shrub and told me to rub them into the skin "until the juice runs out". It did the trick. Next morning there was hardly a sign of the work of the Portuguese Man o' War! This was my first encounter with African bush treatments – something that over the years I learnt to respect.

We were on the move again. It would be a good three years before I caught sight of the sea again now that we were moving into the interior. We headed inland on the long run up to Johannesburg via Ladysmith, first to meet the Rev. Blaxell, a grand old mission man of the old school, whose apparently controversial views, some years later, earned him a short spell in gaol. He was the driving force of the hospital, hostels and community centre he had started for African blind at Roodepoort on the Rand. He and his wife with the English manager, Fred Vanham, were developing original methods of communicating with Africans who were both totally blind and profoundly deaf.

In the Fifties there was a surge of impressive work developing in Europe and America, but much of what South Africa had to offer was overlooked – not on political grounds, but it seemed a case of geographical isolation. Looking back at some of the fascinating work which has been accomplished in the deaf-blind field, the work at Roodepoort, its utterly demanding patience and initiative, amidst the tawdry surroundings was so much more quietly original and solid than the glib headline-seeking experiments which often fell flat on their faces in the West. It is significant that while laurels and plaudits were being liberally handed out quite rightly to Helen Keller and her helpers, at the same time, in an obscure African township the same devotion and patience had led to impressive results as well. All this was in the very early Fifties.

And so the last long leg of our journey loomed up before us. We called in at Pretoria to meet officials of the Bureau for the Prevention of Blindness, a South African based concern. Within the next few months I was to learn that some of the facts and figures which its Director Bill Townsend plied me with were absolutely sound and represented a devastating state of affairs as far as the causes of blindness were concerned in the tropics. He contended from the figures he had collected with his professionals who were working all over the country, that probably ninety percent of blindness in the tropics was actually preventable. This was the core of the problem he said. It seemed to reflect the position which Europe faced in the mid-nineteenth century. A large blind population was caused not so much by accident or congenital defects, but by infectious diseases, smallpox, ophthalmia neonatorum (blindness of the new born), measles and venereal disease. This, in those distant days, represented the basic blinding facts of life. Higher standards of hygiene, new drugs and techniques have meant that the incidence of blindness amongst children in the United Kingdom has dropped dramatically to a level where the blind population of the country has now taken on a *top heavy* aspect. People are living longer, therefore cataracts, glaucoma and conditions to which old age predisposes, explains this situation. Meanwhile as far back as 1948, the blind child population in the United Kingdom numbered only around twelve hundred cases, but the onset of a condition known as retrolental fibroplasia, caused by the administration of excessive oxygen to premature infants and the new born, had made this figure rise for a time to worrying proportions. These days the amount of blindness amongst children in 'developed' countries seems to have stabilised to a hard core – those suffering from congenital effects and, to a much lesser extent, accidents.

The Prevention of Blindness Bureau in Pretoria had provided ample food for thought. It was the devastating statistics their professional researcher produced, both about certain infectious conditions and their maltreatment by the unskilled which were alarming in the extreme. It was with these salient facts in mind that we pushed on to our destination, the Luapula Valley – the Valley of the Blind, which still lay almost two thousand miles away to the north on the remote Congo border.

After Pretoria there were no more professional stop-overs, or lectures to State or voluntary organisations for the blind. It was now a straight-forward journey to Biét Bridge, the crossing point of the Limpopo and then across into what was then known as Rhodesia. A slow and laborious journey on roads which at that time were mainly sandy trackways. Once across the border we were on the strips, narrow concrete paths, just wide enough for car wheels to adhere to. The strip system road took us through miles of bush which, in those days, was famous as elephant country. The road was posted with signs warning travellers to stay in their cars, to be on their best behaviour and to remain quiet if they found a herd was blocking the trackway! Elephants kept out of our way the day we passed through this area. The only other safety sign which, to us, seemed much more relevant at the time, was concerned with the poor state of the bridges, some of which crossed steep-sided ravines and were constructed from 'green' poles cut out of the bushland. For the unwary they could sometimes be a death trap. Our progress was painfully slow, but just as dusk was falling we reached the Victoria Falls and Livingstone where we stayed the night. The Zambezi was in full flood when we crossed the Falls bridge; the car which had been battered by 'corrugations' and grit had its first thorough wash from the heavy downpour of spray through which we had to pass. On either side of the Falls there were superb rainforests and wild flowers.

There were now only a few more night stops ahead of us as we plunged onwards across northern Rhodesia, now Zambia, and headed for the bushlands of the copper belt. Here we broke our journey for three days and stayed with Charles and Monica Fisher, two charming and splendid people who, both in the medical field and in the broader aspects of life, were helping a young and rugged country to reach maturity. To this they both gave much of their time and skill. Charles had lived in the country, apart from the time he was overseas as a student, from infancy. He told me once, with a twinkle in his eye, that he was one of the first people to cross the then unfinished Victoria Falls Bridge, which was completed in 1902. He added quickly, "It was in the arms of my missionary father (he followed a path of steel planks laid for workmen), I was just one year old." Monica came out later in the mid-Thirties and worked as a medical missionary with the University Missions in a remote part of the countryside.

Charles was first a surgeon, one of considerable renown, but he was as well, a man of great and varied attributes; fearless game-hunter, particularly when an African's cattle were attacked in the villages; a marvellous diplomat; a skilled farmer; at one time a pilot and a friend to all.   Essentially a modest and self-effacing gentleman, Africa was his homeland, something he was immensely proud of and to which he was profoundly loyal as well.   He died at the farmstead which he had designed and built, carved out of the bush overlooking the fast flowing Kafue river.   In his day he was another of those living legends and will long be remembered by all races. Monica, brave and charming, is still making her contribution to a land she adopted and loves so well.   As always, utterly fearless, a fluent Bemba linguist and a committed fighter for the underdog, she had taken in her stride the immense and inevitable changes of the last few decades.   Cathleen and I look forward to her Christmas letter each year with pleasure.   It always brings the tang of adventure, excitement and the real Africa as well to our Irish doorstep.   She writes of the birds, the wealth of flowers after the rains; sometimes about the unruly crocodiles on the Kafue, of cattle thieves and once of a python which tried to make a meal of their pet Staffordshire bull terrier, but didn't quite manage it.   Charles and Monica between them saved the day.

The story of the Fisher family is something of an epic.   The early missionaries who had responded to Livingstone's call to work in central Africa, were dying off like flies.   Walter Fisher, a doctor, set out for Africa in 1889, in response to an urgent plea for medical help. He walked into the country and arrived at the upper Zambezi from Lobito Bay.   At the time, explained Charles Fisher, his father found that the Africans were living in dread of the slavers and had fortified their villages with stockades.   His father's main problem was to make contact with them.   Visitors to the stockade had to crawl through a long tunnel guarded by an African with a large axe at the far end.   "It was difficult enough", said Charles, "as my father could hardly speak the language.   The breakthrough came", he went on, "when my father managed to do a successful cataract operation on a district Chief.   The next time Father Fisher crawled through the tunnel, he was welcomed as a friend."   Walter Fisher married Anna Darling, an Irish girl who was a mission nurse.   Anna came from Longford, in Southern Ireland.

Charles Fisher recalled that amongst the Lunda tribe in those days a baby would be buried alive with its mother if the mother died before it was weaned.   This was because tribal custom considered that the infant was largely to blame for the mother's death.   Anna Fisher stepped in and saved many of these orphans and arranged for them to be fostered by female sorcerers – women who had sometimes been sentenced to death by the tribe because their 'magic' had not been effective enough. The mission the Fishers established near Mwinilunga was almost at the source of the Zambezi. These two intrepid adventurers survived the early days and their mission station and the esteem with which the locality still reveres their memory remains to this day.[2]

Our stay with the Fishers was drawing to a close. At least we had managed to scrub off the red dust and grit of the journey, to get the car serviced for the most strenuous leg of the trip and, most important of all, to buy in supplies. We would be nearly three hundred miles away from a modern store. Meanwhile Monica had briefed me thoroughly on the Mbereshi mission station and on the villages we would be visiting: Chief Kasembe's, Kafulwe, an abandoned mission station on a high cliff way out somewhere on the shores of Lake Mweru, and Chief Munuga's village. There were many more interesting spots as well. She told me something of the language, the way of life and customs of the interesting people we would be living amongst. Finally, she had added with a smile, "If you survive this deep-end treatment there is a sixty acre bush site for you to convert to the best Centre for the Blind in central Africa." This was pragmatic Monica's vision of the future – a vision which she, more than anyone else, did so much to bring to reality over the long years ahead.

---

[2] Dr Monica Fisher, in her book *Nswana – The Heir* (Mission Press, Ndola,) gives a factual and graphic account of the conditions prevailing near Mwinilunga where Chief Lewinika held court. She writes "…those accused of witchcraft were forced to wash their hands in boiling water. Guilt was proved after twenty four hours if the skin shredded off; the penalty was immediate, burning alive before a screaming mob." She continues, "Before any important event such as the consecration of a tribal drum, a boat, or house, a child's fingers or toes were chopped off so that blood could be sprinkled over the object of the ceremony. The victim was then killed, ripped up and thrown to the crocodiles in the Zambezi."

Frederick Arnot, a missionary of outstanding courage and integrity confirmed this nauseating state of affairs when he wrote in 1887: "…a few yards from my house in Mwinilunga is a perfect Golgotha of skulls and bones."

VE Day at Fighter Command Headquarters, Bentley Priory, was celebrated in appropriate style by those who had, from the days of the Battle of Britain to the invasion of Germany, been at the forefront of the fighting.

This is one of the last pictures of Group Captain Lord Cheshire VC DFC at a public function. He is attending the unveiling of a memorial to the men of 76 Squadron of which he was Commanding Officer. The devastating casualties suffered by the Squadron may have been the catalyst which inspired him to work with the severely handicapped. From humble beginnings, this modest, unobtrusive man has left behind an international network of homes for the handicapped. This photograph was take by Arthur Jones who with the author survived the disastrous night when they were both shot down.
Second from left: Group Captain Cheshire. *Far right:* Group Captain Iverson.

The catalytic episodes which propelled many young men and women into the challenging work with the handicapped were the appalling traumas which World War II had imposed on many of them. In this tranquil valley on a summer night in 1944, the SS executed eleven of the author's 'dizaine' or group. Today the ruins of the burnt-out farm and a simple memorial are a reminder of those frightful days.

Jamestown, the capital of St Helena, lies in a ravine between two frowning rocks; Ladder Hill, with its 699 steps carved out of solid rock *(right)* and Munden's Cliff *(left)*. From the sea, one single road lined with white houses stretches along the ravine inland. St Helena, with a total population of about 4,000, has changed little since the time Napoleon was a prisoner on the island.

Mosi-Oa Toenja, the local name for the Victoria Falls, means 'the smoke that thunders'. Here the Zambezi plunges 354 ft into a narrow gorge. There are three falls; the Devil's Cataract, the Main Fall which is 573 ft wide and the Rainbow Falls. On windy days, especially during the rainy season, the spray rises in five columns to a height of 1,600 ft and can be seen 25 miles away. The Arab slavers called the falls *Musa-i-nunya* meaning 'the end of the world'.

A tribal gathering between Tabora and Kigoma, Tanzania. Nyamwezi warriors have travelled for days by foot to meet Chief Fundikira. The Nyamwezi women folk are famous locally for their ritual snake dancing.

Above and below: Amidst the busy routine of running a large school, a teacher training centre and a clinic, the author and his wife found time to make friends with the local wild life. They included an orphaned monkey and an infant duiker (antelope). Both were reared in the Salisbury household on powdered milk and affection.

Travel into the interior of Central Africa can at times be difficult and hazardous. Apart from earth roads, river crossings – especially during the rainy season – can be difficult.

Two of Central Africa's most colourful pioneers. 'Yangwe' Davison and 'Chirapula' Stephenson, both of whom died in the mid-Fifties, are legendary figures in the transition from the tribal and traditional Africa to the modern day lifestyle. Though feared by some, they were loved and respected by many Africans who knew them.

A victim of a virulent type of measles. The mother of infant Chansa left her exposed to bright sunshine in the hope that it would 'cure her running eyes'. She then took her to the local village herbalist (witchdoctor), whose treatment destroyed the front of the eyes resulting in permanent blindness. Some authorities estimate that over eighty per cent of blindness in some parts of Africa may be due to unskilled treatment.

The cobra shown in the picture attacked a young African. After expanding its hood, it ejected a fine spray of concentrated venom directly at the man's eyes. Fortunately he escaped serious harm due to prompt treatment. Poisonous snakes are present in most parts of Africa; generally they are shy, timid creatures but sometimes their bite can be very dangerous. They are a serious hazard to the blind.

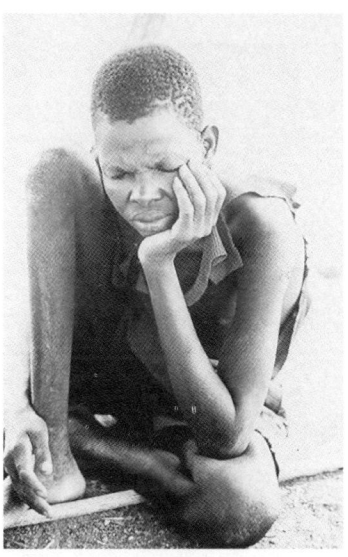

A beggar boy totally blind and badly deformed due to polio or possibly malnutrition. His clothing, part of a tattered sack, rests on his twisted body. He keeps his stick (indispensable to mobility) close to him. Tired, dejected but not hopeless – just hungry; he is typical of the many thousands of similar cases that the Royal Commonwealth Society for the Blind has helped.

The 'Valley of the Blind' in West Africa where the simulium fly has decimated villages. These are the blind left behind after the able-bodied have fled the area. They are led by a man with some remaining sight as they make their daily visit to a distant well.

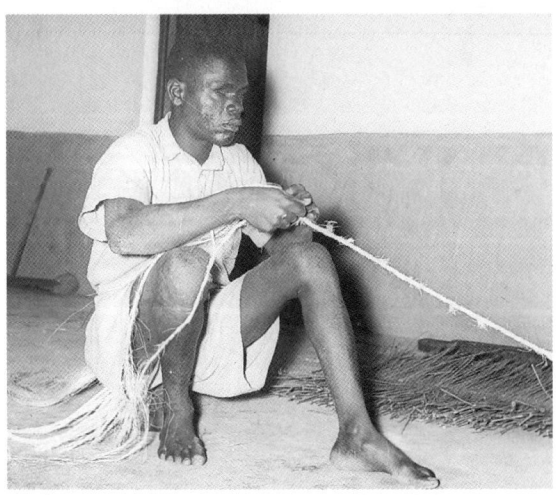

Mwapwa, blinded by smallpox, which, according to WHO, is now eradicated, makes rope from local sisal leaves.

A young trainee teacher helping ten year old Kama to develop 'touch recognition'. His fingers are now being introduced to the first Braille symbols. Within a few months he may be able to read simple phrases in his own language and later in English. Kama's sight was almost certainly destroyed after an attack of measles followed by treatment by a local herbalist or 'witchdoctor'.

Chapter Five

Our first African journey, from the Cape to the Congo borders had become in the early Fifties a fairly common achievement. Certainly, it was a memorable trip and a salutary way of shaking off the stilted life of school-mastering in confined pastures. We learnt to do things the hard way and not to panic unduly when our engine spluttered to a halt miles from any habitation. We met a variety of people, Afrikaans, the proud Zulus, the Malayan coloureds, and the ordinary Bantu still free from the inhibitions of progress and mission school ties. In retrospect it was a harbinger of things to come. Here was Africa, a slumbering giant, a continent of contrasts, of poverty and wealth, of culture and brutality, of immense natural beauty and sometimes frightening starkness.

It was the diversity of humanity and its background which was to challenge the preconceived ideas of many youngsters who came to work in those distant lands in the Fifties. I found that Africa at that time could regenerate some of the things we had lost in our sophisticated society – time to think, and a sense of wonder. Lives which had been blighted by the cosmetics of TV and artificial make-believe episodes found time to gaze in awe as nature, sometimes raw and cruel unfolded in their midst.

*

On reflection my journey had given me a new perspective and the mental and physical preparation for the years ahead and the strange bits of humanity I was to meet. There were the nomadic Kalahari bushmen, some still lingering in the stone age, with no vestige of law, tough little creatures with yellowish withering faces and skins like leather. Contrast these pathetic souls, (who had been hunted by both the Bantu and whites, eventually to be driven into the vastness of the

Kalahari) with the nomadic Fulani tribe, proud, handsome sophisticated people whom we were to meet a few years later on the Chad-northern Nigerian borders. The Fulanis have a long and treasured history of their own. They are ardent Moslems with strict codes of conduct. Until the turn of the century they were essentially a warrior people who, like the bushmen, used bows and arrows, but the Fulani from time immemorial have been traders and took over the desert caravan routes from Tripoli to Katsina, Sokoto, and Kano. The commodities they traded in were salt, beads, and slaves. Some maintain that slavery is still one of their less well known activities. They are tall slim people with lighter skins than those of negroid descent. Their women are graceful, often quite beautiful and faithful – adultery is punished according to traditional laws. Even Katsina, where we lived for a short time, was a crime free area and we never locked our house.

Mallam Barda, a retainer of the Emir of Katsina who was working with me on an open education scheme for the numerous blind children in the area, had explained how this unusual state of affairs had been arrived at. It was a Friday he recalled, the Moslem holy day, a few years before our arrival in Katsina. "A young peasant no more than twenty years old," said old Mallam Barda, had been apprehended early that Friday morning, "stealing from his master's home a small sum of money. He was immediately arrested", he continued, "and taken before the local court and found guilty. As soon as prayers at the mosque were over he was led before the crowd which had gathered in the square and beheaded, cleanly," Mallam stressed, "with one mighty stroke of a huge sword." He described the gruesome scene in some detail, the head rolling on the sand, the blood spurting out of the headless trunk with the arms and legs still writhing and thrashing the air. The unfortunate man had received one warning – that was enough.

It was a tough world in those days for thieves around Katsina but the Fulani were tough people! A few decades earlier they had been raiding desert caravans and the victims who survived were either taken as slaves or were mutilated by cutting off a single arm or leg and left to die. The desert routes were marked with the bones of those who perished and were eventually buried by the shifting sand dunes. Mallam Barda was adept at linking the recent past with the present. "In those days", he remarked to me as if what he was going to say was the most ordinary thing in the world, "the Arab caravan masters who crossed the desert to Katsina employed blind guides; you see," he added, maintaining his serene demurity, "caravans could easily lose their way but the blind have a keen sense of smell and so they could easily pick up the odour from previous caravans, the rotting bodies of men, and camel urine which is pungent and lasts a week and sometimes more. It was the blind who saved many a caravan."

In those halcyon days I knew precious little about either the Kalahari or the Fulani people. In later years I found it difficult to link the nomadic Fulanis with the marauding raiders of yesterday. I found them a people herding their cattle peacefully on the scrub land wastes of the western edge of the Sahara. Here the arid wastes are still tsetse free and horses and packs of dogs grow up hardy and tough and form the basis of a lucrative trade one thousand miles away on the Atlantic hinterland. Here these creatures, after being driven from the dry desert borders to the humid oppressive climate near the coast, are sold for meat and for ritual tribal sacrifices. Here they are subjected to the most horrific forms of cruelty about which little is ever heard outside West Africa. Fortunately I never witnessed the ritual horse slaughterings which were taking place near Oyo when I was in this area. I did, in the course of my journeying, witness the maniacal 'dog beatings to death' which took place almost within the shadow of the Ibadan University. When I made further inquiries about these barbaric activities I was told by a senior political figure of those days, a Nigerian, that the Government was afraid to clamp down on such activities in case there was a reversion to human sacrifices! Maybe that was not exactly true – no one saw anything really wrong in animal cruelty. But, on reflection, how many people in Europe see anything untoward in organised dog fighting, badger baiting, fox hunting and coursing?

*

The stormy evening which found us bumping down a steep escarpment into the Valley of the Blind was a forerunner of things to come. Suffice to say we had left for the Valley well laden with supplies. Our enemies in those days were appalling trackways, shaky bridges and swamps. To us in our innocent enthusiasm Africa was still untamed, the Suk and Mau Mau uprisings in the east were spirited stories of fantasy and vivid imagination. We had much to learn!

Our journey took us across the Congo 'pedicle'. Here a group of scruffy, ill-disciplined Congolese gendarmes operated an apparently lucrative bribery system in exchange for a pass to proceed further. It was annoying. We had to pay up and the delay also meant that we had to stay in Mokambo, a Congo border outpost. The next day we pushed on along monotonous sandy, winding roads, not a solitary vehicle passed us for the first hundred miles and then one of Musango's lorries carrying dried fish from the lakes in the interior edged by us. Musango, whom I later got to know well, halted and we had one of those delightful informal chats exchanging titbits of news. I asked Musango, an enterprising old African, about the road down the escarpment. He looked gloomy. "You shouldn't be making a journey like that in your car. It will be smashed and the two of you as well." With a cheery smile he waved us goodbye. In clouds of red dust he and his passengers rattled on to the markets of the distant copper belt.

Night had set in fast on the escarpment road to Mbereshi, once we had cleared the *dambo* which brought our progress to a temporary stop. The storm we had seen building up over the distant lakes broke just as we started the descent. In the half-light, a ceiling of dark brooding thunder clouds seemed almost on top of us. The enormous blue flashes we had seen in the distance now appeared to envelop us and, with them, came sheets of rain which turned the trackway into a river. Thunder roared continuously, the blue white flashes lit up the jungle, bamboo leaning over almost flattened. There was a tree down. We squeezed by and then visibility was reduced almost to nothing. The track was now a rushing torrent, nearly a river. We had to keep going. I did not like it. The steep gradient and the flood waters pushing us downwards meant that we were only just in control. Lightning flashes showed up rocks. We slid or slithered past them. It seemed only a case of time before either the engine or the chassis of the car would pack up. On looking back it seemed reminiscent of a bombing run over Happy Valley, the war-time Ruhr. We seemed to be in one endless descent. Where would it end? Would we be whipped away in one of the flash floods Musango had warned us about, or would the puny bridges survive this deluge? Somehow we made it. The rain stopped as suddenly as it had begun. We reached

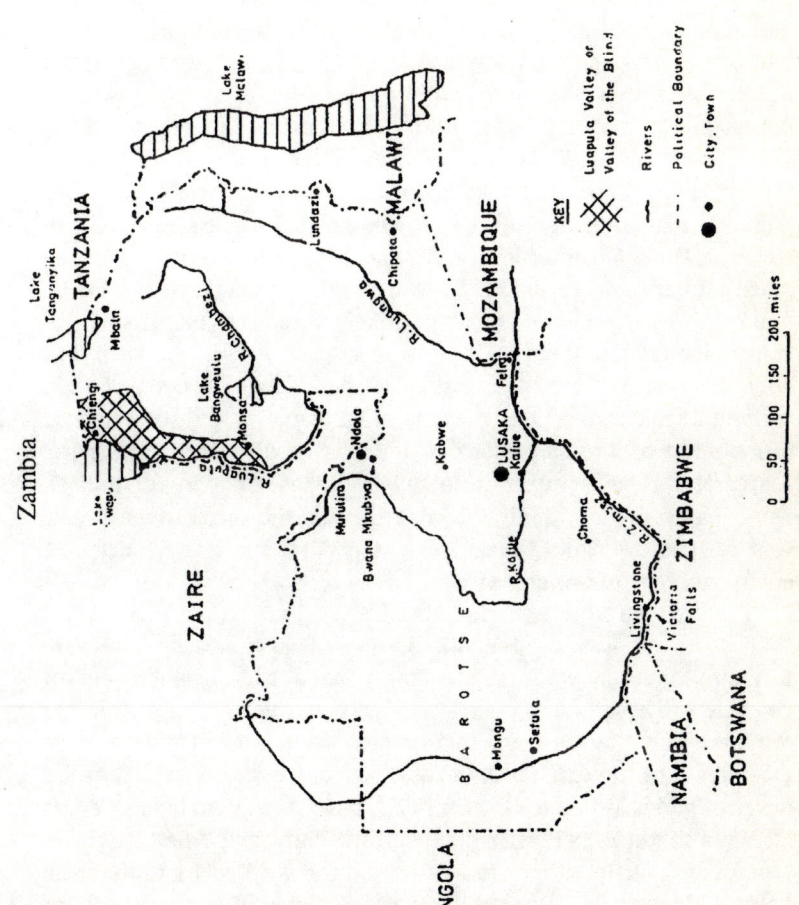

Zambia

TANZANIA

ZAIRE

ANGOLA

MALAWI

MOZAMBIQUE

ZIMBABWE

NAMIBIA

BOTSWANA

Lake
Tanganyika

Lake
Mweru

•Chiengi

Mbala•

Lake
Bangweulu

•Mansa

R.LUAPULA

R.LUANGWA

R.KAFUE

Lundazi•

Chipata•

Feira

•Kabwe

LUSAKA
•Kafue

•Ndola

Mufulira•
Bwana Mkubwa•

R.ZAMBEZI

Choma•

R.Kafue

Livingstone
Victoria
Falls

B A R O T S E

Mongu•
•Senuta

Lake
Mweru

KEY

Luapula Valley or
Valley of the Blind

Rivers

Political Boundary

• City,Town

0   50   100 150 200 miles

the valley floor. Within a couple of hours we were banging on the door of Bev Packer's house, the young missionary with whom we would be staying for some weeks before moving off down the valley.

Bev was a tall, lithe, athletic school teacher who was in charge of the mission. Margaret, his youngish and attractive wife, had emigrated some time just after the war to this outlandish spot. She had lived in the depths of suburban London. Bev and Margaret came into the country the hard way and had to walk the last two hundred miles with a train of porters carrying their belongings. Bev was not outstandingly popular with the Government administration in Kawambwa: his views were in advance of the times and there was a fair amount of unrest in the valley, not that he was directly concerned with this, but some of the activists who erected barricades and threw stones at Government officers were members of his church. Bev had given military service during the war a miss, at least that is what he told me. There were probably excellent reasons on grounds of conscience for him doing so but this, I suspect, did not go down well with the District Commissioner – Colonel Hugh Balydon. I soon realised after meeting Hugh Balydon in Kawambwa, that I had arrived in the midst of a tense personality situation between Bev and the DC Margaret was an extrovert who, whilst doing her share of mission work, enjoyed quite rightly the good life and the social rounds. She was a down to earth young lady; something she proved within a couple of hours of our arrival.

The old two-storey mission house dated back to pre-First World War days. It was a place full of nooks and crannies, hard bare furniture, cracked walls and ceilings and a bath moulded out of concrete. It was under attack. No, this was not a native uprising. We were being invaded on our first night by armies of minute black creatures, the *impashi* ants. They had advanced unnoticed under cover of darkness into the kitchen. The huge mesh wire food safe was already infiltrated and under the light of lanterns and Tilley lamps we found more ants preparing to advance up the walls and into the main house. Margaret and I traced the snaking column of invaders back for thirty or forty yards to one of those huge ant hills which abound in the area. There was to be no rest that night. "Either", Margaret said, "they will take over the whole house and drive us out or we will have to fight it out here and now."

I subsequently learnt that when *impashi* attack, they sweep through a house and consume everything in their way, beetles, flies and even bats, of which there were plenty in the rafters of the house. For this reason some people welcomed them. But there was another side to the *impashi* story. If a tethered goat or dog lay in their path, they were quite capable of consuming it. Some of the old timers, both black and white, can tell fascinating stories about these methodical and persistent creatures. Death by *impashi* was a fairly common fate for those who had offended against some tribal laws. The victim was tied in front of a moving column of *impashi* ants and literally eaten alive. Adultery and rape were punished sometimes by using the *impashi* treatment. One African friend remarked somewhat drily after discussing this invasion, "at least these crimes were virtually unknown until the white people came and interfered with our laws."

The battle raged on. It had started shortly after our arrival at 9 p.m. Midnight was now past but under the flickering lights of our oil lanterns and Tilley lamps, it seemed the crisis was upon us. We had spread barriers of motor oil in the path of the ants, but undaunted they started to build bridges climbing on top of each other and arched their way over. Originally we had tried sweeping and shovelling them aside. It was hopeless. Relentlessly, with utter single-mindedness, which I had found time to admire, they renewed their attack. There was a yell from outside. One of the African girls, who helped Margaret in the house, shouted that she had found a column approaching the front of the house; quite unsuspecting she had walked on the approaching army and had been badly bitten. Bev, who had been out most of that evening, decided that it was time to evacuate the house. He went and alerted mission neighbours that they would be having evacuees. But the tide was turning. Reluctantly we had started burning oily rags and paper in the path of the invaders – it was a dangerous and dirty exercise, the house contained much bone-dry timber and the roof was of thatch. The columns sent out their scouts to look for alternative approaches. They returned. The columns halted and then, almost in unison turned and wended their way through the kitchen door and out into the night. Those columns which were bravely tackling the mud walls of the kitchen had apparently been signalled as well. The retreat was on. Even the column approaching the front door which had been tackled by smouldering wood ash retreated in an orderly manner. They were courageous warriors. According to the Africans whom I met later, very few homes succeeded in winning battles with those gallant little creatures. It was a reluctant but necessary victory on our part.

There was crisis in the Valley. I suppose it had been this way from time immemorial, the incidence of blindness from the shores of Lake Mweru to the rapids of the Luapula at Johnston Falls[1] was quite horrendous yet, it transpires, that attitudes to blindness were much the same as I found out later in many other parts of Africa, in Mali, northern Nigeria and East Africa. An almost deadly and fatalistic pattern of thinking which assumed that such scourges were inevitable and unavoidable. Even a folklore had grown up about the blind and their disability. I found that tribes varied enormously in their attitudes to them, from one of care and attention, inspired by the belief that if you were cruel to a blind person bad luck would befall you, to one of positive cruelty. Blindness to some meant lack of manliness, to others they might be people with special gifts.

There were traditions amongst the Hausa and Fulani tribespeople I met that it was bad luck if when you were on a special mission you met a blind person; you would be wise to postpone your errand to another day. I came across this folklore on the borders between Chad and northern Nigeria, just where the real Sahara begins. A *Mallam*, a wise man (usually a teacher), who had been my guide in the area, told me over the evening camp fire that the marriage which had been arranged between his son a few days earlier and a girl in a neighbouring village had been postponed. Why? I asked more as a formality than curiosity. "Because," said the bearded *Mallam*, "my son was going to the marriage ceremony when he met a blind woman on his journey." There was silence.

"Why", I asked, "has a blind person interfered with the wedding?"

"It is our custom", replied the Mallam somewhat wearily, "that if a man is on a special errand or an important mission it is a bad omen to meet a handicapped person. It is best to turn back. Bad luck would surely have befallen that marriage," he concluded.

Some of the tribesmen around Lake Mweru said (I have been told this by blind people themselves from these areas) that snakes will never attack a person who is blind. How this idea originated I do not know but it must go back into the depths of time. Unfortunately it is

---

[1]Since 1966 renamed Mambalina.

wishful-thinking but some blind people still maintain that it is true. They wander for miles along forest tracks unharmed. Others are not so lucky. Both Cathleen and I had to administer the appropriate snake-bite antidote to some of our blind friends. In Botswana there is a belief amongst some tribes that if a pregnant woman has contact with a handicapped person, the child she is carrying will bear the identical disability of the person she has met. Africa, just like Europe, has a wealth of strange beliefs and ideas.

I saw little of Bev Packer on the mission station. He was an exceedingly busy man. I borrowed a bicycle and bumped along the bush paths visiting secluded hamlets. The extent of blindness in the countryside had certainly not been overstated. At that time even the smallest hamlet had two or three totally blind children. As for eye diseases amongst the adult population it was getting out of control.

Prior to my sallies into bush country I had, with Bev Packer, gone through the local courtesies and etiquette of meeting the Chiefs of the areas I was entering. It was a time-consuming but worthwhile exercise. A white man could make little or no impression on developing special services without the approval of the local Chief. The paramount Chief in the area where I would be circulating was Chief Kasembe, a formal distinguished character whose traditions and lineage were indeed impressive. Livingstone knew all about the Chief Kasembe, skulls of victims killed in the tribal wars decorated the stockades around Kasembe's palace. Livingstone records in his diary, that it was a Kasembe who kept him, Livingstone, waiting for weeks on the banks of the Kalunguishi river before giving him permission to move through Kasembe's country.

Until British rule changed tribal traditions it was customary on the death of a Kasembe Chief for his favourite wives (whose numbers varied!) to be buried alive with the Chief so that he would have their services in the next world. It is believed that this custom continued well into this century, some say up to the mid-Forties, others nearly to this day! On reflection old Chief Kasembe was clearly something of a headache, it seemed to Bev Packer and his mission folk. The Chief had, at some time, become a Christian, but like quite a few others in the modern world of today, was loathe to part with his wives and concubines. But think for a moment of his dilemma, torn between the strictures of European ways of life and that of his ancestors.

Lugard, who did so much to open up parts of remoter West Africa, had a more tolerant approach, to build on rather than to destroy existing traditions and customs. Many missionaries and some colonial administrators were less understanding and compromising. Kasembe had been brought up in the ways of his ancestors – ancestors who were by custom revered. He and his followers had been raised in the world of spirit worship, the powerful influences of animism, of nature and the forest. "Everyday", said a young Bemba man to me, "we talk in our gardens to our bananas and to our mango trees and ask them to produce good fruit. We talk to the spirits in the forest as well." The long-standing customs, sometimes taboos, perhaps the horrifying rites of girl and boy circumcisions which were extended by some tribes into a three day sexual orgy, could not be swept away at one stroke. What precisely happened, if anything, in this sphere with the local tribes I was with, was never clear. I suspect, as I found out later in Malawi and parts of the remoter regions of West Africa, white faces only hear what Africans want them to hear, the tip of the tribal iceberg.

The Chief Kasembe I met was something of an enigmatic character. Kasembe could smile – this was something I had at first doubted but when he did, you could still see his bearing of dignity and pride. He was thin, with a smallish head, and gold rings hung from holes in his extended ear lobes. His teeth were coloured red from the cola nuts he chewed – teeth which he continually ground whilst you were talking to him – a disconcerting habit for the newly initiated like myself. It was his ancestors who, within living memory, had fought tribal wars, sometimes aided the Arab slavers and sometimes fought them. The Chief had fine soft hands. I noticed this as I greeted him in my frugal Chibemba, *Mutende Mwane* – (Peace, Chief) and he replied *Endita Mukwai* (Agreed, Friend). On the little finger of his right hand he had cultivated with care the nail so that it protruded from the fingertip for at least an inch to form an extended type of claw. What this signified I never found out. I recall thinking that few Europeans would be able to produce such a fine specimen with the shortages of calcium type foods still plaguing Europe in the early Fifties!

For a number of reasons: the critical petrol situation which had limited our movements and the fact that the mission was not well situated for establishing firmer contacts with the population in the valley, I decided that we would transfer our headquarters to Kasembe's village. It was something of a traumatic change, but one which we never regretted. We used a neat mud-walled hut with a thatched roof as our home. The mission loaned us one of Margaret Packer's well trained domestic servants, who managed to cook excellent meals and to make bread as well from a small fire made in a shallow hole in the ground. This outside oven was surrounded by stones which became white hot. There were two camp beds, basic kitchen utensils and two cups and two plates a-piece. We were the only Europeans living in the midst of this crowded village community and I suppose we were something of a one day wonder to the locals, who took time off from their crops and herds to visit us and comment on Cathleen's long hair and my fair skin and blue eyes. They were friendly and charming people but very poor.

Bev, who was a popular figure with the staid old Chief, had arranged an audience with him which was to take place in his palace attended by his full council advisers. The purpose was two-fold, to pay homage to the old man and to encourage him to use his influence in supporting the work we hoped to introduce in connection with the blind. It was a long and weary business. We wended our way up to his palace and sat in the great hall. He eventually arrived, sat on his throne and beckoned the visitors to come forward. The proceedings had started. His latest wife, a most attractive acquisition, sat coyly in the background, a delightful little girl with gleaming skin possibly between thirteen and fifteen years old. Bev did most of the talking and interpreting as well. Conversation covered health, the state of the crops, the rains and finally why should a Britisher come to work in the valley amongst the blind? I explained the object of our visit and asked for Chief Kasembe's co-operation. He agreed. To set the seal on matters tradition had it that visitors drank a special tribal drink. Chief Kasembe clapped his hands and along came three clay mugs full of a frothy grey beverage on which floated a multitude of black specks. This was the drink for honoured guests explained Chief Kasembe. We consumed the beverage by degrees, an insipid mixture made, Bev said hopefully, from roots – nothing else he assured me! The meeting was at an end. I invited the Chief and his new wife to our hut in the village. He was delighted. He would come tomorrow.

Chief Kasembe was due to arrive at our humble mud house at 3 p.m. I never realised until that afternoon that time in this part of the world meant nothing. He arrived three hours late with a retinue of councillors, followers and wives which extended for fifty yards down the village street. We welcomed him. He sat down with his official food-taster by his side. His followers packed into the hut and the rest squatted outside. Our resources in cutlery and crockery, which had been augmented that morning by the arrival of a couple of the mission hospital staff who were doing a round, was sadly inadequate. Conversation was stilted and limited but it set the seal on the future, a useful three years of co-operation.

The one interesting point which arose from this meeting was that the Chief's predecessor was apparently a young and go-ahead individual. Once whilst out hunting he had found an infant who was blind. It was abandoned in the bush. This was the customary way of eliminating the weak and in fact most handicapped infants. The young Chief broke with tradition much to the consternation of his followers and ordered the babe to be brought back to the village. It was from that day he started a home for the Blind, a type of refuge. Infants soon, instead of being left for the jackals and hyenas and other beasts to feast on, thrived and were fostered in a remarkable little colony which was still in existence. I suspect that the inspiration for this move came originally from one Willie Lammond, at that time an eighty year old missionary who lived a further seventy miles west of Kasembe. On discovering that the weak and handicapped were offered to the beasts of the jungle, Lammond started his own shelter for them. Unfortunately the young go-ahead Kasembe did not last too long. New ideas perhaps did not go down well with elders who were steeped in witchcraft. The Chief Kasembe I met, an elderly man, was apparently wise enough to retain the services of a capable food-taster. Strange things happen in the African bush. Sometimes it is put down to sorcerers or natural causes. Those who claim that they are more in touch, point the finger at the ancient home industry of utilising plants and their roots to concoct brews which can sometimes cure and can sometimes kill! The Luapula in those days was steeped in witchcraft and some of its inhabitants experts in the use of local poisons.

Before leaving Kasembe's village for a ninety mile move up to the mid-point on Lake Mweru, two small but interesting things happened which gently reminded us that we were still in the heart of Africa. Each Sunday I cycled along a bush track to collect the mail which came up once a week from Luanshya. It was a long run, a very hot afternoon and my progress on the twenty mile journey was slow. Darkness had almost arrived and I had not returned. Belina, the houseboy, came on duty. *"Bwana* has not returned," said Cathleen anxiously.

"I think he is in trouble," said Belina looking appropriately sad.

"Whatever makes you say that?" asked Cathleen with a gasp.

"He was last seen being followed by a pride of lions," said Belina. "Hasn't anyone told Madame?" he added with some concern. I arrived back safely minutes later, but apparently Belina's story was genuine enough. The Chief had ordered a party of his men to follow my path to find, as he put it, either any leftovers or to ascertain the direction in which the lions were moving! The last time they had been sighted was when they were following my cycle reportedly less than a hundred yards distance behind me, ambling along at a steady pace. I was totally unaware of the flap until I returned. This was just as well as I would not have looked forward to the return journey in the evening light.

The second incident occurred when we were leaving Kasembe's village to move up to the lake. I had managed to get a supply of petrol from Kawambwa. We planned a night stop at Mbereshi before moving up to a mid-point on the lake near Chief Mununga's village. We made the short run to Mbereshi at night. The car bumped along the track at a steady fifteen miles an hour. Suddenly the headlights picked up an elongated phosphorescent presence lying stretched right across the track. I was almost on top of it and then it started to move with a wavelike undulating motion. It was a large python. Its head was already in one side of the bush and its tail well hidden in the undergrowth on the opposite side. I deliberately ran over it. I distinctly recall two thuds as the front and rear wheels went over the creature. I stopped and gingerly reversed, expecting to see a dead or writhing snake. It had disappeared apparently unharmed. I suppose it was a fifteen to eighteen footer. These were the length of specimen skins we had seen in the trader's store in Kawambwa; in fact one, he told us, was over twenty feet.

Chief Mununga's village was on the banks of the rapid flowing Kalunguishi river. We had to leave our car under the protection of the local Chief and proceed by dug-out canoe across the river and then march on to Kafulwe, a delightful sandy cove on a cliff overlooking the shimmering lake. The house we were using was a deserted mission station and was supposed to be full of snakes, though we never saw any.

Chief Mununga was a very old man, helpful and polite but fatalistic. The people who were blind must have done something very wrong in the previous life he seemed to suggest: it might be best to leave such people alone. The facts were that the incidence of blindness we were to find reached horrendous proportions. Within a sparsely populated area of a radius of six miles from our base, there were thirty-six blind children of school age. Before I left Kafulwe arrangements were made to start a day school for these children which was something of an innovation seeing they were supposed to have all sinned in a previous life. The teacher who eventually took charge of this development was a brave young man who had a gift for teaching the blind. He brushed off the massive problems which surrounded such work – but what were his problems? No equipment, white ants eating the building, his teachers' pay arriving late and cynical elders preaching doom and gloom. The breakthrough came when Fred Kafwankwe, the teacher, had actually taught some of his brighter children to read Braille. This was real magic, the villagers muttered. There was no going back and Mununga's village with its precious little day school for the blind did much for those who were irrevocably blind.

What about those in this area of appalling blindness who were statistically due to lose their sight because of the ravages of unknown diseases. And why was there so much blindness? This was the question which many people had been asking. The thirty-six children we had found were all over seven years old and had gone blind recently. Why?

In search of some enlightenment, we pushed on higher up the lake to Chiengi which for many years had been endowed by both Europeans and Africans with an evil reputation. The story was that Chiengi Boma, a one-man Government station overlooking Lake Mweru was haunted. It was here that young District Officers were stationed completely on their own and expected to survive the steamy climate, black water fever and other tropical hazards. We camped under the shadow of the Boma, a deserted gaunt two storey building with a wide verandah overlooking the gleaming blue waters across to the old Congo shore and to the east with a possible glimpse of distant Tanzania. According to those who knew about isolated Chiengi, it was the constant steel-blue waters of the lake combined with the utter isolation which drove men mad and resulted in a frightening casualty list. The Boma was closed just before the First World War because of the mounting deaths amongst the single occupants. It was re-opened in the Twenties and closed again in the mid-Thirties having taken a horrendous toll of young lives. The death which caused the final closure was that of a young cadet from the Colonial Service who, according to his African servants, sat on the verandah staring over the shimmering water day after day. He could stand it no longer it seems, and as dusk was falling one day went inside and shot himself. There were a string of deaths, some from natural causes, such as malaria and dysentery, but there were many others which have never been satisfactorily explained. So the haunted Boma stood there in splendid isolation, an horrific testing ground for courageous youngsters of the much maligned Colonial Service, men who were brought up in the tradition of roughing it, and living close to the people. They did exactly that. I often met, during the next few years, young District Officers camping rough, moving on foot or on a bicycle, eating an evening meal alone, often something they had secured out of the bush earlier in the day. In those days they knew their Africa and the Africans to whom they were all things, lawyer, teacher, bridge and road builder, guardian and first-aider. There was mutual respect between black and white.

A few years later when I was back in the Chiengi area the *capitao* (caretaker-foreman) who was looking after the deserted Boma, asked me if I had ever been to Katema Island. This was somewhere in the Mweru marshes quite nearby. "No," I replied, "but why do you ask?"

"It is a crocodile home," said the serious faced *capitao*.

"And why should I want to visit them?" I asked with some curiosity.

"Because *Bwana*," he went on with an awkward look at me, "there are supposed to be blind crocodiles living on the island." At first I thought he was joking, but apparently it was perfectly true. We went over to Katema in one of those unstable dug out canoes. The island was hardly as big as two large football pitches. The crocodiles saw us approach. They have an acute sense of smell and usually excellent vision. They slid off into the water from the sandy beach where they had been basking. According to some people the crocodiles around these shores were harmless ones, but again I think this was an optimistic piece of wishful thinking. During my stay in the Mweru area women and children were taken. Katema seemed full of crocodile nests and there were plenty of eggs in the sand on the point of hatching out.

One visitor to Katema was David Berwick, a naturalist, who in 1951 considered that the crocodile population of the island was at least one hundred possibly as much as two hundred. On this visit he brought with him Mr Bowshill who shot two blind crocodiles on the shoreline. One of them was a huge fellow. Bowshill tentatively suggests that as the lake is very saline around Katema, this may have something to do with crocodile blindness. This seems doubtful. One thing is quite certain, there is no connection between the blindness of the Luapula and that found on Katema! The one point which has always puzzled me is how does a totally blind crocodile feed? I did not stay long enough to find out!

The Chiengi district produced its usual sad register of the severely handicapped and the totally blind but not a hint about the unseen causes which modern medicine should now be able to successfully grapple with. A couple of years later I brought John Wilson back into this area with a tough brandy-swilling South African, Herbert Squires, who claimed that it was the nightly jar of the hard stuff which kept him free of anything, from malaria and bilharzia to leprosy, excluding sleeping sickness, he stressed. "Why?" John asked with a doubtful tone.

"Because", growled Herbert Squires, "the bugs that bite at me automatically become alcoholics and forget what they are supposed to do."

The results of that last trip confirmed our original findings. There were nearly a thousand blind at least between Mununga and Chiengi, a sparsely populated area, just half the size of the Isle of Wight.

It was time to move back to that sixty acres of bush country which Monica Fisher had reminded me about in a letter which took three weeks to find me. It was awaiting our arrival. Could I get back to Bwana Mkubwa as soon as possible? Chiengi had an odd type of fascination for some people. I could understand why, as we packed our kit together to start the long trek along the valley westward. It had a beauty of its own. When discussing this isolated station with some of the real old timers, I remember one remark, "When we came into the country one out of every eight of us died. If you brought children with you (as some missionaries did) their chances of survival were not good. One child out of every three died." This old pioneer continued, "the white men who lived at Chiengi relied on quinine, Epsom salts and iodine. If you felt ill in those days, it was will power which pulled you through." The odds were loaded against you on that station: it could be mental stress, the usual virulent tropical disease and it could be, I was told, that the people who lived between Mporokosa and the lake were expert in the use of poison. Who knows? The silent Boma, with doors and windows shuttered, remained aloof. A native kept the approach path and surroundings clear and advised us to move on.

"It is not healthy." We got the point. We moved back to Mununga's village, found our car and picked up a pleasant and rather plump German anthropologist cum missionary, Dorothea Friedman, and took her back with us to the Mbereshi station where she joined her mission friends. We bade farewell to Bev and Margaret Packer who had been so helpful and then set course for our last outpost, the one at Johnson Falls run by Willie Lammond. It was this eighty year old mission hero of the Plymouth Brethren who was to give us the first clue to the real causes of blindness in the valley, so that researchers and medical terms could come in with some hope of cracking the problem.

Over the years I spent many interesting interludes with Willie Lammond at the mission station he had founded at Johnson Falls. He modestly told me the story of how he came into the country in 1901 from the Fort Jameson area and actually walked from Beira through to Johnson Falls a journey which took nearly two years. On this epic journey he saw the Arab slavers using the dreaded *Kurbash* and *Chikuto* rhinohide whips on hundreds of manacled Africans who were being driven into the slave caravans, where they would be sold on the east coast of Mozambique and in Zanzibar. There were terrifying scenes he recalled, captives with pronged tree forks fastened around their necks, indeed bodies littered the route the caravan was travelling along. The legacy of the Arab slavers, great pioneers in their own right, seems to have been overlooked, but in my day the evidence was still around. Lammond, then a ripe old eighty-two, mentioned a female on the station, who had died a few years ago, who had been carried off as a slave to Kigoma on Lake Tanganyika. She had been freed and spent her last years under the protection of his mission. Farther afield near where I was to set up my operational headquarters at Bwana Mkubwa was Chief Chilwala's village with a stormy history of slaving and one of resentment when the colonial administration flushed the Arabs out of the interior. I discovered three Arab graves a mile or so from my HQ, people whom it was suggested had put up some resistance to the British anti-slaving drive. Willie Lammond was one of those tough Plymouth Brethren missionaries who survived; to underline this point he turned his car over on the bush road a few days after I had left Johnson Falls and undeterred was back driving into Fort Rosebury (now named Mansa) a few days after this incident.

Willie saw things in black and white. When you died you either went up or down, there was no in-between! "Why did you come to Johnson Falls," I had asked him one evening.

"To stop the Catholics getting in," said the uncompromising Willie. "The White Fathers were just the other side of Kasembes", he continued, "and they had come far enough." Regrettably the spirit of ecumenical reconciliation seemed to be adrift as well in that part of the world in those days, but Willie Lammond when he collected his mission folk around him in his room overlooking the river for evening prayers, generously prayed for everyone, unbelievers, misguided Protestants and especially those with Catholic wives! In his garden down by the river he had placed on a pedestal a small Gipsy Moth aero engine. It was in gleaming condition in spite of the tropical rains – all that remained of a light plane flown out from England about 1928, which came to grief in the jungle just across the Luapula river.

William Lammond trained as a carpenter in Glasgow. He was a superb improviser, an inventive man and essentially a practical fellow. He wrote a textbook on the Chibemba language. It was exceedingly popular and useful amongst newcomers. He probably knew more about local customs than any other person in the area. "Why", I asked this sage, "is blindness present in such frightening proportions?" I expected the usual non-committal reply – perhaps poor diet, it could be trachoma, maybe it is a breeding ground for the simulium fly which spreads river blindness.

"No," said Lammond, who had read my thoughts, "there is probably a factor that we Europeans have hesitated to recognise, but which happens to have a direct bearing on matters. In the valley", he continued, "there is a preponderance of simple, but aggravating eye conditions such as conjunctivitis and the less complex complaints which result from the dust, bright sunlight and the flies which tend to irritate eyes. In addition," he continued, "over the years there has been a very virulent form of measles sweeping up and down the valley year after year. What is the result then?" He went on, "I'll tell you. You do not have to seek far. Probably there are none of your exotic eye diseases such as onchocerciasis – river blindness – I suspect it is something much more simple, or shall we say sinister native witchcraft remedies."

Subsequent investigation in the Luapula Valley, proved Lammond's contention right. For one thing we found that whilst measles epidemics were raging, mothers placed their infants outside the huts in the full light of the glaring sun. When they found that the child's eyes began to deteriorate the first person they consulted by tradition (rather than for other reasons) was the local 'herbalist' or witchdoctor. This just about summed up the situation. The 'herbalist', or as some refer to him, the witchdoctor, held sway. It was only when the damage had been compounded by him and was largely irreversible that the child was brought to a clinic or hospital as a last resort. At Chipili mission, mid-way between Fort Rosebury and Kawambwa, the mission nurse showed us a child whose eyes had been treated by white hot ash. Years later, within half a mile of my own bush home, an eight year old girl was brought to the school clinic suffering from simple conjunctivitis. The treatment was straight forward. In the meantime, the local 'herbalist' had offered a rapid cure, for the price of a couple of chickens, which the father tried first against our advice. What was the result? Three days later the child came to the clinic with the front of the eyes irrevocably damaged – burnt out it transpired by an infusion of root potions which were strongly acidic in their content. (We tried to find the person who had administered this fluid but were unsuccessful.)

The expert on this startling state of affairs was Dr Malcolm Phillips, an ophthalmologist who made, in the late Fifties, a special study of the Valley of the Blind. He concluded that treatment of simple eye conditions by the unskilled native 'herbalist' was the cause behind so much blindness. Such facts and findings were repeated on a lesser scale in Malawi and West Africa. Malcolm Phillips was no stranger to Africa. He told me his conclusions. Firstly, over the years, he had secured a large variety of the native medicines which were being applied to eyes in the locality. Of the sixty-four samples which he had somehow secured fifty, on being subjected to a detailed analysis, were found to be corrosive – strong enough in some cases, he said, to burn a hole in material. The substances used were usually roots leaves or berries, but for good measure there were sometimes other ingredients such as bone grit. The method of administering this material Phillips told me was to get a large leaf and fashion it into the shape of a fine funnel and then pour the liquid direct into the open eye. The result he concluded was that the cornea was usually burnt out or disintegrated within a few days.

Dr Phillips made detailed surveys which covered ninety villages in the Valley and the Lake Mweru area. It revealed that one child in every thirty was totally blind and one adult in every forty. River blindness was at one time considered to be the factor which was responsible for the situation. The area with its rivers flowing into the lake, and its dense undergrowth, plus the climate, were conditions which could facilitate the disease. During the following years both Government and the Royal Commonwealth Society for the Blind sent out mobile clinical eye research teams under the direction of Dr Phillips. The findings were to bear out what Willie Lammond had suggested a few years earlier to me, that the indiscriminate use of native medicine was the fundamental cause of so much profound visual disability. Although this had been long suspected it had not been confirmed by thorough professional investigation until Phillips turned up some interesting facts.

He found that in practically every case of blindness the children's eyes had been treated previously by a native 'herbalist'. He confirmed that the assortment of substances used were usually highly toxic and that it was the appalling treatment rather than the eye complaint which hastened the onset of total blindness.

I found that people in those far away places had an implicit faith in native medicines but why? when cause and effect seem to us so patently obvious? John Wilson in his book *Travelling Blind* writes, "The strange thing was that despite the fearful results the witchdoctors and their patients really believed that these medicines or the incantations which accompanied their administration, did good and without them even more people would have lost their sight." If you believe as these people did that eye trouble is not caused by a virus but by the influence of a spirit, or the malice of a wizard, then you go first to the witchdoctor whose job it is to guard you and your family against supernatural peril. Matters in the Luapula Valley have improved beyond recognition. In my day we had to make almost wild guesses to try to pinpoint the aggravating factors which were contributing to blindness. The tribes of the Luapula were great eaters of lake fish. Some reasoned that this might have a connection with visual problems. Others linked it with the staple diet of cassava which, unless prepared properly by soaking so that all traces of acid are removed, can be injurious. (Oddly enough diet has proved to be a partial contributory factor, but not in the way some of us suspected.)

It has now been proved conclusively that malnutrition, especially lack of vitamin A, pre-disposes towards sight deficiencies and it is reasonable to assume that this factor might well be present in the Luapula though famine in this particular area has not been endemic. In certain parts of Bangladesh and other regions of Asia cornea scarring is linked to vitamin deficiency, at least this was the consensus of opinion from ophthalmologists who were working in the 'eye camps', during my stay in that part of the world.

I feel that the old timers like Willie Lammond who had been in the country for over fifty years were shrewd observers. Willie was quite certain in his own mind that the local 'herbalist's' role should be thoroughly investigated. Malcolm Phillips bringing in all the latest ophthalmological techniques demonstrated through his years of research that although there was a combination of aggravating factors present in the Luapula, the real *enfant terrible* was not a virus or diet though they were clearly contributing factors. I recall travelling with John Wilson through the Valley in 1955, in some areas almost every hut had its blind man – two and three blind children in one family, their eyes in a frightful state, disfigured and purulent – a District Officer reported to us that he had counted seventy blind people in one morning. That is what the Valley of the Blind was all about in those days, appalling ignorance leading to unnecessary blindness. It was the story the Bureau for the Prevention of Blindness in Pretoria had told me earlier that almost ninety percent of blindness in the tropics is preventable. We soon learnt that this was true.

It was to be in this area that the Royal Commonwealth Society for the Blind made one of its biggest contribution to third world countries. The Prevention of Blindness and Sight Saving Campaigns are still going on. Massive inroads have been made within the space of three decades into the scourge of blindness, its treatment and, for those who are irrevocably blind, the provision of proper training and educational facilities. These days those who have benefited from the work of this organisation are numbered not in thousands or even hundreds of thousands, but in millions. This is the astounding story of a largely unknown war, a war which in our lifetime will have no end. But at least the Valley of the Blind is no more: the beautiful simulium fly is recognised for what it really is – a deadly carrier of blindness – and the blind, once referred to as the living dead, or the shadows from the dark, are no longer jeered at as the 'useless dead who walk'.

In those distant but exciting days, we were trying to bridge the gap between two modes of life. Many of us who joined in some of those unceasing battles which sometimes brought us into head-on confrontation with tradition and age-old treatments were level headed enough to recognise that our own sophisticated society has its own imperfections. The black arts and superstition are not limited to distant lands, but the gullible in Europe including the 'educated' can be sucked into the orbit of the confidence tricksters, who may claim a special relationship with the unseen world. In 1986 the revelations at an English Court hearing on a black magic case surpassed the sensational claims of some of my most respected and feared *mganga* friends! (A *mganga* is a witchdoctor).

On looking back I can see the broad canvas of the Africa I knew in two different perspectives. Firstly, what was happening in my Africa had unfolded in Europe not so many years ago, old women were disposed of as witches and heretics less than three hundred years ago and we still have the hangovers of that brutal age with us, a time-scale which in the universe is as a yesterday. Secondly, I learnt some of the common threads of African society, that the language of East Africa, Swahili, and of the West African, Hausa, have common elements and indeed some almost identical words, that the customs and rites are sometimes common as well; in the west, Sierra Leone has its sinister leopard man cult and the east, around Tanzania, its horrific lion man cult in the arid plains around Singidia. Both cults are similar. Fertility rites vary in their intensity and expression. One thing is certain that with the exception of the Moslem North, they run the length and breadth of Africa. They manifest themselves in worship rites of different forms; in seeds, fruit and especially in blood as the symbol of life. This is often expressed in the sacrifice of goats, chickens and sometimes in human sacrifices. During my thirty years in and out of Africa, I have come across a number of valid reports relating to the consumption of human flesh for ritual or medicinal purposes – in Malawi, in Eastern Nigeria and near the Zaire-Zambia border. According to my friend Brother Lucien, a fluent Chibemba speaker, there was reason to believe that this type of ritual took place quite near our own home in Bwana Mkubwa. The classic story which I checked out carefully was in the lonely Kirk range mountains of Malawi just before Independence. Some unfortunate individual had been accused of witchcraft. He was the member of a local mission church. When he was questioned, he replied blandly, "I have told you all before, that I gave up eating human flesh over two years ago."

This is Africa in transition and old beliefs and customs die hard, especially when there is nothing to replace them. At the site which would soon be my headquarters for the next three years, the 'lion men' were not unknown, neither were the wizards or the *banyama* who claimed that their spirit could enter into the body of a hyena, a snake or some other unpleasant creature. As one of my Swiss mission neighbours was to tell me, "the African bush will never bore you." In retrospect this appears to have been an understatement of considerable dimensions!

In discussing the forms of cannibalism which surfaced from time to time in isolated parts of Africa the role of some units in the Japanese Army involved in similar macabre activities is often overlooked. Why? Is it a case of a nation endowed with technical prowess and the wealth which ensues, being considered exempt from the more embarrassing aspects of its recent history – one mode of treatment for a sophisticated nation and another for an emergent one?

The Japanese within the last years of World War II inadvertently presented society with a host of documentary evidence and subsequent reports which confirmed that a small but worrying proportion of Japanese troops had with the approval of very senior officers, (at least two Generals and an Admiral), eaten human flesh. Indeed, at the war crimes trials which followed the war an appalling state of affairs was revealed.

We know that the Commanding Officer of the Japanese 18th Army Group found it necessary to issue a statement covering guide lines on cannibalism. A rough translation of one sentence reads:

114

> Whilst it is in order to eat the flesh of enemy dead, all ranks must in future refrain from eating their own countrymen who have been slain in battle.

This directive is dated 10th December, 1944.

Major Matoba, a battalion field commander admitted when asked to explain an order he had issued on 10th March, 1945, (which had fallen into the hands of Allied intelligence,) that "he had eaten human flesh on only about three occasions." The Order being investigated was headed,

Order Regarding the Eating of Human Flesh of Allied Flyers.

"It dealt that day", Matoba explained, "with the disposal of Flight Lieutenant Hall, a Royal Australian Air Force pilot who had been shot down the previous day." Matoba had set down the procedures to be followed with preciseness. These included the following instructions:

> "... medical orderly Sakabe will attend the execution[2]. He will remove the gall bladder and liver;
> Lieutenant Kanamuri will be responsible for the distribution of the flesh...."

Major Matoba after expressing his regret and profound apologies went on to state that Sakabe "appeared to have insufficient anatomical skill for his task and medical officer Teraki therefore completed the job." Major Matoba explained to Allied intelligence officers the reasons he decided to despatch Flight Lieutenant Hall so hastily. It transpires that the previous night he had given a 'festive' dinner. The guest of honour was Admiral Mori who remarked when thanking the Major for his hospitality that he had particularly enjoyed the human flesh which had been served and requested that the next time an Allied airman was executed to save him a little of the man's liver. Major Matoba did not disappoint the Admiral!

But according to Lord Russell of Liverpool who made a special study of Japanese war crimes[3] the Matoba case was but the tip of the iceberg. He cites General Tachibaba who consistently advocated at high level conferences in 1944 and 1945, "that use should be made of executed Allied airmen when food was in short supply." Tachibaba further went on to recommend that when no enemy corpses were available Japanese soldiers, rather than starve, must be prepared to eat

[2]Flight Lieutenant Hall was beheaded over a crater made by one of his own bombs.
[3]*The Knights of Bushido*, Lord Russell of Liverpool, published by Cassells, London.

their own comrades killed in battle.' Whilst the majority of Japanese would clearly reject without question such advice in wartime and it would utterly disgust the present day population of Japan – it is very clear that a small but influential wartime body were prepared to tolerate and apparently encourage such atrocities. Memories of those frightful times can be devastatingly selective and the truth, because of the enormity of what apparently happened over a wide area of the Pacific, can sometimes be dismissed as an aberration of fact. The War Crimes Commission did not take that view.

Whilst much has been rightly made of the mass killings in Europe, history seems to have let the Japanese off lightly. Technical brilliance and Economic astuteness has done little to enhance Japan's standing in the league of those who generously support Third World countries fending off starvation. Maybe it is all too much to expect from a country which in 1945 was probably the outright winner in the stakes for sadism, torture, mutilation and cannibalism.

Chapter Six

I was fortunate. When I arrived in central Africa the bush had not been tamed. It was, with the exception of the scars of one or two mining townships, much as the pioneers at the turn of the century had found it, a massive sea of bush and jungle, broken in the lower regions by crocodile infested rivers and malarial swamps and lakes.

My task of laying the foundations of a service for the blind, and later for other disabilities, had now started. With the help of a work force of a hundred Africans a magnificent site had been carved out of virgin bush. There was a school, a teacher training centre, an adult unit for the blind, staff houses and, lying across this spacious sixty acre site was an ancient tribal graveyard which was, of course, reputed to be haunted! This presented problems. It was covered with a mass of tangled creepers and tall elephant grass. No African would pass through this area at night. Eventually we placed the male and female student quarters at opposite sides of the old burial ground. As there was only one trackway, one which passed through the graveyard, night escapades and boy-girl problems were minimal! It was a brilliant arrangement.

Cathleen and I, in those formative days, were the only white faces on the place. This unique and pleasant little community lay like an island in an ocean of bushland six rough and rugged miles from what was then a deserted village, Bwana Mkubwa. As there were no other place-names I recall seeing on the map of the area, our settlement in the early days took on this name. (Later it was changed to Kangonglwe after the name for a stream which ran through the grounds.)

In those days there were still rambling elephant trails and spoor patterns which occasionally passed through the site. At certain seasons, usually around August and September, lions sometimes ambled past our bungalow but they were never tiresome. Eventually their visits became less frequent as our establishment developed.

There was no electricity, no telephone or laid on water supply. The ample supplies of wood around us provided the fuel for cooking. A thin miserable track led through the thick vegetation broken by rocky outcrops, huge ant hills and wild bamboo. It passed the foot of a hilly green spur called Kaloko, which rose a few hundred feet above the jungle. This was the road leading us to Ndola, our nearest link with the outside world and, at that time I suppose, a tenuous one.

It was Kaloko, that jungle-clad promontory rising out of the bush which was known to Africans for miles around. It seemed to be a rallying point going back into the mists of time. They sang about it, and named their children after it. Its name has for generations been in local folklore stories, in their rituals and tribal dances. They would shout and scream: "Kaloko forever" or "Kaloko will never die", and around they would go dancing and screaming the praises of this revered hill. There were other physical mysteries around us as well. The Sunken Lake, a few miles from Chief Chiwala's village; a depression possibly of volcanic origin where quite suddenly the flat plain is pierced by a vast wide hole at the bottom of which lies a deep dark sheet of silent water believed to be connected to Lake Isiku by a subterranean river. Isiku is a large pool rather than a lake. It was here, according to the Africans who worked with me at our new Bwana Mkubwa Centre, that a huge two-headed serpent lived. He comes to the surface every five years and marauds the district to satisfy his hunger and then retires to the lake for another lengthy period. The story came to light at my establishment because a pile of human remains had been found in the shallows of the lake. All agreed that the grizzly find confirmed that the monster had been at work. Old Yacobo, who had told me the story, sensed that I doubted his tale. "The *Bwana* does not believe us," he told his friends. They sighed. "Ah," said Mwana, "how can you expect a *musungu* [a white man] to understand the things our forefathers have told us. It is not for the *musungu*." His friends nodded their heads in approval and I left them talking in low voices and looking very wise!

Our nearest neighbour, a mile to the west of us was a helpful Franciscan mission. It was run by the Swiss members of this religious Order, who had arrived about the same time as Cathleen and I. They had settled in quickly and within a few months had opened up the bush in the vicinity of their base and built a delightful little church. In the solitude of these surroundings they hoped to start a seminary for

African priests. Well past the mission station the track diminished to a footpath which led down to the Munkunglwe river and this was crossed by a frail timber footbridge. The path led through tall reeds and towering elephant grass to the edge of the bush. Here, in a wide clearing, was the mud and *daga* thatched house of Arthur Davison, known to the Africans as *Yangwe*, the terror.

Arthur Davison was unique in many ways. He came from a good county Durham family and could trace his ancestors back to the time of the Norman Conquest. It was a Davison he told me once who signed, with nineteen other leaders, the death warrant of Charles I or, he added with a twinkle in his eye when the Catholic mission folk were around, "it may have been Mary Queen of Scots". Davison was one of the few still around, who walked into the country. He was a shy man with few friends. I suspect that in his Durham home there had been problems and like many other self-willed lads, Arthur Davison left his home and never returned. He came into the country at the age of twenty-one and through sheer force of personality (he was a smallish man with piercing blue eyes and much common sense) he established an odd kind of rapport with the Africans. They feared him yet they loved him. Like a number of the old timers who came in around this period, he was engaged in prospecting and sometimes trading in wild animal skins. He went 'native', something which was fairly common in those days, taking on a native wife or wives. In my time he lived on his own. The African women he had loved and cherished, sometimes for years at a time, he had sent back to their villages with ample resources in kind and cash. He was now a sick man, but held high in the esteem of the local Africans and in awe by many as well. No one would pass near his house at night. Dreadful things were supposed to go on at *Yangwe's*! An African villager told me, "Those who displeased him he threw down a well at the back of his house." Of course this was not true, but it was all part of the type of folklore which grew up around those early mystics of pioneers who, single-handed, would rule a district almost as large as Yorkshire, until the colonial Government sitting in comfort in Whitehall decided to annex the area. These personalities which seemed to thrive in the adversity of the tropics were now drifting into the twilight world and would soon be forgotten or, if not, tagged either as exploiters (which some were), or as oddities. Men who actually survived the mental and physical tribulations in Africa at the turn of the century were great characters. There were not many still around in the early Fifties because, as Arthur Davison once told me, "When we the pioneers came into this country, we were on our own. Life was nasty, brutish and for some very short." They were a great and intriguing race.

Our Franciscan mission friends were already seasoned bush veterans for they had opened up work in other isolated areas of the jungle. Father Cotting and Brother Lucien rarely thought of their own beautiful cool, clean country – Switzerland. They had embraced Africa and cheerfully proceeded with faith and dignity to try to spread the Christian message. They had their difficulties and terrible disappointments, but they never gave up. Arthur Davison and his lifestyle was at first something of an embarrassment they had to live with, but they tackled the situation admirably, so admirably in fact that when Arthur died at the age of seventy-four he had in his last days become a convert and willed to the Mission most of his property which was considerable! Arthur Davison for all his faults loved Africa and he made sure that the people to whom he had left his land and farms would develop them in the best interests of the African. It was this much maligned old man who had made my work possible, for it was he who had donated the extensive site we were now developing.

Amongst the survival advice the mission veterans had given us was to make sure that we always used powerful torches when we went out at night. Nightfall was the time when the bush became alive – jackals called to each other and hyenas with high pitched wailing cackles joining in the chorus. It was in the cool of the night that the leopards, which were plentiful, started on their nocturnal maraudings, especially if the day had been hot and the hunting poor. Leopards have a great appetite for small dogs. We lost two of our own to them within as many weeks. The first, a friendly mongrel named Rory, was calmly snatched off the verandah one evening and a fortnight later our friendly biscuit-coloured Pekinese puppy was taken in even more dramatic circumstances. Cathleen was up early one Sunday morning and was walking along the bush path to the mission when the peke escaped from the house and followed her. The dog caught up with her and when only a few yards behind was suddenly scooped up in almost complete silence by a leopard. There was a muffled yell and a patch of hair and blood left on the path which told its story. (I now have the skin of the culprit in my Irish home.)

Life was much what you made of it. If you accepted Africa as it was and as you found it and not as you may have thought it should be, life could be almost magical and magnetic! If you found time as well to appreciate the exotic bush flowers which pushed their way through the dry iron-bound laterite soil after six months of drought, the colourful bird-life, weaver birds building intricate nests suspended from threads over a stream, duiker (small antelope) bursting through the bush, creatures hunted both by man and beast, Africa could get into your blood and become almost hypnotic.

Duiker are strange dainty little animals. Cathleen raised a kid duiker on a bottle when its mother had been killed. It became a great pet and Cathleen named it Cissie. She grew up with the household which at the time included our latest dog, another peke named Sherry. (Sherry survived bush life and came to England.) One day Cissie disappeared and we assumed that she was another bush casualty for she never failed to keep close to the house and answer to her name. Almost a year passed when, one evening, we had just returned from our usual walk, but who should come trotting out of the bush in her typical dainty fashion but Cissie! There was a touching reunion as she went directly to Cathleen who had reared her and put her nose in her hands and on her face. She was now much larger and with a shining fawn coat. After five minutes of mutual affection she gave a whimper and dived off back into the bush. We never saw her again. Wildlife and nature can tick over in a curious and touching way in a hostile world.

It was about this time that I started to get the school and training centre for the blind and the unit for teachers and social workers dealing with the handicapped into some shape and format. There were over a hundred and twenty blind youngsters drawn from all over the country, plus a large African training staff with equally diverse backgrounds. The challenges I had been seeking in distant England were just about to descend on me! I had a lot to learn, lessons which have stayed with me and enabled me to survive. For example, I learnt that, with the best will in the world, people drawn from widely differing backgrounds, of race, language, religion and traditional cultures rarely gel into cohesive units, not at least until some degree of maturity develops. Suspicion and jealousy usually predominate. Tribal animosities run deeply in African life, sometimes they go back for generations and sometimes for centuries. A high degree of preparation is therefore needed before launching into ambitious multitribal schemes. I also learnt that Africans, at least in the early 1950s, expected a European in charge of a large establishment to be all things to all people. In practical terms at my establishment in the bush, this implied checking that the school cook didn't burn the *bwali* (porridge) or steal the children's and staff rations, being a lorry driver and mechanic, even weeding out characters who were busy applying 'spells' which threatened the mental stability of individuals and sometimes of members of minority tribal groups.

One of the most successful teachers turned out to be a 'sorcerer' and the influence on the whole complex was quite appalling. Much as I liked the man, it was quite clear that he had been playing nasty little games with susceptible people and he had to go. Years later I met him in the capital, Lusaka. I think whatever magic he was alleged to have been able to work must have been pretty successful for he was now holding a very high Government office and in rank was my superior! He died a couple of years ago a very wealthy man. Another passing crisis occurred when a staff member was alleged to have been having an affair with somebody else's wife in the local village. Adultery is a dangerous pastime in tribal Africa, and it was by sheer good fortune that this individual missed being carved up. If some of the relatives had indeed laid their hands on the culprit he would never again have been in a position to offend against female society! Matters on a different level included trying to find water for a campus which was reaching a strength, if employees were included, of nearly two hundred. The *dambo* from which we collected our black-grey water was an atrocious place. The water had to be meticulously boiled and filtered, but at periods of drought even this supply dried up. To keep the community together we had to drive our Bedford lorry with a gang of labourers and a dozen old petrol drums and bale out water from a distant stream. We managed to get by until the rains broke and then other problems came to the forefront, at times the trackway into our supply centre, Ndola was impassable; on another occasion the fuel system in the lorry packed up and it took the best part of a day to get it working again. Repairs in bush country under the midday sun were not easy for novices like myself.

There was one other misfortune which occurred. A smallpox epidemic was raging. The health authorities in Ndola came out and vaccinated everyone, but unfortunately one blind young man who was in hospital at the time was inadvertently missed out. Smallpox was still lingering in the area and sure enough the boy, who had been missed, turned up at my wife's clinic with the tell-tale signs on the palms of his hands and on the soles of his feet. I remember the lad well. Cofitula was his name. He was something of a loner, the only one of his tribe at the school. He came from distant Mwinilunga, a destitute who had wandered from village to village. He had managed to just about survive. Few understood the language he spoke, but he was one of the calm and tranquil types so different from the angry Lunda lads, whose hardships had contributed to the blind in the area being looked on as tough and aggressive. Not that I blamed them for their attitude to society, for they had certainly suffered badly and been treated with contempt by the tribe. Cofitula did not recover. I was sorry to lose this sad and innocent youth. The soothsayers waxed mightily about his demise – no it was not smallpox, but a 'spell'! I missed him.

The school labour force was reduced to twenty-five when the main buildings had been completed but even this was insufficient to keep the bush back and to clear new areas. The African workers were mainly likeable local rogues who had a great sense of humour, especially when they tried to pull a fast one over you and failed. They were loyal but not too hard working not, I hasten to add, through their own fault, but because they did not have sufficient food. In addition to the wages, we issued a meat and mealy meal ration. This meant that the men at least had basic food even if they went out and spent the rest of their wages at the weekend on beer in the village. In the labour force there were a few 'outsiders'; two hard working lads from Lake Nyasa and a sly little sorcerer Nyeleti from Katanga. The watchman, an elderly but delightful fellow called Kachasu was something of a 'real herbalist' and could deal with simple complaints. Now and again he tried his hand at curing snake bites - at least no one died.

The remarkable thing about this heterogeneous mixture of society Cathleen and I were living with, was that on the whole we were a very peaceful and happy community. Every month we had our communal camp fire, with special treats of sweets and sugar for the youngsters and meat cooked over the fire. There was a whole series of tribal dances, songs and acts, including one which sometimes featured the *Bwana*. In that encampment we could go out all day and leave our house unlocked – something we did frequently and only once was anything ever touched. That was when our houseboy, Noah, stole two girl-guide uniforms. He was going through a bad time with his wife so I suppose it was partially excusable. Around where we lived Europeans could walk in perfect safety and this went on in much of the Africa where I worked for the next few years. But in some places this was to change. After I left for East Africa, a white woman was attacked at Bwana Mkubwa and burnt to death inside her car. Other disturbing things happened as well. This was not the Africa that the pioneers had known or the one that Cathleen and I had grown to enjoy and respect. We were lucky, our African neighbours were tolerant and loyal. There was some kind of unwritten understanding. We depended on each other. When African medicine failed, the sick came to our settlement. Our Africans were not the kind of people to hold grievances either, even though I had landed one young man in prison for a serious wounding offence against another lad. He came and saw me afterwards. He had served his time and our relationship was back to normal.

Mulandu is the Bemba word for dispute or row. *Mulandus* usually developed over misunderstandings connected with cattle or land. Usually these disputes were taken to the local Chief. Sometimes they came to me first for advice and we managed to arrange a settlement or patch up a problem about a dowry for a wife. Sometimes employees, especially the teachers and social workers, whose homes were between two hundred to four hundred miles away, had *mulandus* to settle and needed help with funds for their journey. It sometimes happened as well when relatives died. By custom the bereaved had to go back to the village to conform to native tradition and observe certain rites. Not once did an employee fail to repay the money he had borrowed, nor did I have to ask for it.

Money was still something of a novelty in the bush country. I can still recall the true tale told me by Father Dominic, one of the Franciscan mission members, about the African villager who was urgently in need of money for his family. Apparently the African had never been to school, but he managed to write a brief letter, or got a friend to write it. The letter he addressed to God. Then he posted it. The local African postal clerk, when he saw to whom it was addressed, decided that the best place to find God would be in the nearest mission station! This is how it came into Father Dominic's hands. The letter was a simple request for £5 to pay for food for the poor man's family. Father Dominic considered the matter and, as he knew the man and his family, decided that he would help him. He considered that £3 would cover the items that were needed. He enclosed £3 in an envelope and with a short note posted the money to the man. A few weeks later another letter arrived addressed "To God". This time it was not a request for money but a timely warning to God, it read:

> Dear God,
> Thank you very much for the £3 you sent me the other day. Next time you send me money, please do not send it through Father Dominic as he kept £2 for himself.
> Thank you God.
> Your loving son,
> KATATA.

There were other heavier and more harrowing aspects of life in those free and easy bush days. One of our workmen – I remember him as a quiet inoffensive fellow – came to me very early one morning and asked to speak *quietly*, as he put it, to me. I brought him into the office, a thatched hut. He looked nervous and worried. "Can *Bwana* let me have a large cardboard box?" he asked.

"Yes, certainly," I said. "Let us go down to the store." We found the size of the box which suited him.

"Has *Bwana* another box about the same size?" asked our friend. We found him one. I was curious and said, "Juma," (I think that was his name), "are you sending something to your village?"

"Oh, no *Bwana*," Juma replied, "I have big trouble with me."

"What has happened?" I asked. Juma unfolded the story. His wife had given birth to twins the previous night and they had both died. He needed the boxes to bury them in. The word "twins" in much of Africa has varied and sometimes sinister connotations. I asked no more questions and merely sympathised with him. When he had assured me that his wife was well, he went on his way.

I was puzzled about the whole affair particularly as no one on the campus had commented about the deaths which had taken place. Usually a death was the subject of much wailing. That evening

Cathleen and I walked over to the mission to discuss some other business and I happened to mention the tragedy to Brother Lucien. "Would the mission be burying the twins?" I enquired.

"No," replied the Brother who spoke Chibemba fluently and knew a fair amount about local rites. "The chances are," he continued grimly, "that they have already been buried, well before sunset." He went on, "According to the man's tribal customs he may, with his wife, have to return to the grave tonight, disinter the bodies and consume certain token pieces of the flesh to expiate any wrongs or evil the twins may have left in this world on other people. This will, according to the tribe, mollify the spirit world." Brother Lucien was not a man to make dramatic statements unless he was reasonably sure of his facts. I learnt a year later from a source well connected with tribal rituals that the things he had foreshadowed had actually happened. It was a hard world to understand in those days, at least for newcomers to Africa!

As a result of the experience of conditions in the Luapula and Mweru regions it was possible to identify the two outstanding problems concerning blindness. The first covered its prevention and cure, a matter on which the Government and RCSB collaborated very closely and was clearly of the utmost priority. The result was the introduction and extension of Ophthalmological services including the use of mobile clinics. Suffice to say that great inroads have been made into the frightful state of affairs which existed in the Fifties. The second conclusion which reflected on the development of services for those who were already blind, led to a rethink on Government policy. Blindness existed in concentrations, in Barotseland, the north-east of the country, and worst of all in the Luapula and Mweru regions. I don't think officialdom realised at the time quite how bad the situation was. Like most governments in those days the easiest and most expedient method of dealing with the problem was to create a national centre for the blind. (Our centre at Bwana Mkubwa originally had this purpose in mind.) Experience has proved that big institutions may be prestigious but they are not always practical propositions. The idea of transporting hundreds of handicapped from their homes, people drawn from entirely different backgrounds, tribal loyalties, religions and tongues (there are over forty different languages in Zambia alone), seemed to run against important principles – those of building on existing patterns of local community life.

In those days most of us found that bureaucracy and the hordes of the bumbledoms (that dwelt in splendid isolation in offices) had no place in a vibrant young country, so it was easy enough to alter course before much damage and expense had been incurred. Some of us learnt as well how to blend the good things of African life, of which there were plenty – patience, a respect for nature and the ability to live a full life in difficult surroundings, to name a few – into the work we were trying to foster. It was an almost idyllic situation – at least some of us thought so – to live without shops, cinemas, TV, fast cars and the shallow tinsel arrangements to show that one was one up on the neighbours. Certainly our neighbours apart from the mission and poor old *Yangwe* Davison, pondering over his adventurous past in his mud thatched house, were non-existent. But on reflection we were never lonely. How could we be with an African village half a mile away augmented by the labour force from the school building team programme.

I suspect that in some respects it was a perilous position for some of my African staff from distant places like Barotseland meeting up with the indigenous natives, who milled around this area and were much influenced by the recent past, of old Chief Chiwala, his antics and the Arab slavers. Tribal disintegration has now been happening over most parts of Africa, but from time to time something gives and then the trouble starts.

I found that the catalyst which fanned the smouldering latent fears into reality were the tribal dances and heavy beer drinking sessions which occurred mostly at weekends or on some special occasion such as a marriage. The village announced such social occasions with day long drumming. The drums seems to arouse some primeval instinct. I noticed how our own men and women responded as the sounds echoed across the forest. Eyes brightened, those who had felt gloomy went around with a lighter step, most of them were looking forward to a session which at weekends would normally last a full and continuous forty-eight hours. As we lay in bed listening to our neighbours enjoying themselves, the thud of tribal dancing, the beat of the drums, the screams of ecstasy as they worked themselves up to a crescendo of excitement, it was calculated either to thrill or frighten you.

The aftermath of these occasions was our main concern. The local brew was quite devastating. It was generally distilled from millet. Its victims sometimes lay paralytic for days on end. Fights and stabbings seemed to be part of the weekend entertainment. This is where the inter-tribal mix, which formed part of my own establishment often came to grief. Cathleen's clinic, which was used by the neighbourhood as well as our centre, was kept busy patching people up. The missionaries have tried for years to stop these bloody sessions, but I suspect that they have increased rather than diminished as the economy in rural areas improved.

It was for these and other reasons that a change of strategy was considered necessary. Government in its wisdom had advised – one presumes for administrative and financial expediency – a large national multi-training, purpose-built complex, one which we had now almost created. After close consultation with those who knew the country well, I put forward a plan for decentralisation with the training component based at our present establishment and half a dozen up-country satellite units; fortunately this was immediately approved.

Decentralisation in rural Africa, as far as work amongst the handicapped was concerned, implied working in the midst of small communities to remove innate prejudices and to demonstrate by example and achievement that the blind are trainable, that they are part and parcel of the community as well and have a right to exist side by side with those who can see. These ideas were alien, and in those days were revolutionary, type thinking! It often ran against tribal attitudes and age old sentiments. I frequently heard expressed the opinion that the blind are the 'dead men who walk,' or 'they are the forgotten people, the living dead'. Even an understanding colonial Government considered that the immensity of the problem in certain parts of northern Rhodesia suggested that the solution was at present beyond existing financial resources.

This was only one side of the story. What did the blind think about their status in society? In some areas of Africa, particularly in northern Nigeria, the blind from time immemorial have formed themselves into local bands, or groups with their own blind Chief called a *makafi*. They formed pressure groups for organised begging and, in the Moslem North, were listened to with a fair degree of respect by the local rulers, the Emirs. Over the years in a number of parts of Africa they banded themselves together in quite formidable unions.

The majority of blind people who came my way from the Luapula country or from around Mweru were often hardened and embittered from the treatment they had received. The fact that they had survived at all was a tribute to their toughness. The problem was to convince the majority of the blind from rural Africa that with a little training they could at least enjoy a fuller, more useful and independent life. The starting point was to gain the confidence of each individual so that with kindly but firm training the bitterness and rancour which most of them felt against a sighted community, no longer dominated their lives. It was a task for enlightened teachers and social workers (who now formed quite a large team), to help them forget their past lives of stagnation, misery and squalor, by placing within their grasp things that they could do, work and pastimes that they could enjoy and, the quite novel respect they might win from their own community, by demonstrating some of their new found skills. "Mwamba can read and write but Kamba, who can see, can do neither," said one perceptive villager. This was the kind of thing which impressed the Chief, the local headman and villagers and was probably the start of a new attitude towards the blind.

Why were the satellite schools and training centres which we established from our Bwana Mkubwa base in distant places like Sefula in Barotseland, Mununga's and Kasembe's (there were others as well) successful in breaking down the massive barriers of prejudices and ignorance about the blind? Attitudes which sometimes expressed themselves in rank cruelty and sometimes at the other extreme (with a few isolated tribes) in kindness. The training units we established up country were simple places, often only mud and thatch buildings staffed by willing but inexperienced staff, who had only the briefest of training, but they became grafted into community life. This was the component which led to success. They flourished because they eventually linked up to the old extended family system. Once it had been shown that the blind were not the hopeless and helpless fraternity which society had always considered them the rest was straightforward. The secret was to take the community with you. The blind were not different, they were not an alien group, but they were, if you moved them hundreds of miles from their own community where language and tribal customs were those of strangers. It was a case of straightforward logic. Let the villagers see the whole system of training unfold and even take part in it – that was the first step. They were fascinated.

In the past the blind child and blind beggar had sometimes been taken to distant mission schools to return home many years later to find that they were strangers in their own homes and environment and their own families could not understand the ways in which they had been trained. Simplicity was the keynote of our up country work. Simple buildings, attainable objectives, work and crafts closely aligned with those of the locality. Somehow these ideas worked, thanks to the excellent type of African professional we recruited and trained for these duties; people who were on their own, but were reliable and resourceful and who saw that training the handicapped called for initiative and not the straight and level type of thinking beloved by some of the red tape type characters. It was all a challenge but great fun as well. These rural training units took the blind along the road of literacy through Braille (we published Braille books in the local languages), but more important they learnt to grow their own food, cassava, maize and nuts – elementary subsistence farming.

I am sure that much of our type of work rested on inculcating a positive attitude of mind, that of self-help, of independence, of proving to their sighted brothers and sisters that they were not the beleaguered creatures which society had labelled them. It was the young and informal staff who with tact and masterly competence and confidence guided both young and old away from the beggars bowl to acceptance by their community, to marriage – in some cases a few eventually married people who could see. Looking back, this was something of a social revolution.

There were plenty of disappointments as well. The old hands resented the self-discipline which comes with learning, some drifted back to begging their way around the countryside but, provided our staff retained the thrust for all round development and inspired the blind, we seemed to be winning a battle which was at this stage still a gamble. The majority who came to us had found that there was a substitute for begging which brought other good things as well as a basic livelihood.

The spirit of our staff training unit at Bwana Mkubwa was successfully carried far afield into our distant bush schools. Because of the time factor, the staff training I was able to give these young people spearheading the attack on blindness, was rudimentary in the extreme. They took with them a particular message, that of partnership. This is the key to success in African adventures of this type. Partnership with the blind and partnership with the community. The 'them and us' situation, the bane of many similar establishments in Europe, was banished. The Bwana Mkubwa message of partnership found expression in what I term, when working with the handicapped, the companionship element. Teachers and social workers in those days, (as in Europe), were not always renowned for their ability to improvise or initiate. The African men and women on my staff seemed to be of a different mould, ready to have a go and quite delighted to be chosen to spearhead a completely new type of service in distant parts of their country. They sought to inculcate confidence by bringing in the human touch into every aspect of their work. I am sure that this was the most valuable weapon in our armoury. It won over village communities and whole tribes. This was the component which at the end of the day, eliminated suspicion and indifference. I think it is true to say my African colleagues set the standards and attitudes of a new humanity and approach towards the blind.

In many regions of the developed world, the handicapped are big business. If you don't believe me go to an international conference and see for yourself. Administrative and financial efficiency there must be, but there seems to be a Parkinson's Law in operation, so that the Headquarters of organisations for the disabled, which one might have expected to find slim and lithe, are crammed with flunkeys filling up forms to paper over the gaffes and cracks in the edifice made by an elite corps of seniors.

I suppose it is a sign of the times. The Royal Commonwealth Society for the Blind and its counterpart, the American Foundation for the Blind, were two of the few organisations which seemed to get it right. These organisations with a worldwide coverage operated with literally a handful of home based people – the rest of the staff were put into the front line overseas.

The sophisticated no doubt will laugh but in those days we saw ourselves more as brothers and sisters working together to establish services in difficult and cynical countries. I suspect we had something in those days which was rather precious, the warmth of a service that was personal and which really cared. In Britain and maybe in other developed countries, this simplistic approach may now be missing. It has often been long lost in a tide of self-generated bureaucracy, but recently I caught a glimpse of a caring society in my own western Ireland. Long may it last. Learning to live with others then was the theme of our training in Africa; a training which was socially orientated and the academic side gently restrained to the basic 'three r's' which for the blind, were difficult enough but attainable. We even managed to put over the hard lesson that the blind can sometimes give, in various forms such as music and service to others, as well as receive. It was a hard lesson for one or two of our professional beggars, but one which they accepted when they realised the type of giving which could soon be within their grasp.

A few years ago I revisited Bwana Mkubwa. The changes since my time had been imaginative and worthwhile. The Principal – Mr Mubita – an old friend who came from Balovale, asked me to recall some of my impressions of those distant days. (Mr Mubita had been a staff founder member.) He had posed an interesting question. After a moment's thought I selected three Chibemba words which indicated the extremes of life we experienced in those exciting times. Firstly, there was *banyama* signifying the difficult stage of building up the establishment. During the first few months of my stay the rumour had gone the rounds that the *Bwana* was a *banyama* man. This is a dreaded person who at night is capable of changing into another form and feeds on the local population! Fortunately this rumour soon died a natural death but it denoted the more depressing side of developments and did not make life easy. But there were happier times to remember – the shouts from the blind lads of, "*Ni Kuno, Ni Kuno*" (I'm here, I'm here), when they were playing a simple type of football with a bell inserted in the ball. The pitch was a small one and the game and rules easy enough. Accurate listening was the secret of success and the only words the players were allowed to shout to break the silence were "*Ni Kuno*". The fact that blind Africans were now playing games, going for long distant jogs and climbing ropes and trees, heralded the new approach we had all been waiting for. The echoes of "*Ni Kuno*" from the playing field indicated that we had crossed another bridge on the road to normality.

A third phrase which gave the tone of our training centre was "*Waiseni mukwai*," (Welcome friend). It was the job of the blind youngsters to show visitors, the Chiefs, their councillors and villagers around the centre. They always started this duty with words of welcome which seemed to impress those who had made up their minds that it would be quite impossible to teach the blind anything worthwhile. Visitors, and there were many, were shown the huge complex by a blind boy or girl who welcomed them as a member of the family with the word *Waiseni*. Once they had done the rounds, our visitors would sit under the shade of a tree and watch the daily routine unfold or visit the classrooms and listen to youngsters reading and writing Braille in the local language. Those who had made a long journey would sometimes stay the night. At the end of the visit with true tribal courtesy we would all shake hands, the visitors by tradition would 'clap hands' three times and express their thanks with *Twatotala Mukwai*, (Thank you my friend) – perhaps it is all magic – who can tell?

Those were great days moving from the difficult ones of the *banyama* stories to the cheerful ones of "*Ni Kuno*" and the community linkage of "*Waiseni*". To our African staff and to myself those were days of moving into the unknown world of the African blind. "Days", as Makasa, the Headmaster said, "of fulfilment."

Chapter Seven

"If such a fearless woman as Elizabeth I took precautions against being bewitched, one should not be surprised that the Bantu of northern Rhodesia fear witches," wrote John Munday, in 1953, a missionary who for very many years worked with the Lala tribe. He maintained that, "there is a fear of witchcraft all around us in Africa." Munday made a close study of the subject, certainly not with the idea of eliciting sensational or confidential information but rather of trying to understand the fear it sometimes injects into African society. Many of his findings with the Lala were relevant to the tribes I had contact with, especially those who hailed from the north-east of the country.

Most of the people who came out to central Africa after the last war were entirely ignorant about African life. I was one of them. Those of us who were designated to work in some of the remoter regions were usually taught the local language by an African, but the finer points of local life such as customs, traditions and attitudes were somehow overlooked or at least covered, of necessity perhaps, in a superficial form. I saw some of the strange things going on in the Luapula, the *muti*, medicine, handed out to people with sore eyes and some of the incantations which went along with some forms of healing, the folklore which centred around the various forms of disability and its relationship to a previous life. All this came into more direct focus when I took over the building up of the Bwana Mkubwa settlement. It was particularly accentuated because here were men, women and children from a dozen different tribes, often speaking different languages and dialects. The age range was equally varied and food and habits were also diverse. It was in one sense an interesting melting pot of humanity dominated unfortunately by the fear of each other. Tribal attitudes and thinking gently simmered under the surface and quite suddenly would explode with accusations, usually unfounded, of petty theft or utilising 'charms' or 'spells' to protect one against one's enemies. 'An alien's' spell had to be neutralised by one's own tribal *mganga* or witchdoctor. Strangely enough it was not as complicated as it may sound for after a month or two things settled into a routine and with work and training to take their minds off many of the native's latent fears, we all settled down into a fairly useful and pleasant daily life.

My mission friends were great respecters of native law and tradition though it was always a constant obstacle in the development of their own work. They taught me the wisdom of being tolerant and understanding. The old timers, Arthur Davison and his brother Tom, (who came eventually to live near us) had not spent fifty years in Africa and more for nothing. They were a mine of information so were other pioneers like *Chirapula* Stevenson and *Chiana* Harrington. It took some time for it to dawn on me that African folklore – some call it magic, and others 'witchcraft'– was real enough, indeed a perpetual part of local existence. My reservations about these activities soon disappeared as I realised that this was an integral part of African life and had to be lived with and largely accepted. Much of this 'magic', which came our way, was harmless enough and often aimed at being helpful. It was used for example to influence crops, to protect the storage of grain, to influence the examination board for a school-boy sitting an examination, or to help a friend find a job. If you were going on a journey you could make sure it was going to be a safe one if you put three stones in the fork of a tree at the commencement of the trip. If your hands and feet tingled, it meant you would be going on a journey and that there would be a good meal for you when you arrived at your destination! An African would use a charm to protect himself from robbers or to prevent a hang over! All this kind of magic was 'soft' and often quite innocuous.

The characters to watch were the *mgangas*, the full-blooded witchdoctors who differed fundamentally from the native herbalist. Both dealt in charms and spells to some extent, but the herbalist was an intriguing individual, frequently a benevolent old man or woman who could probably cure some things from his inherited knowledge of bush folklore but, unintentionally as well, there could be quite a grave risk in entrusting oneself to his care. The *mganga* is still a much feared individual who deals in charms and 'hard' fetishes, his hut is often surrounded by animal skulls, pieces of mouldy fur and claws of differing shapes and sizes. He trades on fear. The *mganga* is a great psychologist whose techniques centre on the unknown, and an ability to exploit the slightest weakness that an individual may reveal. I have known him to inspire fear in some of the bravest and best educated of Africans. To me, the witchdoctors always seemed a law unto themselves yet, traditionally, in many tribes, witchcraft was a capital offence which only seems to have ever been invoked against feeble old men and women who may in earlier years have been in the 'business'.

Some *mganga* make extraordinary claims and instruct those who consult them to do some equally unusual things. My contacts in the Luapula and Mweru districts were no exception. The net result was that the blind who came from that area were susceptible to their influences. Other residents of the school coming from tribal areas to the west and centre of the country brought along their own brand of witchcraft as well. Some *mgangas* claimed that they could make themselves invisible, others that they could enter at will into the body of an animal (usually a wild one). Whilst some of the things they traded in were simple enough, a root of a certain tree tied to one's leg protected you against crocodiles, and similarly another type of root was a protection against snakes, there were other activities which were not so innocuous.

Blood was seen as the emblem of life and subsequently it has always featured in some of their rites, usually the blood of a cock or goat, but sometimes it appears that this was not always sufficient. The leopard and lion cults in West and East Africa respectively, followed some revolting practices which involved murder, but it seems that in central Africa the *mganga* may order the person he is dealing with to consume the flesh of a recently deceased relative. At about the time I was beginning my work at Bwana Mkubwa there was a case before the magistrates court where a couple were found guilty of consuming human flesh. The case was reported in the local press almost as a 'filler' item. The final lines read, "The prosecutor said that the pair disinterred the body of a recently buried child. They cut off the feet and the head; the brains and flesh of the feet were then put into a pot and cooked and they ate them." The man got eighteen months and the woman nine months. The incident was linked with the advice of a *mganga*. Whether it may or may not have been a widespread activity, it is difficult to say. The fact is that it did happen from time to time. I came across evidence of this in Eastern Nigeria, Malawi and the Luapula.

Arthur Davison considered that an African, including a highly educated African, may in some cases go to extreme lengths to placate the *mganga*. "Didn't we see it in the Mau Mau uprising?" he asked. "The Kikuyu tribe, the most intelligent and educated of the lot, being tied to the most bestial of tribal oaths?" But Arthur Davison could see things from another standpoint as well. His words still echo in my ears. "Most Europeans", he said, "do not fear native medicine but very few Africans are prepared to ignore the words of a strong witchdoctor. My advice to you as a newcomer", he continued, "is to listen, to observe, and to respect a way of life which neither you nor I can ever pretend to understand. Maybe," he went on, "the more we see of it the more confused we become." I was sitting with him outside his thatched house overlooking a green carpet of jungle. Davison was a sick man and only had a year or two longer to live, but he loved Africa and loathed people who derided Africans and their way of life. He was scrupulous in seeing both sides of the 'white' versus 'black' cultural divide. "It does not augur well for a white man who is liable to blame a misfortune on the fact that it happened on Friday the thirteenth, or who touches a piece of wood as an 'insurance' against mishap, to laugh at the natives who, after all blend with nature and an animistic way of life with more graciousness than most Europeans could ever display."

Davison was now on his favourite theme. "After all," he said with some emphasis to underline the point he was going to make, "not far from where I lived when a boy, across the Scottish border at Kirkcudbright my distant ancestors were supposed to have burnt an old woman in a tar barrel because she was said to be a witch. Who are we to throw stones?" he asked. The strict stern men I met from time to time, the people who opened up the country were sticklers for fair play! On looking back one could not fail but to be impressed by their courage, by the hardships and utter loneliness they endured month after month and year after year, and the constant dangers from man, beast, and disease. They were an exceptional breed. I found their stories factual and modest for here was history which they alone had made and moulded. There was no brash media coverage, for the world did not know where they were, what they were doing, or why. Those who lost their lives were hardly missed let alone mourned. It was a fantastic era. Here within the space of less than sixty years a mere half-dozen loners, perhaps a few more, with their loyal score or so of native askaris smashed the slave trade, banished tribal warfare and established an administration which lay the foundation of services in the medical, social, and educational field which are still largely in place today.

The men who achieved the 'impossible' were drawn from diverse backgrounds, employees of the Chartered Company[1], missionaries, hunters, adventurers and traders. They all had one thing in common, courage and the temperament to overcome adversity and to go it alone.

But it was all a terrible price. As one treks up and down the wilderness of present day Zambia there are the lonely mounds marked by a heap of stones. Near Mwansaswe's village lies Captain Everett killed in 1911 by a lion. In Luputa's village up on Lake Mweru lies Mr Kelsey who died in the same year who, as the man who buried him remarked, "was rather foolish, he followed leopard into long grass." Between Mkushi and Serenje lies the lonely grave of Dr Greathead, a victim of sleeping sickness in the early 1900s and a little further on near Mutunoni's village D.A.C. Russell like so many other pioneers lies buried, a victim of blackwater fever. The death roll between 1896 and 1911 must run into many thousands.

But those who survived, what tales they had to tell! In faraway Sefula in Barotseland I met one of the daughters of the famous François Coillard of the Paris mission. (He came into the country in 1878 and set up his mission at Sefula in 1885.) His daughter had a fund of stories one of which referred to the famous 'crocodile doctor'. The story goes that when this witch doctor led people or cattle across the Zambezi fords they were never attacked by crocodiles if they paid him a small fee or a gift of a chicken. Those who failed to do this were 'at risk' and records confirmed that those who neglected the old man were often taken by crocodiles. Folklore had it that this particular *mganga* could sometimes be seen at night crossing the river on the back of a huge crocodile!

Another great survivor was Monsignor du Pont of the White Fathers who came with Father van Oost to the Lake Mweru region in 1896. The powerful Bemba Chief, Chitimukulu, threatened to slaughter them both if they so much as dared set foot in his kingdom. Unperturbed they built a mission station in the form of a fort at

---

[1]The African Chartered Company was superseded when, in 1911, the British Government assumed responsibility for the area.

Kayambi which is still standing on land just outside the Chief's jurisdiction. A few years later the brave Monsignor turned up at Chitimukulu's court unheralded and gave the old Chief such a shock that he forgot about his terrible threats and eventually made the White Father an honorary Chief! There were the brave handful like Bobo Young engaged in the war against slavery who with just fifteen askaris was besieged by hordes of Bemba tribesmen and Arabs for six days at Chiwala's village near Bwana Mkubwa. This brave little party held their own until they were rescued by another loner, a young Scot named McKinnon. The men who were busy making history in an unexplored land were usually not the type who took easily to the pen. The one poet the era produced was an Australian, E.C. Mills, a renowned pioneer and hunter. He says it from the heart.

> I'll tell you of far flung *dambos*
> Where the countless game herds roam
> I'll tell you of broad deep rivers
> Where the Saurians have their home
> Of age old paths through the jungle
> Made by the mighty beasts
> I'll tell you of war drums beating
> Stories of cannibal feasts.

*

We had only been at Bwana Mkubwa for about three months when the first case of witchcraft blew up out of what I had supposed were peaceful and tranquil waters. Everything about the case seemed to have been arranged in a way to produce the most dramatic of effects. Both the hour and setting could have been a little unnerving if Arthur Davison and his brother Tom had not given me a review of their own experiences and the way in which they handled situations.

It was the case of a quiet and quite well educated young teacher, one Robinson Mwa, (Africans in those days often used two names, one European and one African to confuse the evil spirits). Sunday had been a restless day and as I did my final round of the settlement, I had sensed that there was an air of tension about the place. Those who were usually the first to chat were silent. Normally there would be a few smiles and jokes, but not today. The weekend drinking and drumming in the nearby village had come to an abrupt halt earlier than usual. Cathleen and I went to bed early that evening. About midnight I was awakened. (Our own situation as far as home comfort was concerned, was not conducive to heavy sleep. Our furniture had not arrived and packing cases served as makeshift tables and beds.) There were stirrings in the African staff houses half a mile away across the *dambo*. I drew aside the mosquito net and went over to the window. At first I did not see anything but heard the restless murmurings from afar drifting across the bush. Cathleen joined me just in time to see a long winding torchlight procession breaking out from along the bush path and coming up the hill towards the house. There was now a beating of drums and cymbals. It was a large delegation heading directly towards 'us'. By the time we had slipped on some clothes the long procession, with flares and torchlights made of burning rush was forming up outside the front door of the house in a large semi-circle. It was a large gathering for this neighbourhood, staff, villagers and a sprinkling of school children, but no women.

The low chanting and intermittent sounds of sobs, wailing, sighs and groans suddenly stopped. I opened the door. We were carrying pressure lamps which lit up most of the scene; faces were beaded with sweat; bodies only partially clad and fear was written over many faces.

The sudden silence was prolonged. I waited for an explanation. It was not forthcoming, not at least until I asked for it. *"Chinshi muleyafywa mukwai?"* (What do you want my friends, what is the trouble?), I asked. I was answered by a tall lean teacher – not a Bemba man, who choked out the words,

"It is Mwa".

"What about Mwa, has he *mulandu*, trouble?" I asked, as I surveyed the host of petrified faces and tried to identify Mwa, one who was normally a cheerful individual. He came from Mansa in the Luapula region.

"He is bewitched," the crowd groaned almost in unison. "He is dying," they moaned. This was, I realised, with my inexperience, a difficult situation. If one made light of their fears the whole establishment would desert the place immediately. It had nearly happened once before over a cook who was alleged to have introduced bad *muti* into the food.

"Where is Mwa?" I asked, "Let me see him and I will tell you if we can help." There was a stirring in the crowd and Mwa, normally a healthy individual, was dragged from out of the midst of the crowd supported by two fellow tribesmen. He looked dreadful, his normally shining healthy black skin had almost turned, it seemed in the half light, to a dull lifeless yellow. His face was drawn and his eyes red and bleary. He was shaking profusely.

"I am dying *Bwana*," he gasped. "They have bewitched me."

At this stage Cathleen stepped in,

"The man is ill, maybe it's malaria. We'll soon see," she said, looking at the sagging Mwa. This did nothing to reassure the crowd. The wailing started again and Mwa responded with a frightful groan and fell to the ground. Murmurings – loud murmurings were going the rounds and mutterings about 'magic', the work of a *mganga* and other facets linked with tribal matters. Meanwhile Cathleen established a curious state of affairs. Mwa certainly had a raging temperature of around one hundred and three, but his heart beat was ticking over at a leisurely eighty. She checked these factors three times. Meanwhile a series of what appeared to be incantations had now commenced amongst the crowd inspired, I was told later, by the idea of trying to identify the person who had bewitched Mwa. When this chorus started I decided that things had gone far enough. Mwa showed all the signs of dying, but in a moment of more lucid communication had asked me to inform his parents in Mansa that "an evil spirit had been set upon him and was the cause of his death". "Nonsense," I said in exasperation. "You are going to hospital this minute and they will soon sort out your illness."

"No, no *Bwana*," he screamed, "the white man's medicine is no good for the trouble which has befallen me." The gloom of death settled on him again. I realised that if he died his death would be linked with the training centre and the 'bad spells', which apparently were around, would be blamed.

Things looked quite ominous. I insisted that Mwa would have to go to the hospital in Ndola, otherwise his presence would upset the whole establishment. Mwa was hauled into the back of the Bedford lorry and placed on a mattress and I made myself ready with the usual gear for a night drive through the bush. I was on the point of leaving when I noticed a complete stranger had climbed into the lorry with

Mwa and had driven the companions who were escorting the sick man away.

"What are you doing?" I asked sharply.

In the light of my torch I saw a wizened unshaven character, thin, certainly an untrustworthy individual, I thought to myself, but I may have been wrong.

"Stop *Bwana*," he said, "I know this man, he is from near my village at Mansa. I can cure him." Instead of lying down in the semi-coma he appeared to have drifted into, Mwa stood up in the lorry. "*Bwana*," he said, "this man has the means of cleansing me, I do not need white medicine, it must be from an African." Mwa now seemed to be quite normal. There was no sign of fear, no temperature, no sweat and a normal healthy bearing – his skin had taken on its normal sheen.

Mwa still went to hospital as a precaution. He refused to be examined and walked back the fifteen miles to the training centre after discharging himself.

"What was really wrong with you?" I asked the much happier Mwa. "Why were you playing tricks?"

"Oh, *Bwana*," said Mwa, "there were no tricks being played, a white man could not possibly know. It was a terrible experience. I was bewitched. I know I was," he said emphatically. "The man who arranged for me to die was one whose daughter I may have treated badly. The man you spoke to on the lorry before we went to Ndola was one called Bua-Bua. I had never met him before," said Mwa, "but he is a *mganga* and he agreed to release me from the spell so that I can go home to my village and be made clean. He was the one paid to bewitch me, I am sure." I was sure as well, for Bua-Bua had disappeared!

It was a long and complicated story. Mwa went back to his home two hundred miles away where he stayed for three weeks, submitting to a whole series of rituals which as he said to me, "rendered his whole body better." The man called Bua-Bua who looked something of a scoundrel actually came from Katanga, but the results of the consultation and advice he gave Mwa seemed, I suppose remarkable. The symptoms of the raging fever appear to have subsided within three or four minutes, with a few well chosen mumblings and incantations whispered into the sick man's ear. Was there something more to it? No white person would ever know for sure what really went on during those vital moments. Mwa's companions left the *mganga* stranger with him without a query or word of protest. I suppose that deeply engrained tribal beliefs and rituals were starting to unfold.

I discussed all this a few days later with the mission folk and with old *Yangwe* Davison. *Yangwe*, a man of few words, just snorted, "Let nothing you find in Africa, young man, ever surprise you. The day it does, you should pack up and go home." The mission hypothesis was that the *mganga* Bua-Bua had been hired by an irate family to seek out Mwa. Once he had found him he arranged for his food to be doped with poison, (there was evidence to suggest this may have happened). Prior to the journey on the lorry to Ndola the *mganga* arranged to see Mwa on his own for a few brief moments. He probably gave him some form of antidote. Brother Lucien who knew a few things about this side of African life was convinced that this might be the answer.

The Mwa incident was a salutary lesson which underlined the importance of understanding and tolerance. We were surrounded by a multi-tribal society and it was inevitable that strange incidents like this one should surface from time to time. This indeed was the nature of the comparatively large establishment and my job, which apart from supervising training and starting up-country schools, was essentially to hold together diverse strata of a sometimes primitive society.

It was a strange task. I could not establish any degree of sympathy with the scoundrels who called themselves *mgangas* but I could with people like old Kachasu who, apart from being our night watchman, was a 'herbalist' of some local renown. He showed me the mangwe leaves which in solution are good for conjunctivitis and are also used sometimes for stomach-ache. Certain root infusions he offered me are an excellent sex stimulant! The snake bean which grew near us and which he used yields fish poison, yet humans can still consume the fish it kills without ill effect. I often watched him under the setting sun treating the aches and pains of his patients with varying degrees of success. He was one of the rare ones, who was prepared to share his knowledge with a white man. I now wish I had been more attentive. I found that the 'herbalists' from Bembaland were reluctant to talk about their work. I could understand why – they are supposed to be experts in the use of poisons.

I was fortunate. There were a handful of Lala tribesmen at Bwana Mkubwa and, if one walked through the bush country with them, they were able to tell you the name of just about every herb or plant that could heal, poison, ward off evil or danger, be used for food or for making mats and string. They pointed out the reeds useful for making *amatanda*, (the mats used for sleeping on in their huts), the bark called uluslishi with which strong rope can be made and the trees used for making canoes. It seemed that after centuries of bush wanderings they had been handed down a store house of information about the countryside. The Lala treated the plants as almost personal friends and often 'talked' to them. It opened up a world which had some sort of remedy for most complaints. For cuts and open wounds the buds of the leswama bush were used, for asthma some used datura leaves, but others the leaves of a parasite plant: boswa wa scrologa; for abortions the people in the south along the Botswana border used an infusion from the matlakanye leaves.

Around Bwana Mkubwa and certainly in the north-east of the country, herbs are found which if rubbed into the breasts of an elderly woman will stimulate the mammary glands and cause milk to flow. Cathleen and I heard about this and never took it seriously until we saw this actually happen in some of the villages near where we lived. Probably the women looked much older than they really were (they seemed beyond childbearing age), but on at least one occasion an elderly grandmother raised a week-old orphan using this method. Up in distant Kasama one of the White Fathers used a native cure for snake bite. He showed it to me. It appeared to be juice from a certain type of leaf (I forget the name) applied with a small pumice stone. The juice and specks of stone were supposed to react together to produce something which neutralised the venom. The Nyamwezi herbalists in Tanzania, have a well-known snake bite remedy, but are reluctant to tell strangers its secrets. This reminds me of the bushmen in the Kalahari desert who have not yet revealed the antidote they possess for the deadly arrow poison they use. (It is taken from the Acoranthea venenata shrub).

An authority on native herbal remedies is Dr G.H.J. Teichle. He was well over sixty when I met him. After completing his medical training at well known universities in Germany, including Tuebingen, Rostock and Hamburg, he had spent all his working life in central and East Africa, except for a brief spell at the Tropical Diseases Hospital in London. He has worked mainly in mission hospitals. (This was interrupted for a period during the war, when he was interned in Rhodesia, but he has always had close associations with rural Africa.) In the Seventies I stayed with him frequently at the Mochudi mission when I visited Botswana.

From the little I had seen in the Luapula and at Bwana Mkubwa it appeared that native herbalists could literally either kill or cure their patients, but for all that, native medicine may, in the right hands, have something to offer and should not be entirely discounted. Dr Teichler, who agreed with this view had, through much of his professional life, been obliged to work without the help of the modern synthetic drugs. An experienced old herbalist introduced him to a wealth of medicines extracted from the African bush. Teichler told me that the only time he had ever had tape worm was when he was interned near Salisbury (now Harare) and the normal drugs were not available. He managed to secure the bark of the monoga tree and after crushing it and making up a fairly strong solution drank the liquid. He was well satisfied with the results and said that there were no side effects, fasting was unnecessary and the action of the herb was quite rapid.

I suspect that this set him on the track of studying bush remedies. His conclusions are interesting. Whilst some of the material from the bush can be positively dangerous to life and to sensitive organs like the kidneys, eyes and ears, there are some plants which provide satisfactory cures for a wide range of ailments provided that they are administered by skilled professionals. His one fear is that with the growth of western medicine some of the old and proven bush remedies may be lost to posterity. Some, like a powerful poison found in the jungle, buphane, (used for the tips of arrows) contains a deadly convulsant substance but Dr Teichler concedes that like heart medicines and other alkaloids, it might, if examined scientifically, have its uses in small doses. He found another poison named cant haridin which is often used in the Zambian bush when a woman has been made pregnant by a man who is not her husband. According to Teichler it could kill the foetus but its side effects could often be appalling. In small doses patients may survive. He told me of a case where a person was brought to him and was obviously dying after being given an overdose of the substance by a 'herbalist'. He decided to go and interview the 'herbalist' who had given the medicine to the woman. The 'herbalist' was indignant and declared that it was perfectly safe. He said he would prove his point by drinking a large quantity of it himself. He did this and died within a few minutes in the presence of Teichler, who was powerless to help him.

Dr Teichler, realising that I was particularly interested in the connections between blindness and native treatment, said that he had come across two local remedies which were directly connected with ruining the eyes: the juice of the Morekuru plant, when poured into the eyes, would almost certainly destroy sight. A 'cure', equally appalling, used by some herbalists was euphorbia. He has found that discharging and swollen eyes would sometimes be treated by boiling the roots of the moloti tree (a type of teak), the patient would then drink part of the infusion and the remainder would be bandaged over his eyes, preferably with a piece of thin ostrich feather. (The ostrich is introduced into the treatment because it can see great distances.) Dr Teichler's 'herbalist' contact claimed that he used this treatment with some success but Teichler, whilst acknowledging that the moloti tree has useful properties, has reservations about applying the infusion. But the 'herbalists' can and do treat a wide variety of illnesses which range from malaria to gynaecological conditions. If a child is lying in a wrong position in the womb, the roots of the mfetola tree are boiled and given to the woman, and for retained placenta monolola roots are used in an infusion. Dr Teichler comments that sometimes donkey manure is burnt and the patient squats over it but this he considered a highly dangerous method especially because of the danger of infection, particularly from tetanus.

So the 'herbalist' in the African bush has, for better or for worse, a wide range of natural resources to draw on, if they fail or cause complications, the patient as a last resort goes to a hospital and may die, but the herbalist is not connected in the native mind with the cause of death. Some of the medical fraternity who have spent most of their life working in bush hospitals, whilst keenly aware of the dangers and lack of hygiene associated with some unorthodox treatments accept that the African herbalist has still inherited some valuable secret herbal cures and that there is a case for much more in-depth research.

Another aspect of African life I came across is the part reincarnation plays in native thinking. At the Bwana Mkubwa settlement this appeared to be a common thread which was accepted in its various forms by the different tribal members. Even the new high-flying jet Comet, which was on its proving trials in Africa, when it passed over the Mbereshi – Luapula area, was ascribed as the spirit of a long dead Chief looking down on his people! But there were real fears which caused serious concerns amongst rural people. The crocodile lurking in the swamp was supposed to be the reincarnation of a human being who still had to avenge a number of grievances. In some parts of Africa there were (and almost certainly still are) secret societies such as crocodile cults leopard societies and hyaena and lion cults. Their purposes vary but the common theme in the region where I worked both in central and East Africa was that a dead Chief or sometimes a *mganga* could either enter into the body of a creature or make himself invisible. The lions which still wandered through our training settlement in the early days were, so my African friends told me, really some powerful persons in disguise, probably a Chief. The lion cult seemed to dominate life in the region where I was working mainly because lions historically had a very bad reputation as man-eaters. They never gave any trouble at Bwana Mkubwa – as civilisation encroached on their domains they retreated, but they were something to be reckoned with in remoter regions, hence the understandable fear with which they infected small communities. Sometimes lions did attack humans without killing them. When I was near Chikwawa, a hot and humid place, a lion continuously attacked isolated villages, ignoring the cattle and going for the human beings who were then dragged out into the bush and left. It never killed anyone and was eventually shot by a Game Warden who had been hunting it for weeks. (It was found consuming a wild pig.) Apart from the curious behaviour of the lion, the natives were reported in the old *Nyasaland Times* as having their own explanation for the reasons which prompted him to ignore so many appetising meals! The article stated:

> A lion believed by villagers in the Chikwawa district to contain the spirit of a dead man was shot recently. It had attacked a number of people and dragged them into the bush without killing them. Over a period of two weeks it attacked a large number of people. One attack was made on a woman outside Chikwawa Boma. It caught her by the shoulder and

she grabbed the post of the Boma verandah. But the lion kept on tugging and broke off the post before being driven away. The fact that it has neither killed cattle nor one of the human beings it attacked, has led to the widespread belief that a human spirit had entered the animal and it was taking a 'mild' vengeance on those who had not been kind to it.

This lion was a lone male, a really big fellow and I remember that it was left on show at the Chikwawa Boma for the rest of the day. The Game warden who eventually shot it had been hunting in the wrong area, but he had heard the distant drums giving out the wild animal raid warning and he moved into the area and found it.

Unfortunately most of the lion population in the north of Zambia were not as gentle as the monster at Chikwawa. The lions in the Bemba and Lunda lands were the subject of many a fearsome story told around our monthly campfire when the whole of the training centre and village came together. Some of the stories may have been true, but others had all the hallmarks of legend and folklore. The origins of some stories probably came from the long string of casualties which had been suffered over the years, but amusing things happened as well. I recall the time when one of the larger villages had arranged an open-air tribal dance to celebrate the Queen's birthday. "Lions," stated the local newspaper reporting the incident, "'knocked the rock' when they broke up a village dance last week with their roaring. When the roaring lions started prowling around the open-air 'ballroom' the dance broke up abruptly and the dancers fled for the safety of their homes. Added to the noise were the roars of the hippopotamus from the nearby river."

In the early days the man-eaters of the Luapula and Mweru areas were, according to some hunters, more to be feared than the lions around Tsavo in when a hundred and twenty workers were killed during the construction of the Mombasa-Nairobi railway. The Davison brothers, who were certainly not given to exaggeration, could tell a few stories about life around the region which compared with some of the Tsavo slaughter. Mporokosa and the district down to Mununga's village always had a bad reputation and still did in my time. Arthur recalled a lion which roamed around the district between Kafulwe and Chiengi. The natives called him *Chiengi Chali*. This one animal is reputed to have killed between eighty to ninety people, including two European officials who were trying to shoot it. There is the story that one Government officer climbed a tree to get out of *Chiengi Chali's* way but the lion, a male in its prime gave one mighty leap and knocked the wretched man off the branch he was holding on to. He was badly mauled but rescued, only to die a week later from blood poisoning.

Tom Davison, tall, lean and laconic, was now in his Seventies and often he would recall one of the most frightening experiences which came his way in the lion country around Mporokosa. He was out prospecting and had with him eleven porters. He had, incidentally, just discovered a rich vein of copper, it was not developed, he said, because of communication problems. For the last few nights lions had been worrying his camp. The camp was due to move on the next day at an early hour so the Africans had turned in for the night. They made up a good fire and slept around it in the form of what Tom described as a tight semi-circle. Tom was busy writing up some notes on the day's work before he joined them. "I noticed," he said, "that the fire had died down, but for some reason I did not bother to throw on more timber. I was tired and joined the sleeping natives around the fire." He continued, "It must have been about 3 a.m. I was dozing when there was a piercing scream and I sat up to see the outline of a huge lion dragging away one of the natives from the very centre of the semi-circle. I believe the lion had the poor chap's head in its mouth. The camp arose with one accord. There was pandemonium. Some dived off into the bush, a few found their spears and I grabbed for my gun. It was too late, the damage had been done and," he continued, "the next morning we traced the bloody trail to a hillock less than half a mile from where we were in camp and found a few remains of the unfortunate fellow."

The lions in the Fifties were still creatures not to be treated lightly. Up at Chipata where there is a school for blind children with which our training centre had connections, a totally blind ten year old boy was taken in the middle of the afternoon from the school play area. Certainly the school was deep in the bush but on the whole daylight attacks were uncommon. The only trace of the child was an arm found in the school garden.

Chiana Harrington often told the quite true story of how he was in camp in the Luapula area, somewhere I believe near Mansa. He had

had a hard day. After drinking a long sundowner and relaxing, he shouted to his camp cook to bring his meal. The cook acknowledged his call with an, *"Endita,"* but nothing happened. After twenty minutes he shouted again but there was no reply. He got up and went to investigate suspecting that the cook was having difficulties with the camp fire as the wood was wet after a shower of rain. The cook's *insaka*, or shelter, was about twenty yards from where Harrington had been relaxing.

"Imagine my horror", said *Chiana*, a veteran from the 1898 exploration days, "when I found the soup, the tray with my meal on, scattered around with other utensils. There was a piece of shirt soaked in blood and spoor was leading off from the bush path into the jungle." The cook had obviously been 'snatched' as the Africans described it. "After that," said *Chiana*, "I needed something stronger than a long sundowner to strengthen my nerves for the night. Apparently, even though the lion was tracked for some distance, hardly a trace of the cook was ever found."

For years, isolated Chiengi Boma, the tragic place where so many young Government officials seemed to end their lives, had a bad reputation for man-eaters – one lion was said to have killed sixty villagers over a two-year period. Local people were never keen to go lion hunting, not only because it was a hazardous task but because of the old fears of reincarnation and that they might inadvertently kill an old Chief in the guise of a lion! This story must have started years ago when an old Chief of Mununga village lay dying. He told his wailing councillors that if he died at night his spirit would enter the body of a crocodile: if he expired in the half-light of the dawn or dusk, they would hear him calling to them in the form of a hyaena, and if it was during full daylight they would recognise him as the roaring lion which encircled their villages. The result of this legend was that for years (until the Government Game wardens came on the scene), no lions were ever killed in the area. I am told that the old log book in the Mporokosa Boma (which is now lost), records the deaths of victims who died from man-eaters in the Thirties and the casualty rate is an indication of a serious local situation which came about. In the mid-Forties between Mporokosa and Kasama there was a lion which was never caught, who had an odd way of leaving behind his identity. It bit off the legs and arms of its victims and left them behind!

In the Fifties things had quietened down. Cyclists along bush tracks were still attacked, but usually managed to climb up a tree and wait, either for the lion to go away or for somebody on the same path on seeing their predicament, to give the alarm. One of my teachers in the Luapula spent a harrowing twenty-four hours looking down at a bad tempered lion who first destroyed the poor man's bicycle – it was mangled and in pieces – and then patiently sat gazing up at the tree and, apparently for a diversion (or in anticipation of things to come), occasionally started to claw the tree, a method of sharpening its claws. This chap was eventually rescued almost in a state of collapse after a traveller had spotted his plight from afar and then rushed to Kawambwa Boma to fetch a rescue party. A District Officer and three of his brave Boma messengers arrived, the messengers decked in their full colourful red and blue uniform, "Bright enough," the DO remarked to me drily, "to persuade the lion to move on". The twisted remnants of the poor fellow's bicycle were put in the back of the Land Rover and he was taken on to his village where he was greeted with considerable rejoicing.

"It must," said one sage, "have been the spirit of Chief Chama in the lion. He was known in days gone by for his dislike of the white man's machines."

These days you can wander through the bush country without ever seeing a sign of wild life. In the Fifties and Sixties life was still interesting. The Africa I knew at that time was full of wonder, but not as wonderful as the Africa *Chiana* Harrington and my friends the Davison brothers and *Chirapula* Stevenson knew and came to love.

Those were the times when one could feel that one was almost within hailing distance of the greats. I met an old, old African on the banks of the Kalunguishi who, as a small boy, could clearly recall Livingstone in camp, waiting for Chief Kasembe's permission to pass through his country. There was another old man, one Bereston Gwaza, who lived near Kitwe and was approaching one hundred. He remembered, as a very small boy, his father who, when he was living in Nyasaland[2], went to see Livingstone at a village near Zomba.

He said to me,

"We lived at Limbe, *Bwana*, there were no cars, no European houses and no electricity and only two white people." David

---

[2]Renamed Malawi

Livingstone was at that time establishing a mission station near Zomba. This would be between 1859 and 1863 so Gwaza would be about five or six when his father went to see the great missionary.

The opening up of this massive area of Africa can be traced back to 1798 when a Portuguese expedition, consisting of about twenty-two people under Dr Jose Lacerda, was attempting to cross Africa. They endured tremendous difficulties and problems. Lacerda reached as far as Kasembe's where he had a fairly hostile reception. He died there a few days later on 18 October 1798. Between 1850 and 1870 it seems that about thirty Europeans including, of course, Livingstone, penetrated this area. Mrs Reader, the wife of a trader-hunter is recorded as being the first white woman to come to this part of Africa. (This was in 1862 and it must have been a journey to remember.)

From 1870 to 1902 there was a steady trickle of prospectors, hunters, and missionaries coming in from the south. The policy was generally to avoid bringing women and children into this part of the world, but the Protestant missions did not always follow this rule, hence within this brief period the child mortality rate was between thirty-three and thirty-six per cent. (The adult rate was in the region of ten per cent per annum.) The children were largely cut down by malaria, yellow fever and the various types of virulent dysenteries. The men working in outlandish places suffered grievously and were eliminated by anything from sleeping sickness to black water fever. The bush graves I sometimes came across were a timely reminder of all this – a lone DO who died whilst on tour and was buried by askari with a heap of rocks over his body to avoid disinterment by animals.

In the pre-1902 days small groups of Europeans were sent out by the British South African Charter Company to establish trading posts. These were really small forts. Even the missions had to fortify themselves The mission run by the White Fathers between Mbala and the Mporokosa was constructed along fortress lines. I spent the night in the mid-Seventies at this mission station and found time to chat with one of the white Fathers who had established the outpost. He was approaching ninety-five, a Frenchman, who told me that he had been back to his native country only once. The dangers in those early days, he said, came from the slave traders (the mission was on the slave routes) and from time to time was in fact attacked. From my bedroom, there was a small slit through which one could obtain an excellent view of the miles of rolling bushland and sight one's rifle with a good field of fire and fair degree of protection. I had never realised that the mission people had to resort to arms for their own survival. I briefly visited Fort Monze, a pretty typical outpost of the olden days, now covered in dense undergrowth, seven miles from the new village named after it. Two hundred yards from the old fort under a huge fig tree lie, the graves of five British lads who died within two years of each other, of fever.

Those were tough days but a surprising number of people stuck them out and survived, never to give in to this wild intransigent country. Amongst them were young men who, as one old adventurer put it in delicate and diplomatic terms, left for their country's good, or in some cases were paid to stay away forever from their home country. Some were in debt, but others, the majority, were young men seeking to get out of the rut and to find adventure. Most of them found it. The Africa I was swept into still had some of these ancient adventurers scattered around. There were only a few. They lived as independently as ever in their thatched bush homes, valuing their freedom from, as one put it, 'the herd'. Now in the evening of their lives some were watching with apprehension and others with fortitude the Africa they had roamed over, fought over and got drunk over, slip away into the vacuum of historical indifference, or found themselves labelled by the holier than thou brigade as 'cheap exploiters'. Some were, but the men I met were courageous and cared for Africa and the Africans.

Bill Collier was typical of this breed. He was a prospector, who arrived in Africa at the age of eighteen, in his words, "with hardly a penny." He admitted that he was a chancer but that he was one of the fortunate ones. He arrived in the Bwana Mkubwa region where I was now living and gave the area its name. He called it after the person who had helped him most. This was a lonely District Commissioner named Jones. Jones was known by the Africans as the great master – the Bwana Mkubwa – hence the name. Collier discovered traces of copper in this unmapped territory so gave it Jones's African nickname of Bwana Mwubwa. It was in 1902 that he discovered copper in workable deposits. These were to become the great Roan Antelope mine. The story goes that he had observed natives using ground copper as a treatment for open wounds. He asked a native to show him where they obtained the powdered mineral. He was told to follow the Luansyha stream. Towards the end of the day, after a fruitless search, he shot an antelope for the evening meal. At the exact spot where it fell was a huge vein of copper!

Chiana Harrington[3], (*Chiana* means small fellow) was another young explorer we met. He had been a lowly clerk employed by a large firm of corn merchants in Market Lane near the Corn Exchange in London. He recalled that on his way to work from his home in Hertford he used to purchase a half-penny newspaper every morning. He became intrigued by the developments then being reported in Mashonaland. The British South African Company had been granted a Charter to trade and settle the area and it was now raising a pioneer force to establish a base in Mashonaland. *Chiana* went to the Company's office in St Swithins Lane, London, and obtained a place in the column which was being raised, "not", he confesses, that he knew where Mashonaland was, "nor," he added, "could anybody else tell me, except that it was somewhere in central Africa." He was a talented young man. After completing his tour of duty with the British South African Company – a tour which included the march into Mashonaland and the establishment of Fort Salisbury (named after Lord Salisbury one of the supporters of the Company). He was assigned to the Lake Nyasa area and also a district northwards towards Lake Mweru. At Karonga, on the western shores of Lake Nyasa, he had had a run in with the notorious Arab slave dealer Mlozi, when he was helping Sir Harry Johnson (Johnson was Governor of Nyasaland) put down the slave trade in the area. Harrington recalled that Mlozi was captured, tried on the spot, and hanged immediately! *Chiana* pointed out in mitigation for this rough justice that Mlozi had murdered hundreds of local people, which was, of course, true.

One of the Arab rogues who escaped at the Karonga showdown was Nasoro bin Suliman, who went by the African name of Chiesesa. Harrington alone with his twenty native askaris traced him to the banks of the Kalunguishi river. The Arab, Nasora, was a tough

[3]*Chiana* Harrington, *Chirapula* Stevenson, and *Yangwe* Davison were typical of the pioneers who as youngsters left the comparative security of a London office for, as *Chirapula* once remarked, "adventures and hazards mingled with freedom, sunshine and the open air." He recalled, "in those days we did it the hard way, we had to pay our own fare out from England to the Cape, it was £11, second class. It took five days to reach our base at Salisbury. We were then taken on to the pay roll of our employer's the Chartered Company at the rate of five shillings a day (25p) plus when out in the bush one shilling and six pence 'hard' living allowance."

customer, but Harrington's spies found out that his men were deserting him and they finally located his hideout. *Chiana* was on the way to confront the very last slaver in this part of the world when he met Nasora on a white donkey coming forth to surrender. *Chiana* recalled that it was a dramatic moment. Nasoro merely said, *"Bwana, Chiana, ni me kwisha"* – Little Master I am finished. The kernel of this story is that modern Africa had still living in its midst for many a long day, and certainly in my time, the white men like Harrington, who finally put paid to slavery in central . In my day the present and the past sometimes merged into one. The old pioneers with whom I chatted in the Fifties, spoke of the slavery they had seen – they spoke not in the language of a dry textbook but from personal involvement.

After the Nasoro business, Harrington specialised in the administration of the countryside around Lake Bangweulu and right up to Chiengi. With a handful of askari he ruled an area bigger than Wales which included three distinct tribes, the Lunda, the Ushi and the Chisinga, whilst in the swamps of Bangweulu, he said, "lived the water dwellers, the Watwa, the people who were the original inhabitants of the country, but had been driven out by other invading tribes." Harrington's observations on the area are interesting. He described the people as pleasure loving, much given to beer drinking and dances. Like Dr Teichler, Harrington had faith in some native herbalists. He commented, "They are very good in healing open wounds and sores. Their knowledge of herbs is passed from one generation to another along the female line." He became an authority on 'witchcraft' and dealt firmly with a *mganga* at Chifunauli's village, who claimed to an audience whom he was inciting against *Chiana*, that he could make himself invisible to this white man.

Harrington's account of this incident which came my way through one of the Davisons is, I suspect, typical of the methods with which these lone pioneers handled difficult situations. The *mganga*, "a dirty looking scoundrel", according to Harrington, had caused a lot of trouble in the village and it was time, in Harrington's words, "that I moved him on." The village headman was paralysed with fear. "The half dozen askaris I had with me", said *Chiana*, "refused to handcuff the fellow, saying that if they touched him their arms would wither!" The *mganga* sensing that he was winning the battle of nerves, stepped up insolently to Harrington and threatened him. "I stepped close as well", said the small lone European, "and then I brought the heel of my studded shooting boot with full force down on his toes. The *mganga* yelled and screamed and fell down and the askaris seeing that I had better 'medicine' handcuffed him!"

One memorable afternoon Arthur Davison, who could by now hardly walk, brought along to our bush home *Chirapula* Stevenson. I suppose it was something of a unique occasion. These two 'ancients' and comrades of Harrington's rarely met but, now in 1955, we had the unique privilege of having the last two men from the pre-1902 days under our roof, pouring out yarn after yarn and reminiscence after reminiscence. *Yangwe* Davison was the quiet taciturn one, who listened, but whose own experiences were weird and almost incredible to modern society, but were indelible etchings of true history. *Chirapula* Stevenson was the out-going one. His African nickname meant 'the one who beats' and comes from the time when he set out alone with a company of twenty askaris.

He was the first magistrate appointed in Zambia and, on his own admission, kept order with a large stick and a good slice of personality. (He was then twenty-four.) *Chirapula* started life working as a postal clerk in England and then at the age of nineteen graduated to become a telegraphist. He went out like Harrington in response to the British Chartered Company's developments in central Africa, but as well spent a short time in the diamond fields around Kimberley. It was in August 1900 that *Chirapula* headed north into what is now Zambia. He was of medium build, a good looking young man with fair hair. "My hair", he told me "was my passport to success. When", he continued, "I arrived in Lalaland with my twenty askaris I was greeted with great reverence. They even kissed the ground where I stood. It was only after some days that I realised that the Lala tribe considered that I was the answer to a long standing prophecy made by a forgotten witchdoctor or Chief that the blond God Luchere after wandering to the edges of the world, would one day after many centuries return. I, *Chirapula* was hailed by the Lala as the long awaited Luchere."

The result was that *Chirapula* was free to travel the length and breadth of the land between the Zambezi and Luapula rivers. He, like a number of other white pioneers, including Arthur Davison, married into the local tribal systems. Both men built large and weird mansions. Davison built a ramshackle house on the outskirts of Ndola where he housed some of his wives. *Chirapula* built a huge palace at

Kapiri Muwendika where, in his old age, he amused himself growing pineapples and gave interviews to some of those flighty authors from America and Britain, who tended to write with authority on a country which they had only visited for a few weeks and in some cases for a few days! *Chirapula's* last wife was a member of the Lala tribe royal family and this endeared him more than ever to the Lala tribe.

Arthur Davison died in 1955. *Chirapula* followed him two years later. *Yangwe* Davison was buried in a lonely patch of bushland between the mission and the settlement I had been developing. I was one of the bearers privileged to carry him to his final resting place. There were only a handful of white faces. I think I counted no more than five, including Tom his brother, but there were huge crowds of Africans. They had come to pay their last respects to a man they feared yet loved.

It was the same with *Chirapula* Stevenson, the cortege was led by his last wife Loti, his children and numerous coloured grandchildren followed and amidst a beating of drums, natives arrived in their hundreds to bid this brave old man farewell. Two hundred Lala tribesmen kept the night watch over him and he was buried the next day at sunset without a coffin, his corpse resting on an amatanda mat draped with a Union Jack. So, within the space of eighteen months, passed two of the characters who braved, yet loved Africa, and who were loved by hundreds, perhaps thousands of Africans – people who feared them but still worshipped and respected them.

The last of the greats had gone. They had left behind the flavour of an Africa which within the space of a mere sixty years, even less, had seen them and their colleagues succeed in banishing tribal warfare, the Arab slavers and finally they had helped diminish the malignant influence of the Witchdoctor. They were adventurers, hunters, explorers and, some may say, exploiters. Yet it was old *Yangwe's* brother, Tom, who said to me when we threw the last bit of laterite soil onto the bush grave, "Before they venture to criticise such men, let them remember Africa as they found it." A thought-provoking statement. At the end of the day the multitude of weeping Africans who had gathered to show their attachment to *Yangwe* and *Chirapula* must surely have shown at least a glimmer of the testament of truth, a truth which the professional denigrators and armchair critics may not always have wished to see!

A few weeks after burying *Yangwe* Davison, my tour of duty in this wild and desolate country with its lovable people expired. The breakthrough in services for the blind had been made and Africans, many of them totally blind, were soon to take the lead and carry on the work in a magnificent style. This was all in the 'master plan.' Quite frequently as the years went by I revisited Bwana Mkubwa and the up-country schools and training centres and eventually returned as the Ministry of Education Adviser on Special Education in the Seventies.

Great things were being done, the blind were growing crops, some had qualified as teachers and social workers, one or two had even gone to university. Together we had sown the seeds of confidence in the Luapula, around Mweru and in distant Mongu, that the blind are no longer the 'living dead'. But more important still the Valley of the Blind was no more – research and mobile clinics from Government and the Royal Commonwealth Society for the Blind had made sure of that.

Chapter Eight

My first spell of long leave was drawing to a close. In those days we did a three year tour of duty followed by six months home leave. This arrangement, apart from becoming sometimes rather tedious, could be quite expensive as well.

Britain ten years after the holocaust was in some ways still gloomy and its cities cheerless and run down. Perhaps it was my reaction after a different type of life where freedom and independence of action were essential elements in getting things done. Cathleen and I spent a few weeks in Germany and the Ardre Valley. The French and Germans had already finished picking up the pieces and were all set it seemed, for a devastating economic drive. We caught a glimmer of the commercial punch they were packing, something which was clearly evident to the more discerning. I discussed this new-found industrial zeal with some of my French and German friends. Generously they pointed out that British and American bombing had in fact done them, in some respects, a good turn by removing obsolete factories, machinery and railway systems, so that their war-torn countries had the opportunity to rebuild and refurbish along the most modern lines. A new era of industrial efficiency had begun, but I suspect that there were other components which brought about the success story of countries devastated by war. Already in central and East Africa I had seen the ready-made British markets slide into the hands of our continental competitors who were pushing their products with success whilst the supine British business moguls were relaxing and chatting up their customers in an almost offensively patronising way. I do not think Britain has ever really recovered the ground it lost during those vital first ten years. It seems that the vanquished at the end of the day managed to stay the course better than the victors!

I found there was much that was still very special to Britain. The West Country in the April sunshine seemed almost magical, blooming, fresh and glowing. The soft mizzling showers, the new sheen on the firs and birds singing in a springtime chorus. How different to the screeching bird life of the jungle and the constant 'tick' of the millions of ants. There was freedom from the tangled bush, the red aggressive earth and dust which covered you after a few miles along a road. And now, here we were with moist morning dews and chilly but invigorating evening breezes. Exmoor was fresh and gleaming, the Somerset countryside green and friendly. There were no mosquito nets, no daily doses of anti-malarial prophylactics with their weird side effects, just the 'burr' of a rich Somerset accent and crisp clean air. We even ventured out swimming along the murky Burnham shore line and sometimes headed off to our favourite little backwater on the Dorset coast at Eype, a minute hamlet tucked away in a shallow ravine. Most of those peaceful little haunts along this shore are now overshadowed by sprawling urban developments. It was too good in some ways to last. In any case it was time to go back. Africa was calling!

I met Sir John Wilson at his home in west Sussex in July for a briefing on my new assignment. He had just returned from a short tour of East Africa where in Kenya and Uganda plans were well advanced for medical and supportive work in the remoter regions of these countries, where blindness due to trachoma, a fly-borne disease, was prevalent. In those days flying out to Africa and back could be quite an ordeal – chugging along in a cramped propeller-driven aircraft with frequent stops for refuelling, was a tiresome business. Britannias, the new turbo prop machines, would soon be available and this would cut down the fatigue and flying time considerably. It was around this time that Airwork (now part of British Airways) ran a four-day service out to central Africa, using twin engined Vikings. There were night stops at odd little places, like Juba, Lake Victoria and Valetta. John had plenty of stamina and never let such minor things like long distance flying bother him! It was the time, he told me, when some of his best ideas were born!

"Well, Geoffrey," he said, sporting his recently acquired East African suntan, "I thought it all over coming back in the plane back from Kampala, we have been offered a large estate and a complex of buildings in the centre of Tanzania. I think they were originally set aside for rehabilitating Mau Mau prisoners, but now that the trouble in Kenya seems to be less critical it will be a good place for a repeat exercise along the Bwana Mkubwa lines." He waited for a response and there was none. "Now come on," he said, "this is a most intriguing little job, just up your street."

"Where exactly is this latest acquisition of yours?" I asked in, I imagine, an expressionless voice.

"Oh," said John, "it's near a place called Tabora, about seven miles out along the road to Lake Victoria. The Lake is a couple of hundred miles further on." I had had visions of my next tour of duty being a soft posting out to the West Indies, but no such luck. "They are not ready for you yet," said John blandly, as if reading my thoughts. He started running his fingers over his Braille notes with increasing enthusiasm. "Really," he went on, "it's a great opportunity." Clearly I would be going out to East Africa. Breaking new ground was a challenge which most chaps like to take on before they sink into a comfy mid-thirties syndrome. There were one or two snags – family matters. Cathleen was pregnant, but she had about seven months to go and my father was now on his own; my mother had died a few months earlier but, when Africa gets in one's blood, I suppose one becomes rather selfish.

We talked late into the night, discussing the trips we had made together and with Herbert Squires in the Lake Mweru region. We had in-depth discussions on the Tabora assignment. I felt that it was going to be a rugged trip but entirely different to my last mission. It was. "Tabora," said John, "cannot be approached by road from the coast, but we'll get a Land Rover up to you on the rail line," he added cheerfully. He then explained that a single track line ran from Dar es Salaam right up to Tabora, six hundred bush miles away and then on to Kigoma on the shores of Lake Tanganyika another two hundred miles further on. The shaky railway which snakes its way from the humid coast to the plateau had been built by the Germans in pre-World War I, days as far as Tabora, formerly a staging post on the Arab slave route to the coast. It was unreliable and in the rainy season was out of commission for days and sometimes weeks at a time, because of bridges being washed away.

World War I halted the progress of the line to Lake Tanganyika and it wasn't until 1927 that the line was completed. Unreliable as it was, this one link was to many a valuable lifeline. John poured out a whole host of statistics, names and attainable objectives with the final instructions, "Whatever you do establish a base, get things going so that those who follow you have something to build on." The next day

I called in at the RCSB office in Victoria Street, London, and took away a further bundle of maps, notes and reports which I planned to read on the three week voyage via Suez to Dar es Salaam. But, briefly, what kind of components would make up the scenario over the next few years? On reflection they were impressive.

In the years to come the whole of East Africa was to be one of my favourite and most exciting areas of operations. It could hardly be otherwise, a colourful azure coast line running from Dar es Salaam by the ancient forgotten Arabian city of Bagamoya and through to Mombasa and ancient Fort Jesus. These days the Kenyan coast is dotted with idyllic resorts like Malindi.

Far from the coral reefs, the white beaches and palm-lined tropical shores lie the savannah lands and then massive mountains like Mount Elgon and Mount Kenya and finally still almost beyond reach even today the remote Ruwenzori Mountains, the fabulous 'Mountains of the Moon'. To the far north lies the Shifta country where nomadic tribes still pursue their pastimes of feuding and cattle raiding. I spent an uncomfortable few days at Egoji a few years ago. This was a lonely mission station providing services for the blind. The Government administration had been having a rough time and had recently been shot up. The mission was located on the one low hill in the area. On a clear day when there was no wind to disturb the sand and dust, you had a splendid view of the shimmering Shifta country and I wondered how people had the energy and will to fight over such scalding desert wastelands, but tribal warfare was apparently not a thing of the past by any means. In the north it was the Shiftas, then it was the Suks and far far away in the west against the Ruwenzori ranges, tribal fighting had been going on for years. When I was in Fort Portal some of the victims in the hospital, who had been brought in, had terrible arrow and spear wounds. My work took me to places where tourists rarely travelled. This was the backdrop to some of my work, as I saw it and where I witnessed the spasmodic tribal feuding.

I was to find it was in this context of traditional local inter-tribal unrest and warfare that the aftermath of one of those strange uprisings which have pseudo-Christian connections suddenly came into prominence in the late Fifties. Its repercussions echoed into almost the next decade. The Suk[1] uprising was particularly interesting to me

---

[1] The Suk tribe live near Lake Barrigo.

because the Suk tribesmen suffered a very high incidence of blindness, mainly trachoma and there was high infant mortality as well. Of additional significance was the fact that one of the leading 'prophets' was an old blind woman called Chepkucia. The origins of the sect only went back a few years. It was founded by a renegade mission boy called Masinde and an assistant, one Kipkoech.

They named their organisation Dini-ya-Msambwa[2] and preached subversion but it was not directly linked with the depravity of the Mau Mau uprisings, though sometimes it was obscene enough. Masinde promised his followers that the blind should see and the lame walk. In a country where these disabilities are prolific and people cling to the slightest suggestion of hope these were items destined to provoke emotion. Matters in the early Fifties had taken a turn for the worse as Masinde taught people to sing hymns about getting rid of the Europeans and dipping their spears in the blood of white men to fulfil these promises. This was heady stuff.

There was one occasion when Kipkoech gathered nearly four hundred tribesmen and took them one hundred and twenty miles away from their villages to the top of a hill where there is a small extinct crater and a spring. He told them that the hill would open and they would be able to walk through it and they would find fat cattle grazing in lush green pastures. When the gathering discovered that the hill did not open, Kipkoech told them that it was because there were not yet enough followers and their arrival at the promised land had to be postponed! It is evident that mass hysteria had gripped the Suk followers. When forty native police arrived with four European officers to persuade them to return to their homes quietly, violence erupted. The Suks charged the police and put them to flight. Three European officers were killed. The fourth officer escaped and reorganised the police who had fled and finally restored some semblance of order. The Suks involved in this action fled into Uganda and continued to propagate the Dini-ya-Msambwa cult in increasingly threatening ways. New converts were initiated in orgies held in caves and dried up river beds. The followers were marked by up to fourteen cuts and branded by 'teachers' who wore a blood insignia on their arm, rather like the Cross of Lorraine. Cattle and goats sacrificed during these orgies were always white. The teachers led

---

[2] Religion of traditional beliefs.

prayers and bowed to Mount Elgon. The vows they made were followed by the singing of obscene 'hymns' and drinking. The Special Branch dealing with this cult reported that there was never any problem in finding converts, long life was promised for their children and the blind would soon be able to see.

The story of the Suk, Dini-ya-Msambwa cult is a long and rather sordid tale – sometimes of people who refused to join the movement and were, it is believed, the subject of 'witch' killings. The movement was still much in business when I arrived in East Africa, but for a number of reasons its activities were not highlighted because it was a proscribed organisation. When I asked one member in 1957 the reasons why he joined the cult his reply was to me a pretty typical one. He said, "to get rid of the European, to obtain freedom, to enable barren women to give birth, to make poor people rich, to prevent disease, to make the blind see and to live a long life." I recall that at the time the authorities, apart from handing out prison sentences, did a considerable amount on the positive side to rehabilitate members, with settlement schemes and training in local skills, including animal husbandry. It paid dividends.

One of the characters imprisoned in 1958 was the blind woman Chepkucia, the prophetess; in those days she was a person with considerable prestige. She was sentenced to seven years imprisonment but the authorities anticipated that she would be free by 1961, perhaps before that date. I remember that great efforts were being made by two ophthalmologists (one an RCSB colleague) to try and restore to the old lady some degree of sight. I understood that the cornea was in a poor condition so the prognosis was not too cheerful. It was positive steps such as these which brought a degree of normality back into Suk life, but its implications for the work of RCSB were interesting. The Suks realised that the mobile eye clinics had something to offer and that even if sight could not always be saved or restored there could be some hope in rehabilitation. It is the quiet unobtrusive work like this, carried on by teams of Europeans, Africans and Asians, which at the end of the day gets results. Smooth operators and sometimes hysterical leaders did not always have it all their own way now!

In the Sixties in Zambia there was another female prophet cum pseudo-Christian agitator of the same brand as Chepkucia of the Suk tribe. This woman collected an enormous following in the eastern regions of the country. She was in business in pre-independence days as well but once the country became independent she and her followers became quite out of hand and much more troublesome. Troops had to be sent to the area, villages were burnt down and there was considerable loss of life. As for the prophetess herself, who appeared to exert a hypnotic influence on her followers, she ended up in jail. Her activities were an embarrassment to the Government and the loss of life sustained in the area was considerable, though this fact was never made public. The reasons behind these strange cults are deep-rooted. Much of the traditional way of life has been taken away or eroded and nothing has replaced it. Usually there was a strong element of anti-white sentiment. How the pseudo-Christianity cult becomes mixed up in it all is difficult to understand and is maybe another divisive discussion point.

By 1957 the Mau Mau uprising appeared to have lost much of its momentum but it had been an entirely different and a much more serious affair than the Suk tribesmen unrest, or the type of subversion emanating from the prophetess and her followers in Zambia. These were minor upheavals.

The Kikuyu were, and still are, one of the most educated of the tribes in East Africa, in fact they are often regarded as the intelligentsia of this part of the continent. They are well travelled and even in the Fifties many of them had been educated up to university level. They held down most of the best jobs. The Suks were different. Brought up in the wilderness of the north-west frontier district, which borders the Sudan and Ethiopia, they were largely simple people and easily led by almost equally simplistic leaders. The Mau Mau were anything but simple. Their leaders were men who had been abroad and had come under Communist influence. They returned to Kenya and using the then usual Communist penchant for subversion and deceit, linked it all up with the tribal customs, traditions, and bloody oaths, to become a most petrifying force. The terrible oath-taking ceremonies were the key to their grip on the Kikuyu community. The authorities expected the uprising to spread to other tribes throughout East Africa. This never happened. There were many reasons for this, but one of them is certainly the influence of organisations and Government policies which sought to place a positive image on welfare, medical and educational developments and put them in the front line. RCSB, particularly in its medical role, did much indirectly to stabilise matters.

The leaders of these strange cults were hypnotic personalities. This went for the blind woman Chepkucia, the mission renegade Masinde and certainly for Jomo Kenyatta. I met Kenyatta briefly years after the uprising and his eyes were truly magnetic. Sir Evelyn Baring, the Governor, stated that even in a photograph one could discern Kenyatta's penetrating magnetism. Land was the factor which lit the powder keg for both the simple Suk people and for the sophisticated Kikuyus.

Both Suks and Kikuyu wanted the Europeans out. Some political students of this era claim that greed was the fuel which stoked the tribal fires, but there were a number of Britishers who were actively sympathetic to African aspirations in this direction and showed considerable understanding of these contentious matters. Amongst them was Dr Leakey, an academic with almost a lifetime of experience in this region of Africa. He was well versed in the customs and traditions of the Kikuyu and spoke their language like a native. When Jomo Kenyatta and others faced trial in Nairobi, this distinguished anthropologist acted as interpreter and adviser to the Kikuyu on trial. That he was well disposed and helpful to the Kikuyu was never in doubt. But how was this brilliant man treated by the Mau Mau? That is another matter. His brother was captured, tortured and mutilated and made the subject of horrific rituals which culminated in him being buried whilst still alive, as some sort of tribal sacrifice. His sister-in-law was killed and her home left in ruins. Those who had been the greatest friends of the Mau Mau were often the first to become victims of their cult, whether their faces were black or white.

Today Kenya is the wonderland of Africa and the Mau Mau uprising is rarely mentioned. It is, it seems, an exemplary country where European and African can live happily side by side. How different to that when the Mau Mau oaths started to mesmerise Africans so that, almost in a trance, on instructions from their leaders they would murder their dearest friends and relatives.

The area around Thika some sixty miles from Nairobi was one of the places exposed to the ferocity of the Mau Mau. I sometimes visited the School for the Blind at Thika where the staff, a mixture of blacks and whites, worked together and one could see that the pressures and fears were quite enormous. Away in the thick bamboo forests which skirted that lovely township with its wide streets lined with flowering jacaranda trees were the haunts of the most ferocious of the Mau Mau elements. Fort Hall and the Aberdare mountains as well were riddled with Mau Mau camps. This is where the oath-taking ceremonies were sometimes held, though they had been known to take place in the back garden sheds of European houses in Thika! The Kikuyu tribal oaths made up the powerhouse which drove those caught up with the Mau Mau to murder, to perform ritual sacrifices and to maim cattle.

Whilst in East Africa I came into contact with those who had studied the Mau Mau rising in some detail and were at the time looking for signs of its emergence in other East African tribes. The Mau Mau movement was built up almost solely around evil powerful tribal oaths. Altogether there were sixty-eight binding oaths. These conformed to various gradings. There was one – a recent one – for politicians, one for leaders of murder groups and, as time went on, additional ones were introduced which were more violent and dangerous than the original tribal commitments. In effect it meant that no one was safe. Your Kikuyu servant who may have served you loyally and faithfully for years would, on a command, not hesitate to despatch you. The Batuni oath of 1952 was one of the more recent embellishments which called on those who were initiated with it to:

- kill when ordered to do so, no matter who is to be the victim, even one's father or brother,
- when killing you are to cut off the head, take out the eye balls, and then you are to drink the fluid from them,
- you are to kill Europeans, their cattle and crops and your black brothers as well when ordered to do so.

It is important to understand that these oaths were not merely excitable expressions of hate but they were made to be translated into reality and this is exactly what happened. The cases of ritual murders are almost unending. A young District Officer in the Thika area was ambushed, mutilated and beheaded. The child of a former Chief, Luka, was cut in half, its blood drunk and then the two halves flung to the mother. Often victims were held down and their heads slowly sawn off. In those days the Mau Mau had no time for tribal authority and certainly not for Christianity, so how did the authorities ever start to rehabilitate a tribe bewildered by such evil influences?

It is a long story, but it has been done. It is important to keep in mind that not all Kikuyu succumbed to the commands and pressures with which they were surrounded. There was in fact a very brave and vocal component of the tribe who took up the challenge and at appalling cost fought alongside the security forces. They infiltrated the forest gangs so successfully that the Mau Mau was put on the defensive and finally overcome. This story of heroism is rarely discussed but some of the people I met during my stay in Tabora and again in Kenya, told the tales of operations which compared in endurance and skill to anything which went on in the last war.

Typical of these operations was the capture of Dedan Kimathi in October 1956 near Ndirago. It was the usual joint African-European scheme which led to his downfall. A tracker Gichumu had picked up Kimathi's trail and followed it relentlessly for days. The gang was infiltrated and a successful ambush followed. The credit for this kind of operation was shared by many. In the Kimathi case, apart from Gichumu there was Ian Henderson, who organised the operation and Africans like Corporal Wamjohi, who helped arrest the gang.

One of my Kikuyu friends who was teaching at the large Thika School for the Blind, survived the traumas of the Mau Mau era and eventually came over to London where he joined a short course I was then running in 1963 for senior Commonwealth executives, who were dealing with services for the handicapped. The last time I was in Nairobi this brilliant young blind man was on the staff of Nairobi University lecturing in the social services faculty. It was people like our friend who brought sanity back into a tribe which many said was doomed to be lost forever. They were wrong.

The successful resettlement of the Kikuyu was an enormous achievement cutting across the big divides of life-style and contentious matters of land tenure. The dilemma of the ordinary Kikuyu tribesman was something of a schizophrenic nature, that of blending old tribal ways of life and beliefs into that of an alien society which is rational, coldly clinical and exceedingly factual. It is easy to overlook the fact that modern Africa is still a vast rural countryside, but modern towns and cities like Lusaka, Nairobi and Harare tend to overshadow this fact; indeed, it is possible to be back almost in the Stone Age within an hour's drive of some of these places. This is the crux perhaps of the Africans' difficulties, the time factor, traversing in sixty years instead of six hundred the span from feudal times to the jet age. Helping this transition was the Kenyan branch of the RCSB who took their sight saving work and messages of hope deep into Mau Mau country at the height of the emergency and into the Suk lands.

These brave pioneers headed by modest men like Dr Calcott and Dr Birkett circulated throughout the Mau Mau troubled areas and then carried on up to the north frontier district. These 'save your sight' teams came up with some amazing conclusions. For example, that eighty percent of the blindness they came across was preventable; that there were over seventy thousand totally blind people in Kenya and just over ten percent of them were children; that trachoma and conjunctivitis affected nearly half of the tribesmen in the country areas and that ninety percent of the Suk tribe suffered from some form of eye disease. It was the ability of RCSB to tackle with the other voluntary agencies these difficulties which did much to smooth the path for peaceful co-existence. Medical and allied research which shows concern and works amongst people – indeed in their midst – rather than remain austerely aloof, appears to be the key to one element of rehabilitation. Its dividends in Kenya have been enormous and in Tanzania and Zambia as well.

The only country which failed to respond to this type of approach was Uganda. Idi Amin had turned the clock back. Over the years I was to see the amazing work which had been developed by the Uganda Foundation for the Blind well before his era. I saw it as well during his regime. In fact to get into Uganda was difficult enough and getting out I was to find could be something of a problem as well. I slipped into Kampala to carry out a brief survey of the progress of work in the country. Apart from one African, I had the huge jet plane which left from Nairobi for Entebbe to myself. My passport was seized at Entebbe and the hotel where I stayed, one that had been in the international bracket and largely used by overseas tourists, had now been converted into a barracks facility for the army and their families. The food was of a local variety – dried fish and rice, which is quite attractive. This was the time when Mr Hill, a lecturer at Makakere, was under sentence of death on some odd little charge. I spent my first day working in the British High Commission. The High Commissioner had been withdrawn and a skeleton staff under Mr Henessey ran the office. The previous day he told me that one of the few remaining Europeans had been arrested for allegedly purchasing a tin of baked beans on the black market. It was almost incredible to witness how a pall of gloom and misery shrouded a once beautiful and vivacious city.

My escorts for the fortnight I was scheduled to spend in the country, were either 'not available' or had been substituted by Government civil servants who apart from being nervy individuals had the task of keeping track of my movements. They were kind (or rash enough) to tell me this themselves. It was clear that I was not welcome. I knew Uganda fairly well from Soroti in the east across to Fort Portal far away in the west, and had already sensed the changes in attitude and services for the blind. Uganda, once the most advanced African country in the whole continent, spelt out a sad story of neglect and political intrigue. The people whom I had known at Jinja, the lone little school at Wanyangwe, the teacher training centre at Iganga, were scared and as events have subsequently proved, they had good reason to be. One of the most formidable countries intellectually, with a history which was 'progressive' and disciplined had been subdued, no, cowed into silence. My Ugandan friends were silent and if they spoke it was only to explain briefly the reasons for the silences – fear. At that time, apart from the High Commission and some mission people who stuck it out, I had been one of the few new white faces to come into the country. I had been warned in Nairobi to keep away, but as there were no reports coming through at all from the staff working on behalf of the RCSB it seemed advisable to find out what was going on. I found out. Regression had long set in, thriving clinics, farm training centres for the blind, and schools were either closed or grinding to a halt. The High Commission managed to get my passport back just half an hour before the flight left for Nairobi. Again I had the plane to myself.

This then was to be the extended scenario to my work in East Africa, the diminishing Mau Mau and Suk troubles and, way ahead in the distant future, the antics of a monster whom we are told is still alive and ready to return to Uganda to resuscitate the fires of vengeance and terror. It was difficult enough to extract oneself from the depths of the mellow Somerset countryside for yet another stint in Africa and, maybe, it was as well that the future was to remain shrouded in an enigma of uncertainty.

Chapter Nine

Our ship the seventeen thousand ton *Warwick Castle* was gently edging its way into the harbour at Dar es Salaam after a sweltering August passage through the Red Sea and a prolonged delay at Aden. It was early morning as the ship picked its way from Lighthouse Island two miles out through the intricate channels and reefs, finally squeezing through the narrow neck less than two hundred yards wide into the land-locked harbour of Dar es Salaam, the Haven of Peace. This is one of the most beautiful harbours in the world, a wide sweep of palm-lined shore, the waterline dotted with neat white houses and the old German Lutheran church built in Bavarian style uniting the past and the present.

Unlike much of central Africa and the Congo-Zaire regions, the written history of Tanzania goes back far into the mists of time. There was trade with the merchants of Arabia and India long before Europeans set foot on the east coast. King Solomon's ships are reputed to have sailed round the horn of Africa to purchase gold, silver, and ivory, and traces of early Chinese and Greek civilisations have been found at Kilwa and Bagamoyo. Bagamoyo was the former capital of the region centuries before the German colonialists in the late nineteenth century selected Dar es Salaam, then a minute fishing village, as their capital. But Bagamoyo has a sinister air about it. It was a former slave port. It was to this point on the coast Arabs brought bands of Africans from the interior and sold them to traders from overseas. The slave market is still standing and the mysterious deserted buildings go back to the seventeenth century.

In the season Arab dhows came gliding in from Zanzibar and Arabia. From the verandah of the New Africa Hotel, another delightful German inheritance where we often stayed after a spell up country, we would watch these graceful ships make a landfall. From the same verandah we would sometimes see a young African, still largely unknown, Julius Nyerere, then leader of TANU[1] relax at sundowner time on the forecourt overlooking the lagoon and engage in intense discussions with off duty British administrators.

The New Africa has now been demolished and replaced by a characterless blob of a building, but the old hotel with its wide patio and palm courtyards overlooking the harbour, gave one the aroma of East Africa. There was no air conditioning, perhaps a squeaky fan, and almost certainly the mosquito nets would be riddled by tears and holes which rendered most of them useless. It was here I met a senior Government official John Moffatt, a distinguished Anglo-Irishman who, on the spacious patio overlooking the lagoon, assisted with the help of a cool IPA (Indian Pale Ale) briefed me thoroughly on the set up around Tabora. A three-day train journey lay ahead; the Land Rover I had been promised in London would be put on the train. "Yes," he said, "it is a former Mau Mau rehabilitation centre you are taking over, but it has gone completely wild. The house may, or may not, be habitable but", he added, "I am sure you will make the best of it." It was important, he told me, to get things moving, and so we left behind the 'Haven of Peace', for a haven which seemed to have been taken over not by the Mau Mau but by all the wildlife in Tanzania!

Kazima was the name of our new home. It was a dusty rock, seven miles jeep ride north of Tabora located on a delightful well elevated promontory with sweeping views over the dry brown sun drenched countryside. The track leading up to the Kazima complex had long been lost in elephant grass, but in a sandy nook as the road climbed up to our new home were seven mongooses, waiting to greet us – a father and a mother, plus a playful bunch of youngsters who were not at all abashed at the Land Rover creeping past them. They paused to stare and then continued their frisky games.

The whole area had gone back to jungle. There were massive outcrops of towering rock, some reaching up to sixty or seventy feet in height, and then in contrast were smooth rocky sheets which swept down to the plains. There were wild mango trees in profusion and through the undergrowth I could make out the shapes of a huge conglomeration of detached high security buildings. This gave way to agricultural land which had passed back into bush and still further,

---

[1]TANU = Tanganyika National African Union.

Uganda, Kenya and Tanganyika

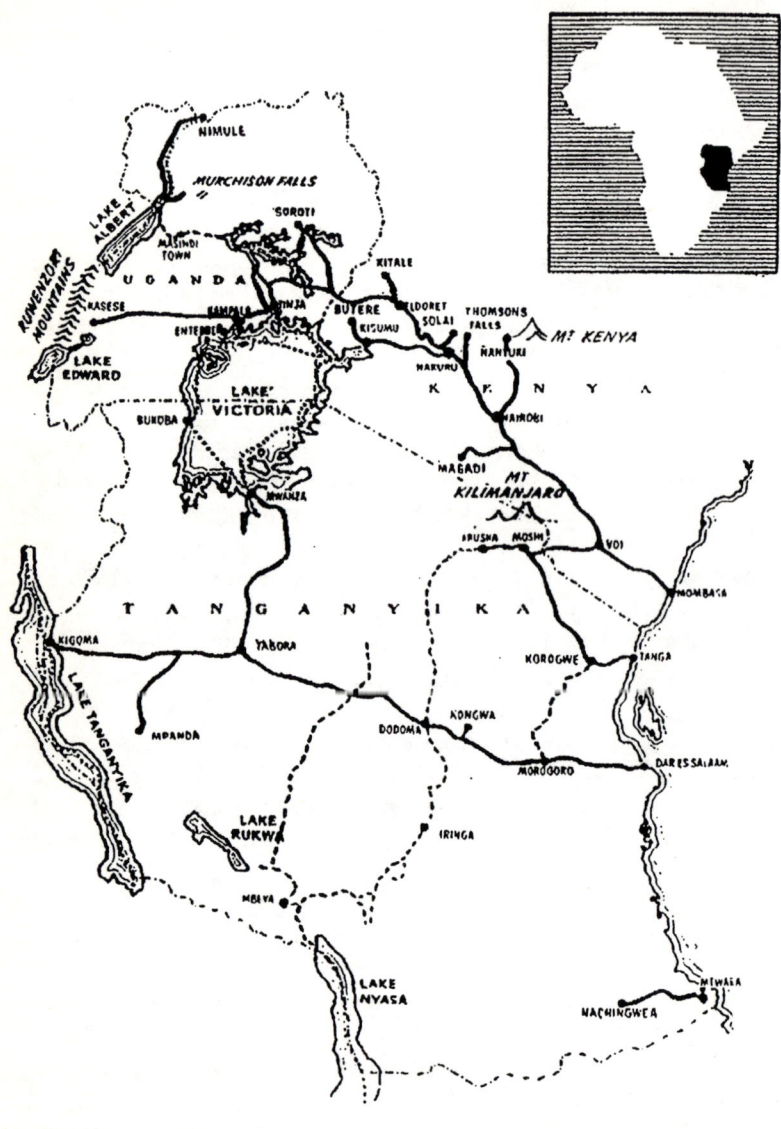

RAIL ————
ROAD ------------
LAKE ············

SCALE

0   50   100   150   200   250   300   350 MILES

down in the valley the signs of where the wild pigs had rooted. This was the real bush country. I had always thought that Bwana Mkubwa had been good African country experience, but this seemed to surpass everything. Our house was a comfy but dirty, very old bungalow, built at the highest point of the escarpment. White ants were starting to make meals of the woodwork and in the nooks and crannies large spiders had weaved the strongest of webs. They lived unmolested, except for one nest of scorpions, who had taken up residence in the soft sandy crevices of the house walls. For good measure, the well-worn enamel bath appeared to be the home of a very thin three foot green snake. We removed the reptile (which could not scale the sides of the bath) by producing some boiling water and it slid down the plug hole (there were no filter bars), and it tried to make its exit through the exposed outlet pipe outside. The Africans with me didn't like snakes either and screamed for the *Bwana* to kill it. This I managed to do but only after breaking the handle of the only broom we had. The Africans considered it a bad omen. Cathleen and I considered it in a slightly different light and one of the practical problems of life on an out station.

One of my main impressions of Tanzania in the Fifties and Sixties was the quite remarkable imprint the German colonialists had left behind. I had met Dick Eberlie in Dar, a young District Officer who had done much to introduce me to East African life on the coast. Dick was an authority on the German occupation of this region which terminated with the end of World War I. When I remarked on the prolific buildings the Germans had left behind and which are still in use, the semi-fortified bomas, the Lutheran churches, the spacious Bavarian style houses, even their hospitals, Dick remarked, "you know, Geoff, these people won and lost an empire within the span of one single generation." What he said was true. Yet within that time they left indelible marks which are with us to this day. Some were quite appalling, like the handling of the Maji Maji uprising. Others in the field of tropical medicine, were utterly brilliant. It was Dr Koch, the discoverer of the TB bacillus, who campaigned against sleeping sickness. It was Koch who introduced Atoxyll as the remedy and the bacteriologist Ehrlich who found the 0.606 remedy against tick and black water fever. These were just a few of the stars in German medical research in East Africa. I think that the German Colonial Medical Services' greatest gift to the country was the vaccination campaign against smallpox when three million Africans were vaccinated in a five-year drive which concluded in 1914.

Unfortunately much of this work was overshadowed by the repercussions of the Maji Maji rebellion. This uprising was indicative of a way of life and thought which few white people can really ever comprehend. "Take nothing for granted in Africa," old Davison had told me. It was a wise maxim which I soon learnt to observe. The intricacies of tribal life can manifest themselves in unusual ways.

The Maji Maji rebellion and its causes have never been satisfactorily explained. A leading German administrator, Dr Derberg, attributed them to, "too many *kiboko* (whips) plus too much forced labour as the root of the trouble." He may not have been far off the mark but Dick Eberlie (like many others) in a paper published by the Tanganyika Historical Society considers the outbreak still to some extent shrouded in mystery.

"What was it," he asks, "that could bring more than twelve separate tribes together from the Ruvu right up to Lake Nyasa – tribes entirely different in habit and character, who were largely traditional enemies, and had never before been united in any case?" The similarities I discussed with Dick between the Maji Maji uprising and the Mau Mau and the minor Suk unrest seemed negligible, except that in all cases, the security intelligence authorities had been dozing peacefully and were caught completely unawares by the pending troubles.

The Maji uprising had lessons for us all, even to this day. The insurrection was triggered off by tribal witchdoctors in the Liwale district of the country. They claimed to have made a special type of water which they said if drunk by warriors would render them immune from the bullets of the enemy. *Maji* in Swahili means 'water', hence in Tanzania this largely forgotten, but bloody episode, has gone down in local history as the Maji Maji uprising. The 'magic' water which the witchdoctors possessed was said to have curative properties as well and was supposed to be particularly good for toothache, sore eyes and even as a charm to provide good crops!

In the colonial era there was sometimes a tendency to underestimate or discredit plausible rumours and the effect they may have on the people who believed them. Indeed complacency on the part of the Germans almost led to their loss of Tanganyika. It was the same story with the Kikuyu fifty years later – of secrecy, oath-taking and then a sudden and bloody campaign. (Even in former Rhodesia this was the pattern. I met Government administrators from around the Inyanga and Melsetter areas who admitted that they had been caught completely by surprise, yet plans for an uprising had been developing for at least three or four years.)

One of the old men who lived on his *shamba* at the edge of our new home at Kazima had lost his father in the Maji uprising. He told me his side of the story. The uprising had been building up for two years. His father took the tribal oath of secrecy at least a year before the fighting started. Husseini (that was my friend's name) then went on to confirm what Dick Eberlie had told me that the uprising was against all foreigners, not just the Germans, but other Europeans, the Arabs and Indians as well. "Why," I had asked, "when it was obvious that the 'magic water' was ineffective, did people still throw themselves against the guns of the enemy?"

"Because," said the wrinkled grizzly old Husseini, "the witchdoctors told us that those who had fallen would rise again, perhaps within weeks and that they would be stronger and better men." This old man, as a boy of about ten, had been herding cattle when his father went to join the rebellion. He recalled the beat of the war drums which echoed around the countryside and the war cry of 'Maji Maji' as his father and other tribesmen went off to the distant battle. Husseini saw the aftermath of the rebellion. Native mercenary troops, some from the Sudan were given a licence to plunder. The Germans paid a fee for every head of an insurgent tribesman which was brought to the Boma in Dar es Salaam. Crops were destroyed, he said, and two years of famine followed. He never saw his father again.

The activities of Dr Karl Peters who was expelled from the country by the German Government, may have contributed to the cause of the rebellion. Certainly he was a hard man who administered the territory with ferocity. He had his black mistress hanged for unfaithfulness and is alleged to have had his houseboy hanged beside her for stealing. He was known by the Africans as *Mkono wa damu*, the man with blood on his hands. There were others who considered that the Arab slavers had organised the rebellion and there are grounds for considering that this might well be true but, at the end of the day, the Arabs suffered more than the Europeans. It seems, as Dick Eberlie commented, that when certain facets manifest themselves, such as in the Congo, Uganda and Rhodesia, frustrating and inhibiting conditions give rise to a Maji Maji situation.

Life at our new home at Kazima was largely what one was prepared to make of it. Tabora was the place we visited at weekends to collect our supplies which came up by train from Dar es Salaam or, at certain seasons, direct by plane on the weekly service from Nairobi. There were two Indian *dukas* at which the Europeans would buy tinned foods, flour and items which would not decompose in the heat. Even though we were at an altitude of nearly four thousand feet the hot season could be trying and the land was parched. Our water which was tarnished with a sickly grey slime was pumped from the Kazima dam and as the hot season lengthened it took on a more turgid syrupy character which blocked the pumps. It was then we were at panic stations.

In spite of the rumours which had first been initiated, that the *Bwana* at Kazima was only interested in the blind, so that he could send their eyes down to the coast as charms, the place rapidly prospered, indeed it flourished to such an extent that a United Nations delegation, which had come to inspect the way in which Britain was carrying out its responsibilities in governing a mandated territory, was so fascinated that it spent a whole day with us. The young blind people who came along were, like those from Bwana Mkubwa, drawn from a variety of tribes. Even the Chief at Singida, one of the most backward areas in the whole country, had sent along some lads. At that time Singida was the focal point of a number of 'lion men' murders, something akin to what was happening in one or two parts of West Africa. There had been fourteen murders near Singida. Tribesmen dressed themselves up in lion skins and then, with the mystic belief of being invisible, attacked the innocent to extract the brain and liver as potent medicine. It was all an unpleasant business, but eventually the cult was broken up. I believe that even within recent times there have again been odd cases of this kind of thing.

Apart from practical crises such as water supplies, the training centre had got off to a good start. We had no mass 'witchcraft' hysteria such as the kind we had experienced at Bwana Mkubwa. Once the bush had been cleared away by hard working tribesmen, Kazima was a delightful and beautiful spot to live in. Fruit was plentiful in the rainy season, our blind men even managed to grow rice on this five hundred acre largely overgrown estate. Millet was plentiful and ground nuts and beans grew plentifully too. We were in fact embarking on work which was severely practical. Survival in this part of Africa depended not on one's ability to read or write Braille, (though in the evenings the blind were taught Braille in Swahili), but rather on one's ability to grow the main staple crops, to keep a few chickens and to build a hut to live in. All very basic but, as far as survival was concerned, essential as well. This philosophy in recent years has been supported by the former President, Julius Nyerere when he was developing his system of Ujama villages, an idea based on family groups and communities building on the local facilities which nature offered.

Our stay at Kazima was pleasant and enjoyable. Weekends were noisy even though we were a long way from the nearest African village. Our bungalow from the heights looked right across the shimmering plain. When the wind was in the right direction one could sometimes enjoy or endure, depending on one's mood, the night-long drumming. These sessions were usually held when the moon was well up. Over the night air the yells, the shrieks of ecstasy, the pounding of feet as the tribal dancing reached its climax came over the two mile space of bushland loud and clear. The native liquor called *pombe* was formidable in stirring up passions and then with suddenness anaesthetising the dancers into a long stupor. Our neighbours were Wagogo and Nyamwezi tribesmen, colourful and great characters at the best of times, but the noise and their tribal costumes was something our animal neighbours took in their stride. They had no intention of giving up their homes in the rocky outcrops and thick bush country at Kazima.

This was the only period in my overseas career when I kept a gun handy in the house. (In parts of north-west Africa along the edges of the Sahara my French escorts had loaned me an automatic, but that was for different reasons – the unsettled nature of the country.) Perhaps the reasons for this precaution can be best explained by referring to a letter written by Frank Rigby, a tough jovial Scot who took charge of Kazima when I moved on to Malawi to undertake another assignment. Frank was not a man who flapped but this extract from one of his letters, records the true state of affairs. He wrote:

At about 11.15 at night there was a loud noise outside
my bedroom window, which was open, but which was

covered by a steel mesh grille. The dog, a
Labrador-Ridgeback, which I was keeping for friends
who were on leave, charged into the room and sprang at
the window barking loudly. I got up and let him out
thinking that perhaps a burglar was outside. He rushed
into the darkness barking loudly. I shut the window and
returned to bed. About two minutes later, his barking
was answered by a soft coughing sound. There was a
scuffle and then complete silence. I opened the door and
called him but there was no reply.

In the morning I saw the tracks of a lion and the
place where it had leapt through the frangipani bush
outside the house onto the dog, killing it instantly at
about 25 feet from the door and then taking the body up
the hill behind the house. The most frightening part of
the whole business, as far as I was concerned, was the
pug marks on the wall outside my bedroom window,
where the lion had stood on his hind legs and watched
me lying in bed!

In my 'hand-over' notes to Frank, I thought I had covered just
about every detail. Verbally, I had warned him that the animal life at
Kazima was in some respects better than living in a game park!

The small security houses built for rehabilitating the Mau Mau
were promptly closed as sunset approached. Unless there were special
reasons or occasions one did not normally venture far afield at night.
Lions and leopards were plentiful, but Cathleen and I normally took
our evening walk, a circular route of about two miles around the back
of the hill down along a bush path which brought us back to the house.
Wildlife came right up to our verandah, sometimes chattering groups
of small monkeys would come up to us whilst we were having tea. At
other times, in the early morning light, Kudu and sable antelope would
nervously graze just outside our windows where the grass around the
house was soft and green. They were beautiful graceful creatures who
were managing to survive in this hostile environment. Their nostrils
were constantly twitching, their ears as well as they paused for alien
sounds and smells. Late at night we would lie in bed and, at certain
seasons of the year, mainly when the rains had left us, we would hear
the muffled grunts of the lions making their regular nocturnal visits to
the nearby water holes, or if they were dry, down to the Kazima lake.

Leopards abounded. They were unpredictable creatures who lurked behind the house amongst the many outcrops of rocks. Once or twice they took a goat belonging to the teaching staff. Coming back one Christmas night from Tabora there had been a frightful tropical storm and the roads were hardly passable, the headlights of the Land Rover picked up a huge fellow, a male leopard who, instead of scurrying off into the bush leisurely turned and had a good look at us. The Land Rover approached to within a few feet of him, he gave a horrible snarl showing a gleaming row of teeth, and casually swaggered off into the undergrowth.

As one might expect, taking on a large run down estate in the middle of Africa, the continuous encroachment of the bush had made an excellent habitat not only for wild animal life but for reptiles as well. John Ionides, the famous 'snake man' of East Africa and later of international fame, visited Kazima whilst I was away on safari, down in Dodoma. He told the African teaching staff that the variety of snakes around the place was probably very interesting, which I suppose meant that they were plentiful and varied. Years later I met this engaging character in Kenya at the Outward Bound Mountain School at Loitokitok. Here at an altitude of eight thousand feet I had assumed that we were now in a snake free zone, but John Ionides managed to seek out mambas, boom slangs and other varieties of reptiles from trees and innocent holes in the ground. Ionides supplied a number of medical research laboratories with snakes. After his visit to Kazima and his verbal opinion about the snake population, I checked up on our anti-snake bite serum supplies!

Most Europeans in the course of their stay in Africa, particularly if they are in the bush, have their own reptile stories. I met, during the course of my work, quite a few specimens and I took Ionides' advice to heart, "all poisonous snakes are dangerous". One of the rarer varieties Cathleen and I came across was the repulsive Gaboon Viper[1]

---

[1] The Gaboon Viper, both in fiction and fact, has a reputation which the late C.P. Ionides once stated, "epitomised the depths of evil". Apart from its hideous appearance, its venom is deadly. It combines both neurotoxics and haemotoxic poisons. This has made the discovery of a satisfactory antidote in the form of a serum, difficult to find. Death can follow within a few minutes. Like the puff adder it is sluggish. It also has the same type of skin camouflage which is highly effective. Casualties usually occur when it is basking in the sun on a bush path and remains largely unseen until it is trodden on. At other times when lying amidst bushland grass it may resemble a fallen

180

– a sluggish evil looking individual with a flat mouth, an olive marked skin, with black markings – it is sometimes called a carpet snake because of the distinct rectangular patterns. Normally it blends in beautifully with the environment and lies in wait for the unwary. It is reputed to be the most poisonous snake in the world and I have heard a number of stories of individuals dying in agony within two or three minutes of a bite from its two inch fangs. At the time of writing I believe an antidote has yet to be developed to counteract its venom. (The South African Medical Research Bureau and Newcastle-upon-Tyne University, under the leadership of Professor John Harris, are two of the many independent bodies carrying out research in this field.)

A good time to find snakes is in the very early morning just when the sun is warming up the sandy roads. This is particularly the case in the cold season. Sometimes when I broke camp early and cruised gingerly along uncertain bush tracks some odd sights came my way. On the road to Shinyanga I came across a four footer lying as straight as a bean-stick across the roadway. It was enjoying the early morning warmth. Usually snakes are, at that time of day, and especially in the cold season, lethargic. I had always made a point of deliberately running over them though this is not advisable as there have been cases where the snakes get entwined in the chassis of the vehicle. That morning I did not have the opportunity to despatch the reptile I had sighted. When I was within twenty feet of it a bird with a huge wing span, probably a species of eagle, swooped over the Land Rover almost brushing the roof and with perfect timing snatched the reptile up in its talons. The snake wriggled and struggled but in vain. I stopped and watched the huge bird methodically gain height and then hover over one of these rocky outcrops. It dropped the snake from a height of about one hundred feet and swooped down again presumably to consume it. (In the mid-Seventies whilst in Eastern Nigeria, I was on the Enugu-Oji river road and I saw a repeat performance but this time the victim was much smaller.)

Most of us assume that snakes do not attack people unless they are provoked. With one or two species this may not always be true. I recall the tragedy of a ten year old European boy who was sitting in the shade under a mango tree on his father's tobacco farm near

---

log. When fully grown its length is up to four feet and its girth at least that of a man's thigh!"

Lusaka, when he was apparently attacked by a green mamba which was lurking in the tree. Unfortunately the child died in spite of prompt and thorough medical attention. There were other cases I noted – an Irish lad bitten in the back of the leg, who, in spite of anti-snake bite serum injection given immediately, died within seven or eight hours. Pythons sometimes have a nasty habit of tackling people. Fairly recently I heard of the case of a native woman who suddenly found herself wrapped up in the coils of one. With the help of men in the forest who heard her screams, she was rescued. Snakes do sometimes consume each other. One of our African men killed a particularly fat stumpy fellow and opened him up to get snake fat for 'medicine'. What did he find but a recently swallowed three foot snake comfortably installed inside, in the process of being digested. He proudly showed us this cannibalistic specimen.

My most unpleasant encounter with a snake was entirely my own fault. It was one of those chilly early mornings and I had made an early start so that I would reach my destination well before dark. I was travelling slowly over the bumpy ground and the side window of the Land Rover next to me was slightly ajar. In a more open stretch of country I came across the typical long black stick. A sure sign that this was obviously a fairly big specimen probably as thick as a man's arm and I guessed several foot long. I was soon to have a better idea of its length! In preparation for the routine tactics of running over snakes, I revved up the engine and made ready to apply the brakes at the moment I was on top of it to make sure the weight of the Land Rover killed it. This time I was too slow. It was a Cobra and not a drowsy one either. It rose with lightning speed and ferocity and in a whip-like movement was in an instant towering above the Land Rover, finely balanced on about two feet of its tail. It made vicious stabs at the windscreen and even at my side window spraying them both with venom. Its hood in all its malignant glory had unfolded and it stabbed again. The fury and suddenness of the attack took me completely by surprise and I nearly lost control of the vehicle, believing, for a moment, that the cobra may have somehow shot through the side window. We nearly overturned but I regained control and just managed to catch a glance of a furious cobra going back into the bushes, no longer standing on its tail, but retreating in an erratic 'hoop-like' manner. I had learnt another bush lesson.

Puff adders seemed to be fairly numerous both at Bwana Mkubwa and in parts of Tanzania, though I never saw one at Kazima. They are similar to Gaboon vipers, slow, sleepy creatures but their skins are of a lighter hue and the markings not as distinguished as the Gaboon viper. Certainly a bite from them can be serious. Once or twice at Bwana Mkubwa they came right onto the verandah where one of our cats had her kittens. It was night time, but the hissing snake and that of the cat as well alerted us that something was wrong. Once one of our cats despatched a couple of small snakes, bit off their heads and was then violently sick, but survived. The women in one of the tribes living near us at Kazima specialised in ritual dances with snakes, entwining them around their bodies. It was a weird performance as the Manyema dancers had painted their faces white with chalk clay.

Usually we never gave much thought to reptiles and in any case at Kazima there were only one or two cases of snake bite. One of the workmen, I remember, got a good spraying from a spitting cobra. Usually they are deadly accurate and aim for the eyes; the venom unless it is washed out quickly (we used fresh milk) can and does cause blindness. Our workman was lucky. He was running away when the snake ejected the poison from a distance of ten feet and it landed on his back. He complained of a burning sensation but perhaps, I thought rather unkindly, this was imagination. I don't know, but he was very frightened. Who wouldn't be?

It was about that time that I watched some of the native tribesmen hunt out quite a sizeable cobra which had taken up residence in a small ant hill near the house. The men had found it whilst Cathleen and I had been in Tabora. We returned to find twelve men armed with sticks and spears surrounding the mound which was covered with creepers and frangipani shrubs.

Anthills in these regions of central Africa are huge earth mounds, twelve or fifteen foot high. They were keeping a respectable distance from the cobra who, intermittently, was darting from creeper to creeper. It was easily visible most of the time. I called the *Capitao* (foreman) over. "Husseini," I said, "I will go to the house and get a gun." He rubbed his grey beard and with a smile said,

"*Bwana*, you need not, today we would like to deal with the *nyoka* (snake), just watch us." Husseini was a man with a local reputation for skills in dealing with little emergencies like this one.

"Alright," I said, "we will watch you at work, but don't take too long." The man had collected a small pile of fresh dark green sisal leaves. They grew abundantly around the place. The leaves were about two foot long and at the widest point about three inches in width. Husseini gave a command and the men redoubled their watch on the cobra. He then bent down and tossed a sisal leaf at the reptile, which was five or six foot long. It rapidly rose, poised in a striking attitude, and then viciously bit the leaf. All the dark green of the leaf visibly turned white. He tossed another one – the same thing happened. This performance continued for about ten minutes until the leaves showed no reaction to the poison. The cobra was now exceedingly angry but it had exhausted its supply of venom and with a yell from Husseini his men moved in and destroyed the reptile. Finally, with one stroke of his panga, the *captiao* cut off the head of the snake and consigned it to the fire in the cook house. This was the traditional way of dealing with these creatures. The only variation I saw of this practice was when the Gaboon viper we had found was not only decapitated but the whole of its body was burnt in a great pyre; "because," we were told, "it holds the spirit of a very evil person." Husseini's method of removing dangerous snakes seems more refined than the clumsy ways some of us Europeans tackled such tasks.

At the time when we were in the Tabora area there were still one or two very elderly natives who had actually been freed by the colonial authorities from slavery. In 1956 HRH Princess Margaret on her visit to these regions met two women, Bibi Sudi and Bibi Chimwai, both of whom had been rescued in 1880 on the coast by HMS *London*. The early explorers like Livingstone, Stanley and Burton all confirmed the importance of Tabora as a slavers' transit camp. Not far from Kazima was the house at Kwihara village where Livingstone and Stanley spent two months together after their famous meeting at Ujiji on Lake Tanganyika.

Tabora was another place where you could almost touch the hand of the past. There was still the scent of cloves and of spices in the old Arab quarters. The Arabs who were now living in Tabora were the direct descendants of those Burton, Livingstone and Stanley had met. There were still the beautifully carved Arab doors on some of the houses and on the Mosque where the faithful prayed to Allah. The 'pure' or, as Burton described them, the 'Omani' Arabs had made the town their headquarters. It was, for a number of reasons, as Burton wrote after he had visited the town, a great meeting place for the slave caravans down from Lake Tanganyika and going down to the coast there were good trading possibilities. It was comparatively safe for them. Long before the railway linked Lake Tanganyika with the coast there was a well defined slave route following the railway's present lines. At the time we were living near Tabora there was no proper road eastwards to the coast so a road journey could only be made by Land Rover. This meant following much of the old slaving route. Here and there were signs of their temporary halts – old defence works, pottery and a few rusting tools and muzzle loading muskets.

It was a desperate journey even in a solid vehicle, grinding along at ten miles an hour (fifteen at the very most) and hoping that the engine would not let you down. It never did. Sometimes the track criss-crossed the railway line and then plunged deep into savannah and sometimes jungle. When I went down to Dodoma where there was a school for the blind, I always aimed to night-stop at Itigi, which was about half way on the two hundred mile journey. This meant sleeping in the Land Rover. The two Africans I took with me usually bedded down as well as they did not like the people in this part of the country. On those trips we came across a wide assortment of game, ostriches and giraffe. I often thought, as we bumped along, that Americans and Europeans were paying fortunes to see such sights and I had a job where it was all free and either on my doorstep or along the routes I travelled. As a matter of form and also courtesy, I always advised the Provincial Commissioner of my route and ETA just in case anything went wrong like a major breakdown. At Buigiri some thirty miles outside Dodoma I found Fred Varley, a Church Army Mission man, who had given up, he told me, a 'soft job' in the UK for a really hard life in central Tanzania where famine was endemic. With meagre funds and a large proportion of faith he had built up a School for Blind Children from nothing. It was a tremendous achievement in a place where improvisation and famine had, of necessity, to live side by side. In future years I often revisited places like Buigiri, but, instead of slogging it out in painful road journeys, the new RCSB Save your Sight and Flying Doctor Service managed to get me into the remotest places with their landing strips hacked out of the bush at places like Mvumi. The youngsters flying those planes were excellent. They included a twenty year old girl who told me, with a grin, that the BOAC (now British Airways) pilots when they heard her on the intercom coming in to land at Nairobi, broke their normally business-like patter to pass the time of day with her and add a few chauvinistic remarks, which everyone took in good part. Unfortunately one of the lads with whom I flew was killed taking off from a bush airfield. The cause of the accident was a fractured petrol feed pipe, one of the hazards a bush pilot faces.

It is not easy to forget the past in Tabora. It is still all around – the huge white Boma, a fort built by the Germans commanding from the highest point great views across the plains, the two small military cemeteries telling their stories of violent death in both mankind and nature. They were badly overgrown in my day. I suppose those who rest under the shade of wild acacia trees, poinsettia shrubs and frangipani far from their German and British homelands, are now quite forgotten as though, as the Bible says, "they had never been."

In my time at Kazima the very old ones could still recollect with something of a festered memory the Arab caravans and their chained captives on the trail to Mwanza on Lake Victoria or down to the west coast to Bagamoya. But the past has had its day. The present and the wild environment were still with us. The future had yet to unfold with its greatest personal challenge: one which is still with us and one which, paradoxically, we would not be without.

Chapter Ten

I well remember the early part of 1957 at Kazima. The rains were late, the countryside parched and desiccated, even Kazima lake threatened to dry up. In desperation the Water Department from Dar es Salaam came along with rockets loaded with experimental rain-forming crystals and fired than at the huge billows of tantalising cloud which formed up every day, all to no avail. But when the rains eventually came in late April, the whole heavens seemed to open up. Just for a brief half hour the ground would soak up the precious liquid and then the searing sun emerged from behind the black rain clouds to give a clear blue sky and scald the steaming countryside again. At least for a few hours we could enjoy the smell of damp earth, the dust was laid low and exotic shrubs and plants came to life with the rich fragrant scents of the tropics.

A few weeks earlier Cathleen had made the lengthy journey of six hundred miles down to Dar es Salaam to await the arrival of our first-born, Anthony. I stayed behind at Kazima where life was busy, hot and dusty, but as the work was expanding rapidly there was plenty to keep me occupied. Everything seemed to be ticking over splendidly. There were no emergencies and everyone was in high spirits now that the threatening rains were about to descend on us. Another United Nations delegation came to have a look at developments and although they made complimentary remarks, I doubt if they had much idea about what we were trying to do – give blind people practical training so that they would be more acceptable in their village communities. They were, I suspect, much more interested in the herds of ungainly wildebeest who had invaded the lower part of the estate where the blind were growing cassava.

It was about this time that I had my first close encounter with a lion. Fortunately the lions in this area of Tanzania were fairly docile. At least, unlike their counterparts in the Luapula and Mweru regions, they rarely killed human beings but nevertheless I, and others, treated the lions around Kazima with a fair degree of respect tempered with a strong element of trepidation. Every evening when Cathleen was with me it had been our custom to make the circular walk with our Pekinese Sherry around the back of the hill past the rocky outcrops, down to the Kazima lake and home. It took about forty-five minutes and we normally started a good hour before dusk. Now I was on my own I still continued this light exercise as there was always plenty of interesting and harmless things to see, colourful bird-life and *dik-dik*, miniature bambi-type deer, not more than a foot high when fully grown. Sherry and I started off in great style over the rocky path which wound in a U turn below the house. Earlier in the day two of the workmen, Rashidi and old Husseini, the *capitao*, had mentioned in passing that the *simbas* – lions – were getting restless. It was, he thought, the drought annoying them. It was a lonely enough walk, certainly remote and wild and I remember thinking at the time you could never really relax and enjoy the manifold things the African bush concealed even if you were patient and observing. My thoughts were abruptly interrupted and the words of Husseini and Rashidi came back to me as an unpleasant afterthought. The dog was ahead of me. Suddenly without any warning she froze and her hair visibly stiffened. I also sensed danger. I picked her up. It was then that I noticed the strong stench of ammonia which came wafting out of the tall brittle elephant grass which grew on either side of the track. This was certain confirmation that we were not alone. I looked gingerly into the bush but saw nothing. I hesitated and decided to head for home, but when I looked back I saw that my escape route had already been cut off, a massive male lion (in its prime I imagined) was staring at me balefully. He had emerged out of the bushland in almost complete silence. His mane was untidy and there were patches on his coat where he had been biting at ticks or some other parasitic insect. I seemed to absorb these irrelevant details automatically and then I realised that the animal was a mere twenty feet away and loping at an ambling pace towards me.

The Africans, who from time to time found themselves in this type of situation, had always told me that there are two basic rules when caught up in such a predicament. "Firstly," Husseini had said, "you must never run, but only walk. Even if the lion is not hungry he will find it hard to resist something which appears to be afraid of him. Secondly," he added, "lions do not like noise, so you must yell and shout as hard as you can. No, you will not be attracting much help, but the lion will think twice before tackling you." With legs of jelly, I walked with my trembling peke in the direction I was originally going, with the lion at the rear of me. Clearly there was no prospect of trying to get back to the house, even though it was only a couple of hundred yards away. I had a long two mile hike ahead provided the lion remained quiet. Slowly and deliberately I set off yelling and shouting at the top of my voice. I constantly glanced over my shoulder. He plodded a few feet in my direction, paused and then slunk off into the bush, apparently quite unconcerned about our meeting. The staff and boys in the training centre who were having their evening meal knew all about the encounter as they had heard my shouts and they started to rally up a hunting party, but by the time they were about to set off, I had completed the rest of the circular walk without any problems and, in any case, darkness was now falling. They thought it amusing and were delighted that nothing untoward had happened, particularly as the following day was Friday. "Why Juma?" I asked, "what is particular about Friday?" He smiled.

"Tomorrow is pay day *Bwana*, so we are all glad to see you back." I understood!

Two weeks after this incident I boarded the one train which left each week for Dar es Salaam. The telegram announcing Anthony's arrival into the world took two days to reach Kazima, the journey I made down to Dar took another three days as the rains had come with a vengeance and washed the line away near Morogora and, to conclude this time-scale to its finality, it took the medicos nearly three long years to confirm that Anthony was a severely handicapped Down's syndrome infant, something which was obvious to the most casual observer at a fairly early stage.

Those were the years when the battles we were engaged in against the scourge of blindness and other serious disabilities entered into a new phase. Indeed it was to be an exciting era when organisations led by the RCSB shook off the strictures of European thinking and set off with a fair share of pragmatic realism and little else, to blaze a trail through the uncharted bushlands of Africa. We had soon discovered that systems which had worked well for maybe a century and a half in Europe and America, had little relevance in the mid-twentieth century Africa which faced us. In the perceptions of men and women of the RCSB like Ronnie Babanau and Grace Ingham-Wright it soon became evident that the duplication of European systems such as workshops for the blind – things which had served Britain and America well, but in an entirely different type of environment, were often recipes for disaster. Some of the soundest advice which came my way was in 1955 from the gnarled and grizzly Chief Puta, whose village was just east of the Valley of the Blind along the shores of Lake Mweru. The substance of what he said in two prolonged discussions was briefly, "Before the *musungu* decides what is good for my people, he must study us just as we study him. He must understand our customs and not despise them, he must listen and go away and consider what the Indunas (elders) have said, he must respect our language and, above all, he must be a man of peace." I think the words of this old man were eminently suitable for a stranger who had yet to win his spurs. The influence of Chief Puta remains with me to this day. I remember his parting words ringing in my ears, "It is easier to destroy than to create." The idea of building on the background, the culture, traditions and customs of the tribes with which we were working rather than attempting to obliterate local culture was the cardinal principle which led to the success of RCSB.

"Always take those you are working amongst with you," was the advice of John Wilson. "Make sure," he would go on, "that what you are seeking to achieve is attainable and then, by example, demonstrate the validity of your claims. It may take weeks," he would add, "more likely it will take months and years." But amidst all these homilies from John and other well-wishers it was clear that the future lay in our work, at least, in partnership between Africans and the Europeans.

Our mutual confidence had been established, the horizons for our work amongst the blind were limitless. The prevention of blindness campaigns have proved this. Who would have thought that the rugged 'eye camps', an idea conceived in a remote little office in the RCSB Headquarters in Haywards Heath would sweep across much of Africa, India and Bangladesh saving the sight not of hundreds but of very many hundreds of thousands of men, women and children? Who would have thought that in collaboration with other agencies the scourge of river blindness, of trachoma and vitamin deficiency diseases causing disabilities would be fought out in the wildest of savage countries with resounding success? In the mid-Fifties we were not to know that the research and experiments our colleagues were undertaking would bear fruit so readily. Certainly there were disappointments, some of them quite disheartening, but on balance the thrust of the RCSB men and women in the medical, educational and rehabilitation fields was stimulating and very successful.

I was to see two refreshing developments in my own area of work – rural training and open education. Rural training was being pioneered near Lagos by stalwarts like Ronnie Babanau. My own efforts in this experimental field were disappointing and it was Ronnie, an ex-St Dunstan veteran from Indian Army days, who made the major breakthrough.

The general principles and development of rural training for the handicapped in Africa were utterly simple. Most of us realised that for many blind Africans, particularly where the extended family system had broken down, the first priority was how to survive. Secondly, once this had been achieved, the problem was how to regain acceptance into the family and community. The answer was in training the blind and handicapped to use local resources – the land and their environment. This has proved to be the catalyst which swept across Africa and Asia and given the welfare of the blind a new look and respectability. It was this step, almost in *pari passu* with another exciting development in the early Sixties in the educational field, open education – the education of the blind alongside those who can see – which was to assist us to solve the almost insoluble, to provide new and imaginative vistas and new hope. These systems which have been widely adopted in third world countries underline the fact that developments between the old and the new worlds are not all one way operations. Far from it. Both rural training for the blind and open education have had their impact in modern countries, including Britain, which prided themselves on the ingenuity of their approach to work for the handicapped. The traditionalists who held sheltered workshops and residential schools sacrosanct have been jolted out of their complacency by the unusual methods we cultivated in the African bushlands and applied with ease in the West. Kazima, along with the work near Lagos and with experiments under Sir Clutha Mackenzie near Salima in Uganda were to be the proving grounds for this new approach.

It is with pleasure that we find that the self-help philosophy, together with suitable support, still provides the weapons system for services engaged in the endless fight to help those in distant lands who are visually disabled. As far as I was concerned, after my initial failure to organise rural training at Bwana Mkubwa the work at Kazima took off. This was to the astonishment of our United Nations observer friends! It was in this isolated former Mau Mau prison camp that we managed to grow the staple foods including ground nuts, keep poultry and cattle and, in the lower section of the grounds near the lake, produce reasonable quantities of rice. Our blind young men learnt basic farming skills the hard way, including thatching and carpentry.

In later years when I was working in a more peripatetic role – one which covered most of Africa and part of Asia, I would sometimes revisit Kazima. It never seemed to change. The bush encroached each year on the same old mud houses and each year it was driven back. The wild life hid amongst the rocky outcrops and in the tall elephant grass. It seemed as if both man and beast had reached an understanding to share the bountiful wilderness with which nature had endowed Kazima and to live out their lives in salutary accord. Long may such an arrangement endure! But there were other faces to the Kazima scene.

More recently I had landed in Dar es Salaam when this picturesque port was in chaos. An attempt had been made to unseat Julius Nyerere, then President of a fragile country feeling its newly independent way through the intricate powder kegs of tribal and racial unrest. He called in the former colonial rulers, Britain, to rescue him from out of the cold. Subsequently a handful of marines from a Royal Naval ship lying off Zanzibar came in by helicopter and drove out the mutinous elements of Nyerere's army from their barracks into the bush. Poor Julius Nyerere, according to one report which was never confirmed, was found wandering in the streets of Dar es Salaam and was promptly restored to the presidential palace on the sea front. Nyerere was one of the great African leaders to emerge from post-colonial days. He was essentially an idealist, a humble man who never allowed power to go to his head. Somehow he welded together diverse sections of humanity, Arabs, Asians, Europeans and numerous African tribes, and made them into a nation. The mutiny which was quickly snuffed out in Dar es Salaam threatened more distant places and one of them was Tabora. Here two dozen marines kept the peace with good humoured smiles and a minimum show of force. I invited two of them to come out to Kazima with me and they had a great welcome from some of my old friends including Husseini and Juma.

My first tour of duty at Kazima had lasted eighteen months and came to an abrupt end. All was going well and life at last was comfy, with regular supplies of water during the dry season and a plane from Nairobi flew in cold store supplies once every two weeks. This was indeed a luxury, but too good to last. A cable arrived confirming that my replacement was on his way and that I was to proceed as soon as I had handed over to swarthy Frank Rigby. He was a Scot who was to become an expert on almost everything to do with tribal East Africa. He was a quiet conscientious man in his early thirties who, like so many others from north of the border, established a happy rapport with the local tribesmen. We saw Frank safely installed in our mud bungalow at Kazima and left him in the good hands of our African staff who soon found him to be an excellent linguist and a great bush ranger – two necessary requisites in those days.

Our next destination was Malawi – then in pre-Independence days known as Nyasaland. We left Kazima with much regret and started off on the long trek south, complete with a nine month old handicapped infant and our little Pekinese, Sherry.

My new assignment was to provide a model training centre for the blind. The country in those days was extremely poor, hence the acting governor of the territory had made it clear to me that the unit had to be cheap to build, economic to run and therefore uncompromisingly utilitarian, designed to meet the needs of a backward community where there was a high incidence of blindness.

These demanding parameters – in those days in Malawi one out of every five hundred people was blind – had some compensations. The site we were given was located in one of the most beautiful and scenic parts of Africa, almost surrounded by shaded tea plantations, lying at the foot of mystic Mlanje mountain, a fearsome ten thousand foot height from which cascaded silver streams, broken by gigantic waterfalls. It was in this lovely five acre setting that plans were developed to remould the lives of countless young blind people who were living, through no fault of their own, lives of abject poverty and helplessness. Many of them we found, like our blind friends in the Luapula and around Kazima, had become hardened embittered characters, deserted by relatives and friends and whilst frequently faced with starvation they seemed to have clung on to life by a strand.

Republic of Malawi

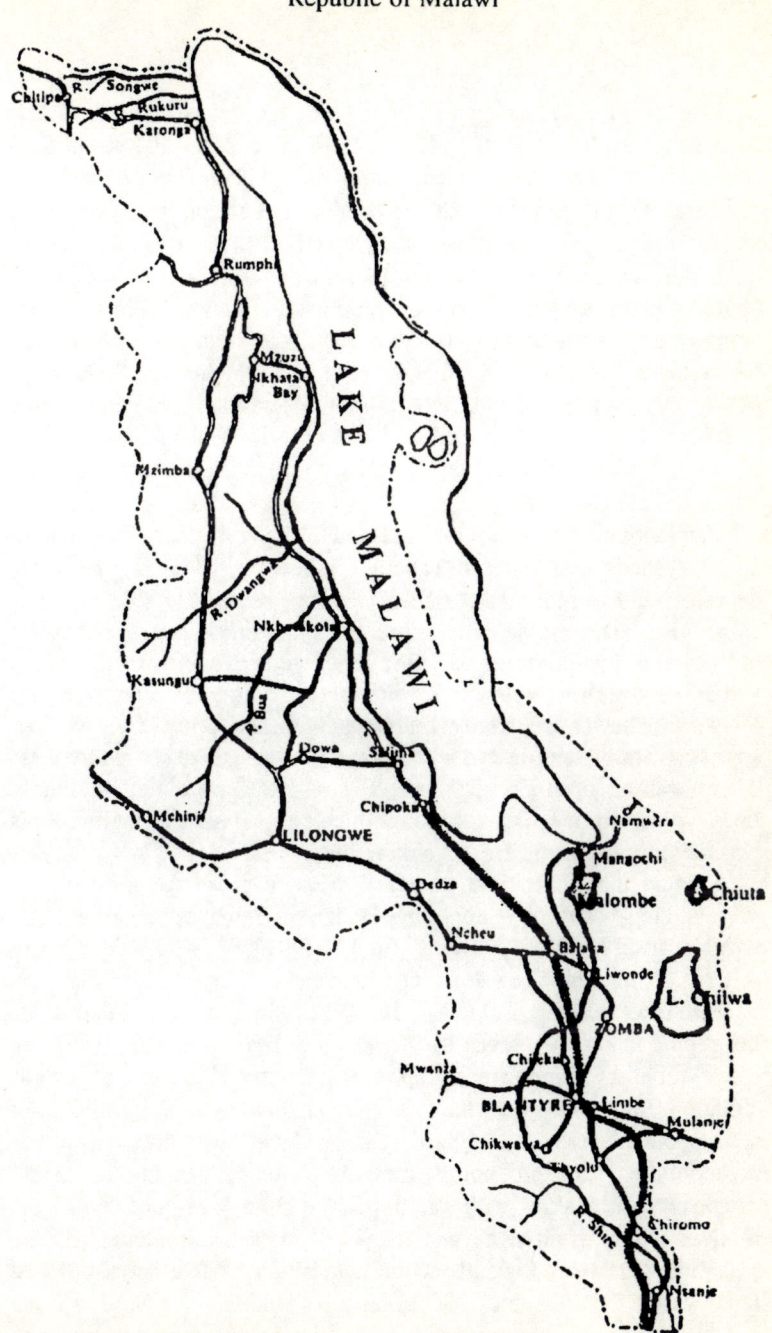

It was not an encouraging picture. Our object was to rebuild their lives using the best features of African life, traditions and customs so that they could be re-assimilated into their villages as farmers and semi-skilled craftsmen. It was reasoned as at Kazima, that if we could teach them to grow their own food and find them a small piece of land, they would at least be able to feed themselves. If as well we could manage to teach them to supply their fellow villagers with simple needs such as baskets, reed mats and light cane chairs and tables, their position in the village would be strengthened. So here, in Mlanje, we were faced with a time limit of less than eighteen months, in a land which, in living memory, had only just emerged from Arab slaving raids and tribal warfare – trying to establish a system and way of life to heal old wounds.

The fact that we managed to succeed in doing this is entirely due to a young dedicated African called Tembezeka, a teacher of great character and commitment. Out of nothing, he seemed able to create something. The simple little units, hostels, workshops, school, were utilitarian in the extreme. He used them well. They were functional and at the cost of a modest sum were erected within two months of my arrival. They were sturdy buildings with the doors and window frames made of steel in order to escape the ravages of the white ants. There was an open-air kitchen and the hostels were run on family lines. Apart from a first aid room which also served as an office, this was the only departure from a simple life.

I found that from time to time Africa, even in the humblest of surroundings, can throw up young leaders of remarkable calibre. (It was a man in his early twenties, Fred Kafwankwe, who started a day school for blind children at Chief Mununga's village, one of the most isolated of outposts in Zambia.) Tembezeka, a quiet individual, knew his people better than some of the old grey beards who sat under the shade of nearby mango trees prophesying doom and disaster for us all. Young Tembezeka soon took up the challenge in a multitude of self-appointed roles, as welfare adviser, local head man, instructor and confidant. He soon got the measure of the opposition. It was the usual story of breaking with tradition. The blind were confused by the motives which inspired anyone to give them a helping hand and the local villagers mumbling about the acquisition of five acres of good land which the 'wizards' had ordained should not be used for ten years! After one or two escapades in which newly planted crops were uprooted and slight damage done to a classroom, we settled down to a happy routine in which the villagers eventually joined us. These social evenings in which they joined took the form of 'camp fire' entertainment. One of the unusual items in this training centre was the small fish farm which Tembezeka made by making a dam across one of the fast mountain streams which flowed by the borders of the school. Mlanje under Tembezeka was a place for innovation and initiative.

But even Mlanje with its sweeping tea estates and curtains of jungle skirting the vast mountain was not immune from the ravages of wild animals. The neighbouring villagers at times lived in dread of hyaenas who, apart from having 'spirit' connotations, sometimes picked off the weakest, the sick, the elderly and children – in one case from the door of their hut. Our nearest neighbour, who lived a mile from us, had a house at the foot of the mountain. He was a single man, Peter de Lapature. He was out hunting a leopard which had savaged a number of domestic animals when the hunter became the hunted. Peter was very badly mauled and was only saved by the brave action of his African companion Edwin Chingwala who very bravely attacked the leopard with a stout stick and managed to drive it away. That morning when it all happened, I was well away from the area where the action was taking place, but the next day, as was customary after such an event, everyone joined up to carry out a massive hunt for the beast. It was some days before he was finally tracked down, a huge specimen with a den in a crevasse on the lower part of the mountain.

In Malawi the past and present sometimes mingle as though they were one. The red hand-moulded brick mission houses of the Church of Scotland were founded as a direct result of David Livingstone's explorations. The Mlanje mission station, significantly plain but enduring was surrounded by eucalyptus trees, neat gardens and fruit trees planted by the faithful pioneers of many yesterdays. They were still providing sustenance. The Livingstonia Mission was first established in 1875 at Cape Maclear, a premonitory jutting out into the azure blue Lake Malawi[1]. The site though very beautiful was unsatisfactory so, after several moves, the missionaries settled in 1895

---

[1]Lake Malawi was formerly Lake Nyasa. Malawi means "the water on which the haze of the sun is reflected like fire."

high up on the Khondowe Plateau, a fantastic location at an altitude of over two thousand, six hundred feet directly overlooking the lake.

The mission complex bears all the hall-marks of its founders, including a single storey Scottish type manse. Sadly, amongst the ruins of its former mission stations can be found the many mounds of missionary graves, a reminder of the perils of those times. The lake part of the Rift Valley, is nearly two hundred and fifty miles long and has formed, from time immemorial, one of the main communication links. The slavers were still using ports like Karonga in the north as staging posts for the journey down to the east coast. At times the placid blue lake can quite suddenly change into a turbulent stormy sea with giant waves crashing on its delightful sandy beaches. The short waves caused by the narrow water confines, reach heights of ten and twelve feet, so tragedies amongst the fishing villages are not uncommon. Apart from providing a prolific source of suitable edible fish, the country has a thriving trade in exporting the minute tropical fish which thrive around Nkata Bay. In the early days small British gunboats patrolled the lake looking for slavers and the Livingstonia Mission also had its own boat. More recently the six hundred ton *Ilala* which can accommodate nine cabin class passengers makes the voyage from Monkey Bay in the south, to Kambwe in the north. It covers on the round trip a total of over six hundred and fifty miles. The entire voyage takes seven days. The voyage provides a great opportunity to see some of the most magnificent scenery in the world and, provided one is lucky with the weather, it can be a most relaxing break. The best time for a lake cruise is between March and June. The lake is then usually calm.

Even with the advance of the twentieth century, old ideas, soothsayers, wizardry, and folklore have a place, albeit a diminishing one, in many African communities. One interesting character I heard about at Mlanje was Mbona the 'rain-maker'. Unusually, our Mlanje district was on the verge of drought. It was then that I noticed small shrines of reeds and a few stones were being erected in some of the villages. I made some casual enquiries and was told that the help of Mbona was being sought to make the rains fall. It seems that Mbona is supposed to have originated from the lower Shire river area several centuries ago. By profession he was a 'rainmaker' of the Lundu tribe. Unfortunately he incurred the wrath of the elders for they, by tribal tradition, were solely endowed with the responsibility of rainmaking in times of drought! Legend has it that during a particularly severe drought when the *indunas*, or elders went through a whole series of ceremonies, including rebuilding the *kacisi* the spirit house, appeals to their ancestors, the beating of drums and sacrifices – he drought continued. Mbona then came on the scene and joined in the ceremony of the day without so much as paying homage to the elders. He entered the circle of *indunas* and leaping shouting and pointing to the sky yelled for the rain to fall. It did – in a deluge with lightning and wind. The *indunas* were aggrieved that they had been upstaged and accused Mbona of witchcraft and challenged him to take the *muabvi* test, drinking from a cup of poison. Wisely, Mbona refused and was forced to flee. (The *indunas* had contended that he was originally responsible for the delay in the rains commencing that year.)

Mbona fled with one of his four wives, Sawawa, his child Sajola and his dog and two precious spears which he claimed were necessary for rainmaking. After wandering on the mountains and bush for years as far as Karonga making rain he was, according to legend, finally caught and killed by his jealous enemies. Mbona, the rain-maker was clearly not forgotten around the Mlanje area even if he was not appreciated by the jealous indunas!

My own work at Mlanje had been preceded by two little mission schools for the blind, one run by Mr and Mrs Creil, near Port Herald, now Nsanje. It was a lonely little spot well removed from humanity high up in the rolling hills overlooking the Shire river. Not a particularly healthy spot, its approach over a rugged track in the wet season was dangerous. In mid-Malawi the Dutch Reformed Mission also had a school at Kasungu, well on the road to the north. Now, in the Eighties, the education of the handicapped in Malawi is often first rate. The foundations laid by the early pioneers have been built on. Now there are exciting developments under Brother Rudolf at Montfort near Limbe. All this from nothing and within the space of a lifetime. With the completion of my Mlanje work, I handed over to Tembezeka and an elderly and much respected local European – Bob Pryor. They seemed to exemplify what we were all talking about in those days, partnership, but unfortunately it was not to last long. Poor Bob Pryor found the pressure too much and dropped dead whilst talking to a group of blind lads in the humble office first aid post. Young Tembezeka and his helpers held things together and when I revisited Mlanje a few years ago, all was well; the mountain was glistening and the rains fell on time with the help, as one youngster said, "of Mbona"!

Blind trainees at the Kazima Centre planting groundnuts. Note the 'spacing sticks' they use.

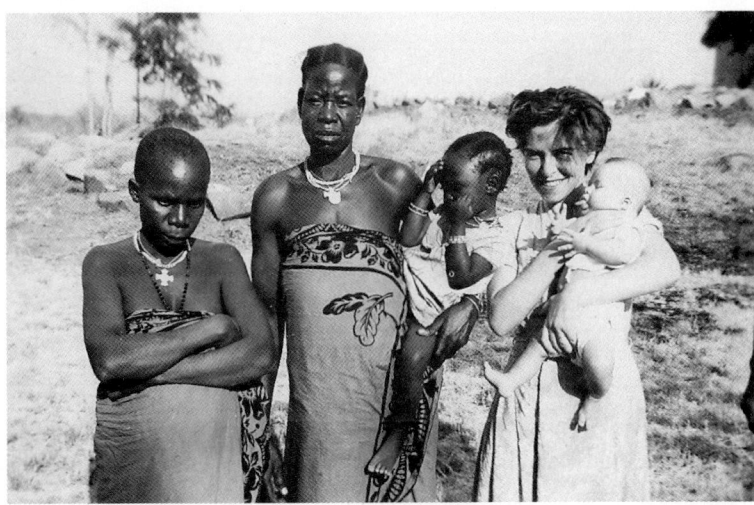

Kazima, a desolate ex-Mau-Mau prison settlement, which for years had been left to nature and wild-life, was assigned to the author as a base for starting services for the handicapped. Here, new arrivals, the author's wife Cathleen and infant Anthony, meet their nearest neighbours, members of the Nyamwezi tribe.

How times have really changed! A few years ago it would have been unthinkable to invite the handicapped to your wedding. Not so in the west of Ireland where this charming bride, Anne Chambers, has a special word and hug for two of the family of handicapped she has been nursing.

The benefits of 'water therapy' for many disabled children are sometimes overlooked. For Down's children, some autistics and others with allied conditions, the simplest of activities such as watching the stream, waterfall, or the gentle waves of an incoming tide can be both soothing and fascinating. The freedom of splashing in a pool or for the more adventurous, being a passenger in a small rowing dingy or even a sailing cruiser, are experiences which some 'experts' seem to overlook.

Horse-riding for the mentally handicapped. Such activities are commonplace in Western Care. They are a source of much pleasure and stimulation. But feeding blue-eyed 'Blackie' (who is looking for another lump of sugar) seems a little precarious!

The Down's syndrome child reacts to 'atmosphere' – a point sometimes overlooked by administrators ultimately responsible for their welfare and quality of life. Here at Roscairn in Co. Fermanagh, Anthony and his mother Cathleen share a light-hearted joke and laughter with two young friends, Sandra and Kathryn MaVitty. At their tender age, they set a shining example in accepting the handicapped in their midst with kindness and understanding.

Learning to swim at the age of seven can be fun for a Down's syndrome child even though he has no speech.

A few years later, Anthony finds that swimming in the deep end under the eye of one of the Western Care staff in the west of Ireland needs effort and courage but is still exciting and great fun.

The East African Mountain School, run by the Outward Bound Trust, was the base for training. Here, totally blind Elud Kiago of Tanzania completes one of the most arduous obstacles in the 'assault' course.

Crossing a semi-dry water course – easy enough if you can see but under the encouraging guidance of Tom Wijenjie *(seen at the rear with his pullover tied loosely around his neck)* confidence is growing. Soon they will be tackling much greater challenges.

One of the Bivouac sites located at an altitude of about 10,000 ft. The area is renowned for its variety of foliage and rare plants. Heathers grow to the height of 10 ft. Here the party rests after a difficult climb. Local grass and branches have been used to construct shelter for the night.

A break on the first bush march to review progress. Mutie *(left)*, complains that he has never worn boots before! But his companion, Palour of Tanzania *(right)*, tells him that he will have no feet at all once he gets on the frozen mountain unless he wears them.

Kilimanjaro, though technically not a difficult climb, claims its victims each year. Hazards include adverse reaction to high altitudes leading to either pulmonary or cerebral oedema, conditions which are potentially fatal. Here, Kisaka from Uganda examines the emergency portable radio.

Charles Gilman, an experienced climber and explorer, plunged to his death when he fell over the precipice into the crater on 19th October 1921. Meanwhile the intense cold and rarefied atmosphere were taking their toll. Two climbers, after gallant efforts at 17,000 ft, reluctantly withdrew. The ice cliffs around the crater rim are the final stage of the climb.

At last Kilimanjaro is conquered by a team of totally blind Africans to show that given proper training and help, the blind are part and parcel of a modern community and can do some things which people with sight are sometimes afraid to tackle.

At a height of well over 19,000 ft, John Lubega of Uganda *(left)* shakes hands with the author who has just radioed to base and told the world that the climb has been successful. As the weather was closing in and snow storms beginning to start (unusual for the time of year) the descent began almost immediately and proved to be a hazardous experience.

Chapter Eleven

I think Anthony could claim to be amongst the most travelled Down's syndrome young people one is likely to meet. Perhaps you may feel that his is a dubious distinction but at least his parents, because the family was so frequently on the move, had little time or indeed inclination to brood over the hand which fate had dealt him. Too much was happening. During his infancy water had to be boiled and filtered, torn mosquito nets repaired, milk was largely unobtainable except in powdered form; if we were lucky there may be a paraffin fridge in the house, and of course, there was no electric light, just the Tilley lamps which became almost unbearably hot and attracted a variety of moths.

Perhaps, fortunately or unfortunately, according to one's experiences, there were no social workers or psychologists coming round mouthing their text-book clichés about feelings of guilt and then hastily running off to the next 'client', (what an impersonal type of terminology, as far as the handicapped are concerned).

It was the momentum of this routine, which included lengthy journeys into the bush sometimes for days at a time when Cathleen was left on her own which, maybe, acted as a balm and concealed the magnitude of Anthony's disability from us. When we did travel together and made a night stop at a bush rest house, it was something of a demanding exercise and involved, according to the area one was in, constant warfare against stink bugs, sand flies, mosquitoes and sometimes scorpions. But somehow, in spite of crawling and grovelling on mud floors and in the sandy wastes outside where myriads of insects seemed to swarm, apart from a slight attack of fever whilst staying near Salima on the shores of Lake Malawi, and a bad patch of dehydration when we moved back to Blantyre, Anthony seemed to thrive.

On balance I suppose we were lucky. European infants seem very adaptable in certain environments, but unfortunately from time to time the tropical climate takes its toll. A six month old infant died at Katsina from cerebral malaria. This was an exception but the massive infant mortality rate suffered by the early pioneers and their families was now a thing of the past. According to Richard Sampson, who researched the exploration movement into what was then Northern Rhodesia, now Zambia, the death rate amongst children was over thirty four percent and this was largely due to malaria, yellow fever, dysentery and allied conditions.

In the early years between 1852 and 1870 only thirty-three Europeans entered the country, but in this number were included, surprisingly enough, Mrs Reader and her child. Her husband, who was a hunter and trader took them to the Victoria Falls. It must have been a perilous journey, but they achieved a notable first, the first recorded European woman and the first European child to see the Falls and enter into present day Zambia. After the 1870s there was an increase in the number of children coming in to this still wild and dangerous land, mainly the off-spring of missionaries. A glance at the records of mission stations and their lonely burial grounds, such as at Sefula in Barotseland and Mbereshi to name just a few, tell their own stories of the faith and fortitude of these courageous, but forgotten families.

In the late 1950s and 1960s, sane objective advice about mongoloids, even if you lived in Europe or America, was difficult to acquire from the medical fraternity. Perhaps this may be the case today though clearly attitudes seem to have changed for the better. It took me some time to realise, even though I had now been moving in the world of the handicapped for some years, that, as the Down's syndrome condition was an incurable one, the clinical interest in such cases sharply diminishes apart from a formal consideration of aetiological factors and the fact that such children are often predisposed to heart and respiratory problems.

A GP friend of mine in the west of England, supported this view and added for good measure that in any case medical student training in the mental handicap area was superficial and hence doctors usually, "Kicked for touch". His words just about summed up the situation which may sometimes prevail even today. The medical syllabus in some universities seems to be in a state of flux. Medical schools are sometimes unable to cope with recent developments and the new technologies, hence a wider understanding of mental handicap conditions remains static and so this non-vocal group remain the 'Cinderellas' of society and stay at the end of the queue. Young medical men and women with the best intentions in the world are unlikely therefore to be well informed on the needs and care of this (at present) irreversible mental handicap condition. I think this situation is understandable, but it is important as well that the parents of severely handicapped children should realise that the medical profession's commitment to what one doctor, unfortunately described to me in England as the "write-offs of society" is of necessity a limited one. Whilst most doctors try to be helpful and do not use such abrasive language, there are a few who are insensitive and treat parents, particularly the inarticulate ones, with appalling disdain. One gentleman told a parent who wished to keep her handicapped daughter at home that "emotionally she must be up the walls". It would be utterly fallacious to suggest that such characters are representative of a busy profession, but it is a fact that there are a few parents who have been treated with arrogance and deplorable manners at a sensitive time by medical misfits.

"My child may be mentally handicapped," said one mother, to a self-styled grandee of the profession, "but I am not, so would you please have the courtesy to explain Mary's condition to me?" This lady was not one of the inarticulate ones!

Perhaps Cathleen and I have been lucky, but clearly other parents may not have been so fortunate. Whilst it is difficult to make general observations, it seems that professionals working for voluntary organisations and certainly on bush mission stations overseas, where standards of service and tolerance take precedence over financial inducements and career incentives, may sometimes have more to offer parents at a perplexing time! Whilst much has been done to explain the consequences and care of the mentally handicapped to the public, it would make life easier and happier for many hard-pressed parents if the medical profession up-dated itself on recent developments. The medical fraternity have their share of temperamental arrogant brethren who orbit around hospitals emulating the deity; few though they may be, they tarnish the image of a largely conscientious professional body who have or should have, something helpful to contribute to parents of newly handicapped youngsters.

But one had to be fair. There are difficult parents as well as difficult professionals. It should be recognised that the painful emotional nature of severe disability and the subsequent anguish of finding that an infant is profoundly disabled often brushes off on the doctor. He or she is being asked to do the impossible, to wipe out the grief and pain, to make good the shock of the bad news and, as the harbinger of these awful tidings over which the medical fraternity has no control, they are subconsciously and ironically the ones who are perversely singled out for blame. It is too facile at such times to sit in judgement on others, but clearly the ultimate solution lies in parents and the medical people working together rather than with recriminations and blame being apportioned to all and sundry.

I have found over the years and more recently in Ireland, that the medium best suited for generating this common-sense partnership, may still be the voluntary organisation. But in these days unfortunately voluntary organisations may not always be as stable and reliable as we are sometimes led to believe. When one sees, as I have done, beautiful seaside homes set aside for the handicapped, unused and allowed to go derelict, sometimes a home doing a reasonably steady job, almost destroyed by the crass foolishness and ineptitude of those who are supposed to stand up for the rights of the disabled, it rather makes one shudder. Added to this is over-administration, lack of professional know-how, the squandering of funds on overseas training and super-comfy offices, whilst their handicapped languish in despair in a home which sometimes has precious little comfort. Are we back to the bad old days of the nineteenth century-type incarceration and indifference? This is the crux of the tragedy – the state for a century and a half failing to grasp the nettle and the voluntary organisations doing the job for them. Of course the Government should take the lead, but it can't do it with half-baked voluntary organisations whose managements may be sometimes weird and intimidating. The cynical used to say in both Britain and Ireland that, 'the handicapped can't vote so don't waste your time soliciting politicians to take an interest in their welfare.' Times are changing and most British and Irish politicians interested in refining their survival techniques realise that a population which is becoming more educated and informed is not likely to tolerate the sordid conditions which may still exist in some state mental hospitals. It is all very well complaining about human rights in distant lands but what are we doing about the rights of the handicapped on our own doorstep who may be still incarcerated in the nineteenth century prison-type surroundings? This is a question which still remains partially unanswered.

The misery and scandal of the state mental hospitals in much of Europe and America has reigned unabated for over a hundred years, largely on the grounds that there are more important medical and social priorities; but of course the real truth is that the mentally handicapped cannot speak up for themselves and hence they have always been at the bottom of the barrel when the 'goodies' are distributed by their respective Governments.

The role of charitable organisations and their work for the handicapped is often an ambiguous one. Some, many in fact, have done sterling work in representing the interests of those groups which are inarticulate, badly organised or isolated and in need of skilled guidance. Most good charities keep their administrative costs down to a minimum so that their funds go to those in need. The Cheshire Homes and Royal Commonwealth Society for the Blind, both worldwide organisations, have impeccable records in this respect, but a few – possibly a mere handful – are positively disappointing and unsuspectingly show a face of administrative greed and rapaciousness.

This is the danger. The handicapped and particularly the mentally handicapped are sometimes big business – something which is not confined to Europe, but can be described as a worldwide phenomena. I think the most hopeful sign (and there are plenty) is the work of the United Nations in this field. Usually regarded as an ineffective and innocuous body, its Charter on *The Rights of the Handicapped* has even made the politicians sit up and take notice. But not content with pious platitudes, the International League of Societies for the Mentally Handicapped, a UN-sponsored organisation based in Brussels has done much to bring mental handicap out of the dark ages into an aura of hope and respectability. This little-known body sets the standards, advises, actively helps distant and impoverished countries to create a spirit of service and care in the 'Cinderella' of special services. The steady flow of its reports and activities which find their way into every land should give us all new hope.

At least Anthony has never had to worry about the problems of creating acceptable standards, attitudes and services for people like himself! In our travels with him we had more mundane concerns. I still recall with some amusement and bewilderment a border post in pre-Independence Rhodesia, near Fort Victoria, where an over-zealous immigration official declared him a "prohibited immigrant" on account of his medical condition. Somehow we managed to get over that obstacle but more problems were to follow. As he was born in pre-Independence Tanganyika, now Tanzania, this caused the South African passport officials much concern until they accepted that he had a British father and an Irish mother. I must confess that the attitudes at the border post near Fort Victoria and later in South Africa surprised me but, like most parents who have a badly handicapped child, there are moments which provide both humour and hurt. This was one of them, albeit an unnecessary one. Another more embarrassing episode was in the midst of the pleasant Somerset countryside when we were on leave. We called in at a village pub for lunch only to be informed by a young flabby, pasty-faced land lord, probably a yuppie blown in from a distant city, that he would not admit people such as Anthony to his house! These days such cutting incidents are becoming rarer thanks to good media and TV publicity. I suppose, on reflection, that these kinds of difficulties will continue perhaps long after racial discrimination has disappeared. There are many misunderstandings about the handicapped whatever their disability. As far as the mentally handicapped are concerned their characteristics, an innate desire to be wanted and loved, shines through the misty world which surrounds them. What are the features, for example, of a Down's child?

Firstly there are physical abnormalities. The head is short in circumference and the frontal regions flattened. When I first saw Anthony some of these features were not too obvious, but the eyes even at his tender age of a few days were noticeably almond shaped and had a downward slope, similar to that of the Mongolian race, hence the old-fashioned name 'mongol' for these type of children. The eyeballs rolled slightly but this has now largely disappeared. His tongue is large and flabby and frequently protrudes, his skin is still soft and smooth, but now at the age of forty, in exposed parts, it has become rough. His thumbs and fingers are abnormally short and 'curled' and so are his ears. He is stocky in build with a fine pair of shoulders. During the first year it was often hard to appreciate that he was abnormal; living closely with an infant one does not always catch on to the less obvious defects which may be quickly noted by a stranger.

It is said by some experts that the mental development of Down's syndrome children reaches a plateau around the age of ten. (I believe that this assumption is quite wrong.) Anthony is profoundly handicapped. He can feed himself, but he has to be dressed, toileted and is totally dependent on others, but a large percentage of these children are 'moderately' handicapped and a very small percentage – one to two percent are quite well developed mentally and may even be able to read and write. This minute category are normally classified as 'mildly' handicapped.

One either accepts or rejects such children, though I have found that with the work and the tact of mental handicap nurses and other workers, hardened cases of initial rejection can be channelled into avenues of great and genuine attachment. But this is a long and uphill struggle if a parent has ideas of perfection!

The Down's child has much to offer a family and this is the message which some of the clinically orientated professions have failed to grasp or choose to ignore. They are delightful friendly children who depend utterly on you. They love attention and respond to a happy home. They bring affection and happiness into a family. Some, like Anthony, are quiet, shy and withdrawn, others are outgoing, but they are all great companions. Music is Anthony's first love; swimming (when the water is warm) is his second; he loves the open air and, when the weather is right, is the first to rush out and get into our small sailing boat. These kiddies, and I always look on them as children (which is professionally wrong), however old they may be, need change and variety. Boredom is their biggest problem. On the west coast of Ireland, as in most EEC countries, they are well looked after in the numerous Day Centres which have been developed by voluntary agencies. Prior to the discovery of penicillin and auromycin their life expectancy was short, but now some reach into the forties and even the sixty age range.

When Anthony's condition had been confirmed it was assumed that if I was to continue my work overseas he would be consigned to the local mental hospital. This was in the Sixties. Fortunately we had other ideas and Anthony has travelled the world with us. His greatest achievement, even though he is unable to talk, is that he can swim. This was one of the advantages of living in a warm climate. Initially at my school in Bristol we had the use of the school swimming pool, which was heated. This was a great blessing. When I arrived in

Lusaka for another three year tour of duty Jeremy, Anthony's younger brother, at the age of eight, was already an excellent swimmer. Anthony was, strange to say showing great promise, but we never expected him to swim. It was in the warm Zambian sunshine that one day at the Lusaka pool Anthony ducked himself twice and swam! Jeremy shouted across the pool, "Look Mummy, Anthony is swimming." We didn't believe him. We never thought it would really happen. Jeremy again nudged him into deeper water and, first, with a serious face and then with a broad smile of pleasure Anthony showed us that it was all quite true. He was swimming and enjoying it. I suppose this is the one day the family will always remember, a landmark in our lives and a marvellous reward to us all.

Even though Anthony is a humble mongoloid his life at times has not been without a spark of adventure. Within the first six weeks of his existence a lioness with a cub, perhaps there were more we couldn't see properly because of the fading light, ambled in front of us. Cathleen and I were sitting on one of those great smooth shelves of rock at Kazima which overlook the plain. Anthony was in Cathleen's arms and, as was sometimes our habit, we came to this point to watch one of those marvellous East African sunsets recede into the night. (In the tropics the space between daylight and darkness is sometimes minimal.) Our peaceful interlude was interrupted when there was a grunt from the undergrowth and two apparitions emerged. We stayed put for a respectable time and then in trepidation retreated in good order. It was about this time as well that on our night journey into Tabora our road was barred by a bad tempered leopard, who sniffed around our Land Rover, bared his teeth and with an ugly snarl decided to let us pass by. Of course Anthony was oblivious to all this.

But perhaps one of the highlights of his young life eighteen months later was to travel from Malawi across Mozambique to Maputo (then Beira) where we boarded the *City of Port Elizabeth* for a six week voyage to England via the Cape. Except for British officers, the crew was Goan. The Master at Arms was also from Goa and significantly this seaman quickly made friends with Anthony. Years later when my work took me to southern India I found that many of the local people had a great understanding and empathy with youngsters like Anthony.

Suppose, just for a moment, that we had taken the easy way out and had decided to incarcerate our handicapped infant in one of these Zombie-type pseudo-prisons built in the 1850s, or earlier, which still adorn the European countryside, what kind of life would he have enjoyed? From what I have seen in early 1970 of these places both in Britain and the Republic of Ireland it is doubtful whether he would be alive today. If you wanted to see how a combination of a grotesque environment and an indifferent staff could produce regression at its worse, the old-type mental hospitals with their uncompromisingly selfish attitudes were the places to see it all. For good measure they were, and some say still are, a damning commentary on a supposedly caring society.

After almost a lifetime of work with the disabled, I had to come to Ireland in 1976 to witness some of the most appalling and heinous standards of care I had come across anywhere in the world. Even the mental hospitals I had visited in Bombay, Calcutta, Lobatsi (Botswana), Lusaka and other third world countries, seemed superior at the time to some Irish or British offerings! Here in the Republic, where in 1976 I took charge of a large voluntary organisation for the handicapped, my predecessor, before leaving, conducted me around a mental hospital. "Just to show you," was the way he put it, "the state some mentally handicapped patients are condemned to exist in." We found them all living under one roof together, with an assortment of seven hundred odd psychopaths, alcoholics, deviants and geriatrics. It was something of a revelation. Earlier we had visited the women's section in which, though not perfect, the staff had worked wonders to make a comfortable liveable place. Old buildings are not easy to up-date. In contrast, the male section of the hospital was appalling in the extreme. It reminded me of the first stages of the elimination camps I had seen during the war – languid disinterest, resignation, and odour. The part we were destined to visit was referred to by some of the male staff as 'the snake pit', although it was located high up in an isolated wing of the hospital. Indeed, it set the tone not only of what we saw on that day in 1976 but of the visits I made two years later to this hospital prior to far-reaching improvements being implemented.

I suspect that my companion wished to impress on me something of the uphill struggle which lay ahead. He succeeded. We were conducted up to the third floor where there was a large dormitory with high windows, no view whatsoever for the patients, bare walls, sparse wooden bench-type furniture, a strong smell of disinfectant and huddled together in one corner three male staff draped in white coats, smoking, reading newspapers, discussing the prices at yesterday's cattle mart. At the far end of the dormitory were the severely disabled sitting on the wooden benches, or crouched on the floor, either hanging their heads down in despair or yelling for attention. I tried to ask a few relevant questions. How often do they get out for a walk? Do the residents have a daily programme of activities? Do they have any outings? There were smirks. The man reading the newspaper lowered it. I forget the exact words he mumbled. They seemed to be, "We top and tail them and feed them." He then resumed reading the racing column of his paper. These were, I reflected, the calibre of people who might have been looking after my child.

But worse was to follow. The 'system' in the male section of this and a number of other Government Mental Hospitals broke down a year or two later because of industrial action and the handicapped were left with a skeleton staff. With an experienced colleague Catherine Pettit, we managed to visit the area reserved for the male handicapped. It was now more conveniently located on the ground floor, but still with high windows, a dark and uncompromising place. What did we find in the dormitory we visited? One white-coated individual sitting on the only chair in the room at a table reading a book. His twelve charges sitting on benches which lined the walls. Utter silence reigned. In one corner was a mountain of soiled sheets and the floor was covered in blobs of faeces. What Catherine Pettit and I witnessed, I was told later, was only the tip of the iceberg.

Some news media and particularly the Irish McGill magazine reported the whole sordid business of life in Irish mental hospitals, in factual detail. Without being emotional it seems a terrible indictment on a country which has been most generous to the Third World, yet on its own doorstep had for years tolerated the sub-standard care of its very own kith and kin, the least able amongst us. It raises many questions. Why did most of the church leaders virtually remain silent? Why did the politicians keep their heads down? And why did most professional people (not all) working in these institutions remain silent as well? Surely there were basic human rights and ethical principles to be upheld? There appeared to be one standard of acceptable service for the mental hospitals and another for voluntary agencies. If my own organisation had dared to offer such a sub-standard service as that which some of us saw in the mental hospitals in the 1970s, we would, quite rightly, have been put out of business immediately.

Unfortunately Ireland seems to have more than its share of cant and double standards. It is fine to talk about human rights abuses in distant places, but apparently not about those festering in our midst, whether it be homeless children sleeping rough and some begging in the centre of Dublin, or the handicapped. Many in this category have no service whatsoever. These seem to be the priorities which really matter. We forget that in rural areas there are still aged parents including widows, some approaching eighty who have faithfully looked after their handicapped child for years. The death of such loyal and valiant people concentrates the mind on short-comings in our own society. This is the situation which organisations like Western Care are trying to tackle with meagre resources but a strong sense of duty and vocation.

Chapter Twelve

The life-line for many concerned parents has been the emergence of first-rate voluntary organisations (mostly religious fraternities) who have in their own right set standards which have acquired international recognition. But is this enough? Some of these organisations can fall victim to their own success; plush offices, generous entertainment allowances and, most cutting of all, distancing themselves from those they serve. This is the danger on the horizon. Beware! From all this it transpires that the world of the handicapped in both Europe and developing countries overseas is surrounded by dividing lines and discrimination – much of it unintentional – which can sometimes be appalling. Strangely, I have found in Europe that the people who can be most vocal in obstructing work amongst the disabled are sometimes the most educated. Why? But times are changing as 'snakepits' are swept away, new places opened, and old hospitals transformed into clean luxurious healthy places, all within the time span of two or three years.

*

In the sandy wastelands of Chad, Niger and northern Nigeria it was the sophisticated Emirs, sticklers for decor and traditional etiquette who, from time immemorial, had numbered amongst their advisers and councillors the *makafi*, the Chiefs of the Blind. This then was one of the reasons why it was to these regions we turned – Katsina, Kano and Maiduguri – to carry out the first experiments in educating the blind (and other suitably handicapped) in ordinary schools. It was in this unique setting, distinctly different to the negroid and Bantu peoples with whom I had previously worked, that I was commissioned by the northern Nigerian Government and the Royal Commonwealth Society for the Blind to initiate an open education research programme. I had spent a few months in America studying the methods they used in integrated education (teaching blind children in ordinary schools) and finally decided that by adapting some of the methods used in the States to the settings around Katsina, the system could be made to work.

The rationale behind these developments was that given basic training and proper support with a specialist teacher at hand, blind children should be able to hold their own in an ordinary elementary school. Africa, with its shortage of money could never afford to build enough special schools and, in any case, was it desirable to segregate these children from the rest of the community? It was an exciting experiment which had to work otherwise the thousands of blind children throughout Africa would have nothing. But most important of all, this system was to become a massive force in breaking down the barriers of apathy and ignorance which surround the lives of many handicapped people. It is this social factor rather than the intrinsic value of rudimentary learning which triggered major changes in attitudes. At present open education is working not only in the humblest of communities, but also at university level, in small villages and large towns, permeating its way into family life with its message of hope and tolerance for handicapped children. It cuts across every strata of African society provided the system is presented in a logical, attractive and persuasive manner. Open education for the blind is now the accepted way of looking after this category of handicapped child in Africa. There are some interesting success stories. Saddiku, for example, who came from a remote village called Batagarawa which is ten miles north of Katsina, managed ultimately to get up to university level and now in most other English-speaking parts of Africa, the open education system has met with a useful, sometimes enthusiastic, degree of success. Suffice to say that with the right support and attitudes and in the right hands, the system works.

I must hasten to add that we do not rate academic achievement as the criteria for success or failure. The real test is whether we can send a blind boy or girl back to their village, a place quite often where they have been ostracised. Are they still able to make good in this hostile environment? This is what the open education system is concerned with, working in the midst of communities so that the handicapped are accepted and helped to independence.

It was following the Katsina experiment that the nature of my work changed. Instead of spending long periods in one place abroad, my role took on that of advisory and consultancy work for a number of international agencies, sometimes in the French-speaking parts of West Africa, such as the Ivory Coast and Mali, sometimes in India and Bangladesh and at other times in the Leeward Islands and Guyana. This meant that Cathleen and the two children had to stay in England whilst I made visits which lasted in duration from a few weeks to almost a year. It was hard on family life but somehow we survived until we were all able to travel out together again as a family.

From time to time, in the course of my work, I lectured on services and plans for the disabled in developing countries. Sometimes, it was in Hanover, or a paper in New Zealand for the Commonwealth Secretariat Conference, sometimes America and most important of all in Asia and Africa. At the time I remember that I was reluctant to mention that my own child was severely handicapped. The reason for this was twofold – firstly, it was a personal matter, and secondly parents of handicapped children are supposed to be unable to think straight or logically as they are emotionally involved! I suspect that this statement has an element of truth in it, but at the end of the day I find discerning parents often know best. It was not until somebody said that it was about time I offered some empathy to parents who were fighting their way through the inevitable traumas of meeting up with disability, that I decided to be a little more forthcoming. Parents look for hope or at least for support from those who have similar experiences. A few years ago there was precious little that they could latch on to.

Often there were only two alternatives. There was the 'put him away' attitude, or to 'soldier on and take your chance'. Cathleen and I had learnt the hard way with Anthony. There was the long slog of teaching him to feed himself. Would he ever be toilet trained? How does someone communicate with somebody who cannot talk? Trying to understand his sign language took years and we are still learning! He can understand much of what we say, he is sensitive to atmosphere, but lives in a world of his own which none of us can really understand. I often ask myself, as he sits watching the trees, the birds and the sea, what is he really thinking? There are some things you have to accept from the start and this may be difficult especially for those who are class or status conscious!

A severely mentally handicapped child can never deliver the goods of social standing and prestige in a society which seems to be money orientated but, oddly enough, it can in a community which has got its values right. Some African tribes are ashamed of the handicapped; what is the difference then between the European parents who reject their child and the tribal African who leaves the disabled child in the bush for the animals? In ethical terms very little. I look on caring for Anthony as another challenge, but one which I honestly feel is something of a privilege. You either run away and desert a helpless individual (and in doing so may consign him to the realms of a Victorian-type mental hospital), or you make up your mind that you are going to stand by him and see things through during your lifetime. *My advice to parents is to do the best for the child, learn to enjoy him, yes, I mean exactly that, and at the end of the day the satisfaction of a job well done is reward in itself.*

These days for many parents in the developed countries who decide to keep their handicapped child at home with the rest of the family, there is usually generous support in cash allowances, home visiting services, and day centre facilities. The whole picture has changed dramatically within the last two decades. It is no longer the lonely path that parents in my native village with their handicapped child had to tread. Community attitudes have changed, there is a feeling of togetherness and, I sense, one of admiration for such parents.

Although parents of the handicapped face, sometimes alone, formidable problems, they are generally the first to acknowledge the blessings and support which comes their way. On the west coast of Ireland where I live we have much to be thankful for: foremost friendly and understanding neighbours. Equally significant, our nearest large community, Newport, has a well established tradition and understanding of the disabled in its midst. Over the years its members have worked both financial and social miracles. It is amongst them that a day centre and two small residential homes for the handicapped flourish. This is where Anthony and the other handicapped in the district are helped, loved and cherished. Both day centre and homes are staffed by people who care and who seek to provide the warmth and affection that only personal contact and interest can generate. These places, to many like Cathleen and myself, are the life-lines which give respite and support in times of crisis.

There are in the system many 'unknowns' and unsung heroes and heroines, both professional and volunteers who inject new hope when spirits start to flag. These are the people whom society can sometimes overlook or undervalue. From this diverse gathering of helpers are stalwarts like Tom and Selina Rochford and their family, who, without fuss or fanfare have for years been fostering Jenny, a once lonely Down's syndrome child. Then there is Agnes Corcoran in charge of the day centre Anthony attends, profoundly caring, and her equally committed staff. Nearby is the residential home where Anthony lives, modern, warm, and friendly run by a young staff whose devotion and loyalty to the handicapped is exemplary.

In August 1995 I had good reason to up-date my thinking about the courage and merits of these largely anonymous faithful who strive to maintain decent standards of care and quality of life.

I had been invited by a French national newspaper and a French colour magazine to comment on a horrendous event which occurred in 1944. Most of the Maquis unit to which I belonged were executed in what became known locally as the Chantereine Massacre. I reminded the news media representatives that only a few weeks prior to this bloody occasion, when the SS and Gestapo had executed eleven of my colleagues on a lonely farm, an event even more reprehensible took place, indeed one which seems largely forgotten and conveniently hidden from public memory.

I referred my journalist friends to two little known concentrations camps, – one near Brandenburg and the other close to Grafenesk. Here within a few days a total of more than fifteen thousand, five hundred and ten mentally and physically disabled men, women and children were gassed into oblivion. (This was only a fraction of the handicapped population who perished in this manner during the war.) These innocents have no memorial. This massacre of some of the weakest in society merits little or no mention by contemporary researchers or historians. Why? It was not until mid-July 1987 that a modicum of justice caught up with the two SS doctors who supervised this outrage. After years of litigation doctors Aquilan Ulrick and Henrick Bunke were sentenced to four years imprisonment each for being accessories to murder by gassing.

As the years pass by many of us seem to mellow when looking back on heinous war crimes. Whilst I deeply respect the youngsters who died at Chantereine and try to keep their memory green I think the incidents at Brandenburg and the Grafenesk camps should not be overlooked. The manner in which these vulnerable souls were disposed of is now almost forgotten. Perhaps it should be a reminder that the dividing line between decency and the filth of the elimination camps and the slippery slopes descending into the gas chambers can sometimes be exceedingly thin.

For me the modern day heroes and heroines are not pop stars, cult figures social celebrities but ordinary men and women some of whom work and live largely in anonymity as carers and protectors of the mentally handicapped. I refer to the marvellous staff of Western Care who look after people like Anthony.

Lurking in the shadows we have the '*en avant garde*' brigade with the philosophy that the badly handicapped are expendable, albeit through 'benign' neglect, rather than the gas chamber. There is not much difference for the end result is the same! We have been this way before. I well remember the words of a young girl who was saved from extermination at Ravensbruck by the narrowest of margins. She said, "the young must not forget that the right to life is indisputable and precious." Like so many others she became one of the largely unknown carers and defenders of the helpless in society.

All this, both as a parent and a professional in the world of the handicapped, makes one very humble. Over the years I have moved in and out of Africa in good times and bad ones, and I have seen the work amongst the handicapped in my adopted homeland in sunshine and storm. From all this I have learnt one golden rule which has helped me survive, *avoid dwelling on differences and concentrate on the things we can do and enjoy together with our handicapped young people, however intense or overwhelming their disability may be*. There are, after all, many components which emphasise the common elements we all share, irrespective of race, religion, geographical location, social standing or disability.

Broadly the mentally handicapped are the same everywhere. Their basic needs are the same. The stagnation surrounding their lives is the same, the distress to parents is the same. The tensions and pressures they create in family life are the same. The mentally handicapped suffer the same frustrations whether they live in a developed or under-developed region of the world and, do not forget, their appreciation of beauty, nature, environment and affection is the same.

I learnt to see the mentally handicapped firstly as part of the whole human family but also as a minority group that may be constantly exposed to discrimination. People, particularly those enjoying a high standard of life, do not always wish to be exposed to those who reflect the negative aspects of existence. But need the handicapped always feel inferior? Every handicapped person, however severely disabled, can teach us something if we are humble enough to seek and then to accept their offerings.

It was thoughts like these which inspired busy men like Lord Hunt, of Mount Everest fame, to find time to back young men from central and East Africa who had been written off as 'second-raters' because they were blind. (This was the social stigma at the time which was holding up many worthwhile developments for the blind all over Africa). And, this is why the Royal Commonwealth Society for the Blind's Operation Kilimanjaro, became a reality. Some claim that this has done much to explode the myths and attitudes which have delayed progress whilst others, the more cautious ones, consider that its most important impact has been to demonstrate that ordinary people can do much to assist the blind to accomplish quite extraordinary things when the situation demands it. I think our approach to disability has much more to offer as well – congenial company instead of isolation, mental enrichment instead of mental stagnation; the knowledge that one is wanted and is part and parcel of a progressive community, instead of being regarded as an 'oddity' that for most purposes is 'dead' or at the best 'inert'; and, at the end of the day, being accepted as a person with feelings and emotions like everyone else.

At about the time the Kilimanjaro project was maturing another development which did much to generate sympathy and understanding for the handicapped was emerging. Some of the younger generation of the Sixties era having worked the excitement, and maybe, exhibitionism of that period out of their systems concentrated their thoughts on the handicapped. This welcome approach made itself manifest, albeit, unobtrusively, in a conference I had attended in Hanover. Young people were asking difficult questions. One concerned the lack of accountability in respect of the murder by gassing in World War Two of the mentally handicapped. As one member of this gathering pointed out, that whilst the holocaust is rightly concerned with Jews, social rejects, political unacceptables, and Resistance men and women, – the voiceless minority, the handicapped who also perished are overlooked and forgotten.

This was the kind of thinking which urged the German authorities to renew their investigations into the activities of a number of former Nazi men and women associated with the death camps where handicapped children had been exterminated.

Broadly, what has been uncovered by researchers is this…

It is estimated that over one hundred thousand mentally handicapped people were murdered in death camps between January 1943 and April 1945. One former Nazi medical doctor, when apprehended just prior to his retirement in 1980, is alleged to have stated that, "these actions were taken by his staff and himself on the instructions of the Fuhrer who considered the handicapped a serious economic burden to the State."

Apart from the Brandenburg and Grafenesk camps the organised murder of the handicapped took place on a far greater scale, at Buchenwald, Treblinka, and Auschwitz. (In one camp both father and handicapped son were used for medical experiments before being slaughtered.)

On May 8th 1996, the fifty-first anniversary of the end of World War II, a simple but impressive service was held in a Hamburg church to remind us all of the handicapped who suffered. It had been organised by relatives, friends of the handicapped and members of the public to let us all know what could happen when we fail to defend the weakest and most vulnerable in society.

At that service, in small caskets were the preserved brains of ten mentally handicapped children which, at the conclusion of the service, were given a burial. Where had these 'specimens' been obtained from? In 1944 and early 1945 hundreds of Down's syndrome children with other equally serious conditions, after being gassed, had had their brains removed by the camp doctors. These items were carefully documented and preserved.

Many are still lodged in the basement of a mental hospital near Vienna and others may be in research centres in Germany. (The Vienna Hospital at the time of writing has hundreds of specimens.)

The misery perpetuated by the Nazi holocaust amongst the most defenceless in society should not overshadow the good and positive things which have been emerging since that period. Certainly, there are some countries whose attitudes may equate with that of the Nazi. China, for example, according to reliable reports, in the late 1980, advocated the elimination specifically of all Down's syndrome infants at birth. Some other countries have sinister records as well but nature does the killing.

But nearer home, and where one may least suspect it there is an enormous and growing fund of goodwill which makes itself manifest in voluntary organisations like Western Care. Volunteers, looking after people like Anthony on the west coast of Ireland, – scenic Mayo, – give up their free time and energy to act as carers, assist with leisure time pursuits including swimming, walking along sandy beaches, and even horse riding. The list is long and is only a microcosm of the picture. Many of us realise that there has been an enormous gap in our education. The older generations were largely oblivious to the needs of handicapped people. These days most schools and youth centres are making amends for this. One teacher said to her class of school leavers, *"If you want to spread a little happiness amongst the handicapped, don't ignore them. When you meet them, say 'Hallo' with a cheerful smile, maybe, add a few words of praise. It will make the child's parents feel great as well. The message you will be sending out to the handicapped will not be lost. What you are saying is, 'No, you are not an oddity, neither are you an outcast, but a valued member of a larger family.'"* She added, somewhat wistfully, *"Tell those who may belittle your efforts, the arrogant and conceited, – 'but for the grace of God go you or me.'"*

If we take the courage to discover that every handicapped person, however grievously damaged, is truly a person and can respond to care and kindness, we have done much to bridge the gap of prejudice and fear which separates 'them' from 'us'. But dwell for a moment on the words of a young friend Mary O'Malley-Medoc, discussing her handicapped brother Andy, now in his mid-twenties, who lives near me. *"The closer we get to Andy,"* she writes, *"the more we discover the gift he is to us. If I wished to say one final thing to anybody about the handicapped it is this: do not presume to offer charity to handicapped people. Seek to find in them the wealth of your own humanity. Have the courage to discover the gift they are to you. Think of peace through perseverance, joy through pain, and love through struggle and commitment. My handicapped brother has been, and will always be, these things to me."*

I think Mary, in these remarkable and courageous words, has expressed the inexpressible which many of us feel.

Chapter Thirteen

'Great things are done when men and mountains meet;
This is not done by jostling in the street.'

William Blake

It was February 1969, one of those rare occasions when the summit of Mount Kilimanjaro was almost cloud free; it was a gleaming icy island peak dominating an Africa which I had grown to love. We were perched precipitously on a sloping snowy ledge which jutted out into the crater. It had been snowing overnight and a thin deceptive frozen surface had formed. I edged forward cautiously and peered into the vast bowl-shaped void below. My boots broke through the fragile ice with a dull crunch and I sank waist deep into the fresh powder snow. It cascaded in a gentle trickle and then deluged forth in a miniature avalanche into the abyss below. It had been a near thing and a timely warning. I retreated to warn the climbing team who lay exhausted a few feet to the rear. Momentarily shaken, I crawled back still aware of the quite incredible beauty which had unfolded before me. Perhaps it was one of those rare moments in a lifetime that always lives with one – vivid and inspiring. Blue-tinged ice cliffs surrounded the crater rim. Undulating snow drifts blanketed the expansive crater floor. The brilliance of a midday tropical sun reflected a dazzling white. It was all so very beautiful. I remember thinking as I clawed my way back, how unreal it was – the kind of thing one imagined as a child made up the Snow Queen's fairyland. White pinnacles rising above tiers of ice-blue cliffs. A cloudless azure sky overhead. Thousands of feet below billowing clouds floating past like great ships and still far far below in the gaps between them, glimpses of the shimmering plains. The silence was broken only by the wisps of an icy wind. Even frozen fingers, frozen breath around our nostrils, frozen camera shutters and the effort of thinking and moving at over nineteen thousand feet on the roof of Africa could not cloud over that memorable scene.

I rejoined the silent group – each man resting, some panting in the rarefied atmosphere, all wrapped up in their own private worlds. Privations and suffering there certainly had been during these last few days but it was a momentous occasion. With John Lubega, the tough wiry Mountain School guide, I tried to describe the scene that lay at our feet. The wide deep crater, its sheer precipices, the deceptive snow blanket that meant almost certain death on the first false move, but no one was really interested. Could you blame them? Almost ten hours climbing with hardly a break, no food, an icy blast that sometimes whipped up the patches of unfrozen snow, and for all but two of us altitude sickness at its worst. And now, an uncertain resting place high above the crater. Kilimanjaro – beautiful menacing Kilimanjaro, the house of the gods, the legendary mountain of the vast African continent – had been conquered, conquered by a team of young East Africans, a team of totally blind courageous men.

It was a magnificent achievement. The climax of years of preparation, an exercise to show Africa and the world that, given the chance, fortitude, tenacity and courage are an integral part of the character of blind and handicapped people. It staked a claim that contemporary Africa could not ignore. It registered a major triumph in the story of man's ability to overcome adversity.

Looking back in the quietness of my Irish country home, I can still sense the serene tranquillity of achievement that often marks great occasions. There was no cheering – at nineteen thousand feet air is too precious – there were few smiles, with wind and sun-cracked faces it was too painful, but the aura of victory after days of battling and weeks of hardship surrounded the young team. We all knew, in spite of our discomfort, that it was an exhilarating moment. Its significance and clarity were now indelibly stamped on the minds of each one of us.

Why did these seven young men drawn from Kenya, Tanzania, and Uganda volunteer to undertake this hazardous enterprise? There were many reasons. Adventure, achievement, yes, even enjoyment. For some it was a personal challenge, pitting one's wits and stamina against a gigantic snow-topped mountain laying sprawled almost across the equator. "How many Africans have actually touched real snow?" I was asked.

"Very very few," I would reply.

"Then we shall have experiences that our sighted brothers and sisters will perhaps never have." This was one more reason – a human one for getting to the top. But there were deeper reasons. From time immemorial the blind and other handicapped people in much of Africa have been looked on as second class citizens, the 'write-offs' of society. (Make no mistake, Western countries are still far from guiltless in this respect.) The Kilimanjaro climbers set out to show Africa and the world that given the chance they are capable responsible people – people who can set standards that sometimes match and surpass those of their fellow countrymen and, when the going is hard, can rise if need be, to unprecedented heights of determination and bravery. Why should they then be condemned to a life of physical and mental stagnation? This then was the deeper reasoning behind the Kilimanjaro enterprise.

This was why on that chilly February day in 1969, we were stuck perilously close to the crater's edge on our final assault on the summit. This was no half-baked stunt. It was a carefully planned operation to show the world the capabilities of severely handicapped people. They were not asking for sympathy, but understanding, not easy money, but the chance to be given suitable training perhaps and a job. They were asking each one of us not to despise their less fortunate brethren who through no fault of their own are sometimes condemned, by both Western and African society, to a nearly vegetative existence. Every day thousands upon thousands of handicapped people, particularly children and their parents face their own Kilimanjaros – mountains of disinterest, despair and even ridicule. Kilimanjaro has already become a symbol. 'Second class people', the so-called rejects of their community, have done something their sighted colleagues have never dreamt of.

This was in 1969. It is now almost thirty years on. I well remember a casual conversation with Sir John Wilson, Director of the Royal Commonwealth Society for the Blind, in his London office. John, blinded by accident at school, is well-known in Africa and Asia for his original work in the development of educational, social, and medical facilities for the blind. A progressive thinker, a man with a flair for action – sometimes unorthodox, occasionally stubborn, but invariably successful – John had long toyed with the idea of a major operation by a group of African blind aimed at breaking down the barriers that stunted so much promising work. In his book *Travelling Blind* he describes his "bush bashing" experiences and analyses the problems that can block progress and dishearten many a courageous man.

Sometimes in his office and sometimes when we were in outlandish places together, conversation would drift to the feasibility of a unique exercise carried out by African blind to demonstrate their capabilities. A number of ideas had been discussed, including a trans-Sahara expedition, but for one reason or another they were not practical enough or sufficiently inspiring for our requirements. It was not until a July afternoon in 1964 that a young Kenyan, Tom Wijenjie, who was on one of the short courses I was then running in England for overseas students, gave John the lead he was looking for. John called me to his office. He came straight to the point. "I've been having a chat with Tom," he said. "He thinks Kilimanjaro could be what we are looking for." Tom had had a fair amount of mountaineering experience. "Of course," added John as an afterthought, "our chaps will have to be hand-picked." And that was the last I heard of Operation Kilimanjaro for at least two years. I left to carry out assignments in Ethiopia, East Africa and Rhodesia.

In the course of my travels I flew over the vast Kilimanjaro range. I was not encouraged by what I saw and concluded that the plan would come to nought. I was wrong. Tom, for his indiscretion in suggesting the mountain as a possible target, joined the expedition and suffered his share of altitude sickness. During the weeks of preliminary training around the foothills of the mountain and in the sun-baked plains below, with tick bites, blisters, and mountain rats to keep us company at meal times (and occasionally trying to share our sleeping bags as well), I reminded Tom of the demise in which he had landed us. "Here we are," I would say, "with hyaenas trying to lick our faces when we're asleep and elephants using our bivouac site as their latrine (the site was covered with droppings) and not a word did you mention about this when you talked to JW about the climb." Tom would grin, his fine Luo features broadening into a beaming smile as he stirred a huge pot of simmering soup over the wood fire. Tom was used to ragging. The group gathered round the fire for warmth against the chilly night and waited expectantly for his philosophic reply. At last it came.

"Well Geoff," he would say, putting more wood on the fire, "I think this will do us all good. It's doing you good already and if the elephants and hyaenas like our company why shun them."

There would be a ripple of laughter,

"But just suppose," added Swato Fundikira, the grandson of one of the most renowned chiefs in the Tabora area of Tanzania, "just suppose no one gets to the top." Swato, like Tom, was one of the instructors. He was always down to earth. "Even we, the guides, can fail," he continued. This was a horrifying possibility. In London we had estimated that between six and eight of the ten climbing team would make the grade. Around our nightly campfire, when the blind lads had turned in early after a heavy day, we would go over each man's performance and always managed to optimistically arrive at a forecast of 'between six and eight'. Swato had put into words that evening thoughts that each one of us had already contemplated but hadn't had the courage to express: the possibility of our own failure as well.

But it was not until January 1968, after John Wilson had been out to Kenya and met the Warden of the East African Mountain School in Nairobi that Operation Kilimanjaro was definitely on. One wintry morning I was sitting in my Headmaster's office in Bristol where after twelve years in Africa I had taken refuge when John, just back from Kenya, gave me a ring. I excused myself to the formidable long skirted teacher whose views on some of our local co-educational problems didn't match mine, and listened to John. He didn't waste words, "It's on. You'll be going up in February 1969. For you, that means the top, and please no accidents. Come up next weekend and we'll go over the details and possible routes." So Kilimanjaro was on. If it came off it would be a major breakthrough into the hearts and minds of countless thousands who looked on the blind as hopeless cases. If it failed it could be disastrous. It could go seriously wrong, it could even end in a ghastly tragedy and damage years of work.

I arrived in Nairobi early in January complete with mountain gear and an unpleasant premonition that something might go awry. Press conferences had been held in London, Nairobi, Kampala and Dar es Salaam and, as one press reporter jocularly reminded me, bad news is more newsworthy than good!

Lord Hunt of Everest fame had given the expedition his blessing. We were beyond the point of no return. Nairobi days were busy ones.

I met Ennos Opiya, young and quiet spoken, but a veteran of African mountaineering. We sized each other up over a sun downer at Nairobi's Norfolk Hotel. Ennos was warden of the Mountain School and we were going to rely heavily on him for advice and training. We got on well. He described Loitokitok, our future base. How it nestled, eighteen miles from the summit of Kilimanjaro at the edge of the rainforest and looked down across sweltering plains to the Chulya mountains, visible on a good day sixty miles away. I heard about rock climbing on the 'Rhino' rock face and four day solo expeditions on iron rations in the mountains and on the plains. "It's a rule with us, no fires at night," Ennos said. "The animals are more afraid of you than you are of them. Yes," he would continue, reading my thoughts, "there are plenty of snakes in both bush and forest. Sometimes lions wander through Loitokitok. At present there are three making themselves a nuisance." (During our stay one was killed by a game warden who, when his gun failed to fire, rammed the barrel down the creature's throat as it was making a flying leap at him.) Ennos rambled on: "Yes, there are plenty of buffalo and elephant as well. Now don't push your luck too far with them. They are temperamental. Oh," he continued, "the mountain, that's an attitude of mind, a mental state. We can make the team fit. But they've got to have the mental stamina to carry on to the bitter end." A few weeks later high up in the snows I remembered his words. Essentially Ennos was an unusual man. He had skilfully avoided a senior government administrative post in Nairobi. Bright lights and city life were not for him. He was a lover of the rugged hills, the open spaces, of wildlife on the plains and the flora that abound on the lower slopes of Kilimanjaro.

At the hub of activities in Nairobi was Alex Mackay, a Kenyan with wide experience in many walks of life. He was an able administrator – the type of backroom expert indispensable to an expedition such as ours, where, for example, the team was drawn from areas as much as two thousand miles apart. They brought with them different customs and traditions and a variety of languages. He saw them all adequately equipped with pullovers and heavy boots (some had never worn boots before) to supplement their Arctic kit. He arranged with Ennos the final selection of ten men and their safe passages from distant parts to the base at Loitokitok. Even the unseasonal rains which bogged down the Ugandan-Kenyan parties in

the Amboseli game reserve and the misunderstandings which led to the
Tanzanian party arriving penniless at Moshi were eventualities which
in perspective passed over smoothly thanks to Alex's foresight.
Working with him in Nairobi was Ray Robinson, an ex-submariner
amongst whose achievements was the organisation of a well nigh
perfect communications system. It eventually stretched from the top
of Kilimanjaro to Nairobi and on to the outside world. The original
idea was safety but it made possible an up-to-date news coverage
which the press certainly appreciated.

With the arrival of the climbing team in Loitokitok I got my first
close-up view of the ten men. They were a hardy looking bunch
averaging around twenty-five years old. They had been selected for
their physique from hundreds of volunteers. The men had passed
rigorous medical checks to make sure they could withstand conditions
that would severely test heart and lungs and, with malaria endemic,
liability to ruptured spleens and livers. I wondered whether men,
even though hand-picked, who had been raised on diets that at least
nutritionally were notoriously meagre, would be able to withstand the
next few weeks. Looking back it is remarkable that only two men fell
by the wayside and another, after a very creditable performance on the
actual climb, reluctantly gave up at sixteen thousand feet. (All were
TOTALLY BLIND.)

Training started a few hours after the team made their 3 a.m.
arrival at Loitokitok. They had been rescued from bogged-down
vehicles some eighty miles out in the wilderness. Tired and
mudstained they got down to work with a will. After a day or so
personalities began to take shape. Two long marches through almost
impenetrable bush where at times paths had to be hacked out with
pangas, set a severe test by any standards. There was a notorious
'commando' circuit at Loitokitok as well. A fall from one of its dizzy
heights and one would be lucky to survive. Andikati, a lithe
long-limbed Samburu boy, was quite at home in the bush. He didn't
speak a word of Swahili, the *lingua franca* of East Africa, or of
English, but his incessant chatter and laughter was infectious and he
always managed to convey his point. I well remember how, with
night fast approaching and another seven miles of rough country to
cover, he would generously pass round his water bottle to flagging
men who, under the burning midday sun, had long since consumed

their own rations and pleaded for more. Kindness, and a physique built to withstand a rough life, were but two of Andikati's contributions to our team work. There was Tofida, a different type, who spoke very good English, and came from Uganda. When he was twelve he had lost his sight. He had not lost his courage. It was on a long bush march that Tofida stumbled and fell into one of the wicked long-spiked scrub bushes that abound on the plains. One of the spikes penetrated deep into the flesh under his kneecap, broke off and left a sizeable splinter for us to extract. It took half an hour with our one blunt scalpel (carried in case of snake bite) and our meagre first aid kit to remove almost two inches of barbed thorn. He didn't complain, but there were others who did. Aluma found the going too hard and did not hesitate to let everyone know. I had my suspicions. It became clear that something was seriously wrong. After pressing enquiries, I discovered that his age was not the twenty-six he had originally given, but forty! How he slipped the screening panel I do not know. Our numbers were reduced to nine. The first mountain expedition far from our base camp was a mental as well as physical strain. Men can and do become completely demoralised. The glamour of climbing a snow-covered mountain may seem attractive from the security of one's home, but the reality of living close to nature with wildlife as neighbours is not the life for everyone. Snakes in the low lying wet areas of the plains were prolific and during our stay in the area there were inevitable brushes with wildlife. One group came within a few feet of a lion sheltering from the heat of the day – a huge male, he was not pleased at being disturbed, but after a snarl allowed the party to withdraw. A few hours later the same group came across a herd of buffalo – probably Africa's most dangerous creatures. Wisely they made a lengthy detour.

On two occasions I set off with two blind youngsters from an isolated bivouac site to reconnoitre a suitable route. We came across an unmistakable odour, a sure indication that we had company very close at hand, either lion or leopard. The boys took it all in their stride. But not all animal life was as frightening. I recall leading the team along an overgrown pathway right up to my favourite wildlife species, the small dik-dik, a gem of a creature, not more than a foot high when fully grown. It was a beautiful little creation! Its fine fawn coat merged into the background of the bush and it stood immobile and then with only inches between us dashed with lightning rapidity for cover. We came across gazelle, giraffe in twos and threes and in the distance heard elephant crashing their way through the bush down to a nearby stream. What did our blind youngsters get out of this? Excitement certainly, plenty of bruises and scratches as well, but essentially the experience of living close to nature. "Listen," I would say, "there are three massive giraffe nibbling at the trees to your left. Can you hear them feeding?"

"Thank you *Bwana*," they would say, "let us listen." At night when we slept in our crude shelters made from branches, jackals and hyaena often circled our resting place. They would get bolder and bolder until my torch picked out a pair of red gleaming eyes and they would skulk off.

Our expeditions were gruelling. They taught us to come to terms with bush life. It was on the last expedition before the final climb that Kisaka, a Tanzanian, distinguished himself. Up to this point he had not found things easy. I was worried about him. It was a humid Friday afternoon and with a small group, three blind lads and three army men (who were training with us) were tackling a seventy foot rock face. Two blind youngsters had already reached the top followed by two sighted colleagues. The third soldier had no head for heights and refused to attempt the rock face. Much to everyone's surprise up sprang timid Kisaka. "Let me show the way," he exclaimed. Everyone gasped. Kisaka who had failed miserably on almost every exercise and had had spells off sick with a twisted ankle and septic legs. He was not bluffing. With blistered feet and hands he felt his way up to thirty feet, rested, then coolly continued, unperturbed by bees, some of which stung him. He carried on with unerring accuracy and tackled the vertical last sixteen feet and its overhang with the same uncanny rhythm and with the applause of his team mates ringing in his ears clambered over the top. Kisaka not only made a spectacular climb (of which I have some excellent photographs) but made himself as well. It was the turning point, in his mountaineering career. It is a story that will be told at the Mountain School for many years to come. One would like to be able to round off this little episode by saying that the man for whom this demonstration had taken place followed suit and made a successful ascent, but this was not to be. (Kisaka himself later joined in the final assault on Kilimanjaro but after a praiseworthy ascent to sixteen thousand feet had to give up.)

The weeks passed rapidly. The team, reduced to eight, was in good shape and morale was high. They were ready to have a go. Progress had in fact been so good that together with Ennos Opiya made a number of useful changes in the final assault plans. We estimated that instead of seven days the climb would take between five and six. This meant less food to carry. We were able to dispense with a number of porters as well because all the team could cope with at least thirty-five pound rucksack loads. Finally, eight blind men, three instructors and a few porters left Loitokitok on the eighteen mile trek that would lead them to the top of Kilimanjaro. Our plan provided for three or four night stops on the ascent. We carried no tents. We planned to use the natural terrain, bush, at lower altitudes, and caves at over twelve thousand feet until we reached a hut at the sixteen thousand foot level. From this point, if all went well, we would change to arctic kit and climb the remaining odd three thousand feet to the summit and return to the hut within twenty-four hours.

I recorded the main events of that dramatic climb day by day in my log book. Three times a day we radioed short messages down to base telling them of our progress. It was some twenty minutes after my slip at the crater edge that the team crawled the last sixty feet to the summit. We radioed a short message to base, short because our batteries were running low, but the real story, the last four hundred feet that took over an hour to cover, the nightmare descent through the eighteen thousand foot icefield with three men semiconscious and sometimes delirious, is something we did not tell. At the time we were, maybe, too exhausted or worried to let our friends know our plight. With night fast approaching we could not be caught at high altitudes in this state, and in any case the next radio transmission was not due until 7 p.m. It was a race against time. My logbook, made up hours after these events took place, picks up the story.

> The snow line was well down and very deep. This put us behind schedule. At one stage we were taking a minute to complete thirty-five small paces. Altitude sickness had already hit the boys and two were weeping, pleading to pack up. All the instructors with the exception of Lubego and myself were in a bad way. They were becoming violently ill. It was becoming touch and go. The descent at one stage was like a

battlefield. Men, including the two porters, lying prone or bent up in agony. Tom and Swato though very ill themselves rallied the troops and helped manhandle the three unconscious boys to a lower altitude.

But for a few moments let us go back in time to the start of the climb. As I turn over the pages of the log book I can relive the joys and fears, the beauty and starkness, the feelings of men who against gigantic odds made such momentous achievement. After a briefing which had all the tenseness of a pending wartime sortie my diary takes up the story again.

Monday 17 February.
Left base at 9 a.m. Everyone in good spirits. We climbed up through the rainforest which is teeming with white monkeys who had a good chatter about us. It was wet, dank and steamy, the path littered with decayed vegetation, the sun cut out by vast creepers. We emerged from the forest into cooler country full of swift-flowing streams. Everyone was walking well. We made camp at eight thousand feet in bivouacs made from the branches of trees. We were rather worried about local wild animals. Around the camp fire that night stories were told about hyaenas. The best was told by Noel (Tanzania) who claimed that people in his area trained them and kept them in their homes. We all slept well, or at least said so. Breakfast was tea and biscuits.

Tuesday 18 February.
We broke camp under a copper coloured sky and started the long haul up to the fifteen thousand foot caves where we spent the night; more streams, ferns and heather that grows in some parts to a height of twenty feet. Everyone was happy and we sang on the march, but turned in early. Altitude effects were starting and so were headaches. Around midnight peals of thunder woke some of us. A storm was raging thousands of feet below.

Wednesday 19th, February.

We cooked breakfast outside the cave. The blind lads had collected wood and filled the water bottles from a stream. The day's march was not long but very steep and rocky. We had left the heather country behind and were passing through rocky country, the kind of thing one might expect on the moon. That day we had sore feet and one or two people started being sick from altitude. We had an early night and slept in a hut; it was bitterly cold. By now we were all suffering from burnt faces and cracked lips due to the direct rays of the equatorial sun. We came across our first snow. I climbed up the rocks and broke off a giant icicle and showed it to Opio who was suffering from a headache. He was so startled that I think he forgot the pain. It was at this point that Kisaka (Tanzania) asked to drop out. He had climbed gallantly but was obviously not fit to go on. We went to bed at 7 p.m.

Thursday 20th, February.

We awoke at 3 a.m. after a bitterly cold night. I was glad to get out of my sleeping bag. Bodies were piled up on each other, both for warmth and because the space was so limited. After a bowl of porridge we put on arctic kit and set off under the stars led by John Luberga. He set a steady pace. We reached ravines, high cliffs, and somehow managed to wend and clamber our way round. Progress up to now had been good. The sunrise was magnificent; the patterns it made on the snow above were always changing. The going was getting tough; we entered the ice fields and then the trouble started – one step forward and three back. Ice axes came out and we zigzagged up the slope. No one talked. Breathing was too difficult. The going became harder in the exceptional snow conditions. Ledges of ice and one or two overhangs. It was now ten forty-five and we should have reached the summit fifteen minutes ago. By eleven thirty we were in real trouble; students were violently sick and most of the instructors were down with headaches but we were only four hundred feet from the top. I looked back at our team. They were crawling up automatically. Two lads asked to drop out, but after a ten minute rest they decided to carry on. Lubega led and I got behind and pushed. The last four hundred feet took an hour and was anxious going. We reached the summit at twelve twenty and the team, after a twenty minute rest, grouped together for a photograph. The wind was high, we were perched on a rocky platform about thirty feet by twenty feet with precipitous snow ravines on three sides. The platform sloped and it would have been quite easy to slide off. The famous crater was covered in snow, the ice cliffs and pinnacles looked like something out of fairyland. We tried to tell the team about it but I know my own description was quite inadequate.

Now that we had reached the summit the will to move down had evaporated; an icy wind was blowing and all of us were exhausted. The mountain had been conquered; as to getting down that seemed an unimportant event. It was worrying but apparently is not unusual; strange things happen at altitude. The descent was something of a nightmare. Roped together, all but two of us suffering from severe cold and sickness, we slithered and struggled down inclines which in places were almost one in one. The point was that after this little bit of drama which did not seem funny at the time, things began to improve and we spent the night at just under sixteen thousand feet in a cave.

Friday 21st, February.

As morale, which yesterday had come near to breaking-point, was better, we decided to make one long march, eleven hours down to base. Though physically I felt fit, and later stayed up until midnight celebrating, I was mentally dazed. The blind climbers' achievement had been so magnificent. They had achieved something never before attempted and which most people thought utterly impossible. They worked hard, they trained hard, and, with great tenacity and courage, they made it. It was a privilege to be with them.

The story of this expedition attracted at the time international interest and was front page news in most African papers. A Tanzanian Government spokesman said that it had done more to awaken interest in the blind than anything else. In Uganda the three men arrived to a State welcome. The boots they wore, worn out and beyond repair, are preserved in the Uganda National Museum. In Kenya, another heroes' welcome and feast awaited the return of their men.

It was Andikati who, as we stumbled and struggled through the rainforest, a mere half hour from base and safety, expressed in words the sentiments of his exhausted team mates. "Whereas," he said, in his lilting Samburu dialect, "we were blind, we are now new men. We have met fear. We have conquered it. Though we still cannot see we have walked through the gardens of the gods and they were not angry. Soon we will be safe. It has been a fearsome and beautiful experience, has it not my brothers?" His words did not need translating. There were murmurs of approval and weary heads nodded in agreement.

*

During my time in both Africa and India I had become familiar with a number of majestic mountains including the massive Garhwal Himalayas range, but none were quite as unusual as Kilimanjaro. In central Africa I had lived at the foot of the ten thousand foot Mlanje mountain. Here the climber is rewarded with lush green mountain slopes, crystal clear icy streams tumbling down its precipitous slopes and, at the end of an easy climb, a flat plateau where unique flora flourish in the plentiful rains which sweep in from the Indian ocean. Like Kilimanjaro and most African mountains of note, it has its own store of tales and folklore which are unique.

234

Further north you meet the real giants, the Ruwenzori range, sometimes called the Mountains of the Moon, a chain of mountains running for sixty miles along the Zaire-Uganda border. The Ruwenzori has four great peaks almost perpetually covered in snow and cloud. Morton Stanley, the explorer, camped on one of those massive spurs which protrude from the main range and was totally unaware of the snow-capped summits towering above him. It was not until his second expedition that he saw the highest peak which is now named Mount Margherita. The approach to this peak and to some others is usually made by following the courses of the rushing Mobuku and Bujuku rivers – at least this seemed to me to be the easiest route. Here at around an eight thousand foot altitude one finds huge heather plants and lobelia similar to those we found on the Kilimanjaro slopes, reaching twelve and fifteen feet in height. The Ruwenzori climb took four days. The scenery is spectacular, almost out of this world, no wonder for centuries the local tribes who lived near the range, christened them the Mountains of the Moon. At the time of my visit tribal warfare which had been going on for years, started to flare up again and became quite nasty. Some of the tribesmen had come in from Zaire. They were small squat and primitive – almost pygmies. They fought their battles with bows and arrows and spears tipped with poison and the Fort Portal hospital was never idle. Much further north-east lies Mount Elgon another mountain with strong tribal and mythological connections. It is a mountain to which the Suk and numerous other tribes pay homage. It stands like a massive sentinel just inside Uganda and fringes closely on the Kenyan border looking over the northern territory. Its lower slopes are well cultivated and, for the fit, it makes an enjoyable climb to its twelve thousand foot peak. Elgon is a dwarf compared with jagged rough Mount Kenya, a challenging climb for only the most experienced, but the real *pièce de résistance* for African mountains is Kilimanjaro. It is accessible to most fit people who have the time and sense to respect a mountain of this magnitude.

The key to a successful climb[1] is preparation, good equipment and clothing and the ability to remain calm when altitude sickness strikes.

---

[1] According to the Mountain Medical Centre at St Bartolomew's Hospital three or four Britons die every year of altitude sickness. Failure to acclimatise to altitude sickness can have potentially lethal effects. Rapid ascents at heights over 11,000 feet may induce 'mountain sickness'. This, in its mild form, is usually characterised by headaches,

Whilst there is nothing technically difficult about the climb, the mountain claims its victims almost every year. Like the Ruwenzori mountains you have to choose your time carefully. Kilimanjaro is considered to be safe to climb only in February or September. The mountain looks innocent enough, but climbing through heavy snow at eighteen to nineteen thousand feet, where oxygen is limited and the cold intense, is an adventure one should not enter into lightly without careful preparation. It is as much a mental test of stamina as a physical one! (I made this point in my report.) There are some treacherous ravines and crevices for the careless and unwary. I found this out soon enough.

Few people realise that there are mountains almost sitting on the equator (within three degrees of it) which are permanently snow-capped. The German explorer Rebenmann, who first discovered Kilimanjaro, noted that he saw something majestic shining through the clouds. At the time he could not understand what it might be. It was not until 1889 that another German, Dr Meyer, climbed the mountain and discovered the amazing truth. It was about this time that Queen Victoria arranged for the mountain to be included in the German East African sphere of influences when she made it a present to her nephew Wilhelm II. For climbers like myself this arrangement can still cause problems as the approach from the Loitokitok base in Kenya has to pass across the Tanzanian border.

In African folklore Kilimanjaro is regarded with awe and indeed reverence. Sometimes it is referred to as 'the shining mountain'. The Masai tribe call it the 'all white mountain' and the Ngagenga tribe look on it as 'the house of the gods'. Like the Ruwenzori mountain range there are several main peaks. Kibo is the highest. It is here somewhere on its snowy slopes that tradition has it that King Menelik of Ethiopia and supposedly a son of King Solomon and the Queen of Sheba buried a huge amount of treasure. What is certain is that the

---

nausea and a pounding heart. Unless you respond to the symptoms by descending rapidly the illness in a few cases may deteriorate into either pulmonary oedema or cerebral oedema, conditions which are potentially fatal. In cases where the brain is affected behaviour becomes abnormal and the climber may refuse to co-operate in a descent to safer levels.

Although the onset of altitude sickness can be insidious the prospect of its more serious manifestation occurring to our party of blind climbers at altitudes of over 19,000 feet were disturbing.

Dr Charles Clarke, Mountain Medical Centre, St Bartholomew's Hospital, London.

mountain has a strange attraction for animal life. We saw monkeys at around ten thousand feet, a small mountain rat a little higher up. Hyaena have been reported at the twelve thousand foot level. Even the remains of leopards have been found at a fairly high altitude on this mountain though we saw little in the form of animal life, except a few antelope, who kept well out of our way. The flowers at ten thousand feet are impressive. I still have the everlasting blossoms I gathered on a previous expedition in my home.

The crater is interesting. The summit is one sheet of snow and ice cliffs but if one peers down into the crater there is a minute section which is clear of snow and ice. Does this indicate that this supposedly extinct volcano may still be in a semi-dormant state? I suspect that it may. The results of volcanic activity are especially evident at sixteen thousand feet where masses of rock in columns sixty and sometimes eighty foot high stand like isolated statues exactly where a massive explosion must have hurled them some centuries ago.

The main hazards on this mountain come from exposure and lack of oxygen when sound judgement at critical stages of the climb is at risk. The most awe-inspiring sight for successful climbers is to witness giant clouds floating past many thousands of feet below. Through the gaps of this stately procession, one can see miles below the expanse of steamy jungle where we had trained week after week. On this expedition there was too much at stake for me to enjoy the scenic fruits of the climb. Our blind companions could only be told about its grandeur but no words in English or Swahili could ever convey the really frightening awe and beauty of what surrounded us. There was a biting wind at the summit – there were sheer drops from the precipitous ledges on which our blind climbers had to rest. Sometimes swirling snow picked up in the wind stung faces even though they were protected by glacial cream.

So what did my blind climbing companions really think about this tortuous climb? I was soon to find out.

With Ennos, the Camp Bursar (a British Army Captain who was later killed in an accident) and John Lubega, we held an informal de-briefing discussion on the whole six weeks training period and the actual climb. It was a revealing exercise considering that most of these lads had been leading a sedentary life and were largely strangers to each other before they came to the Mountain School. The Deputy Warden was so impressed that he took notes in some detail of the impressions of these young blind men. Here are a few of the typical questions which he asked and a verbatim selection of replies he recorded at random at this session.

What have you enjoyed doing most and learnt from the course?
How to live with people happily, (Noel Palour, Tanzania).
I walk better, I swim, I am fitter and happier, (Elud Kiago, Tanzania).
I learnt endurance, (Moses Mutie, Kenya).
For me it is tolerance that I have learnt, (Tofiri Kibuka, Uganda).
I know how to face difficulties better, (Lawrence Saernambala, Uganda).
John Opio said he enjoyed the rock climbing most, (Uganda).

Where do you think you may have done better or even failed in?
I still feel I have not learnt to persevere enough.
On the mountain I caused you too much trouble, (Moses, Kenya).
I nearly failed on the mountain, (Andikati, Kenya).

The general reply by other students was they thought they had managed rather well. (I fully agree.)

What are your opinions of the expeditions?
I found it very hard at first but learnt to walk and climb,
(John Kisaka, Uganda)
The plains expedition worried me. I was frightened of the animals, but now I feel much braver,
(Mathias Gailanga, Kenya).
I enjoyed it all but they were so very tough,
(Noel Palour, Tanzania).
I found the rock climbing very exciting, (Andikati, Kenya).

*What were your impressions about living with the
sighted students instead of with a group of blind men?*
I have made so many friends. Some are leaving me
their addresses so that we maintain those wonderful
friendships,
(Andikati, Kenya).
Our co-operation was good, fruitful and helpful,
(Tofiri Kibuka, Uganda).
I liked them all very much. They were kind. Why must we be
separated again? (Lawrence Saernambala, Uganda.)

Without exception the answers to these questions were ones of
delight at being a member of a patrol or 'family' of sighted students.
My own comment on this point is that the sighted students were really
excellent. There was, of course, the odd exception, but the
sighted-blind student relationship is generally considered to have been
a very satisfactory and happy one.

A question asked all Outward Bound students at the school was
"Did you enjoy a happy relationship with your instructors?" As far as
the blind students were concerned the majority stated that they found
them helpful and indeed in one or two cases 'fatherly'. Comments
ranged from, "Full of praise", to, "You were tough with me on the
mountain but I know it was because you wanted me to live."

The mountain School at Loitokitok is far removed from the normal
channels of communications. The mail, including telegrams, are
largely at the mercy of the road and the rains. Our stay at Loitokitok
concluded with a delightful little ceremony held in the open air where
each member of the climbing team received the highly prized Outward
Bound Mountain School Badge, to prove that he had made it. It was
at this crucial point in the ceremony when a messenger came rushing
up clutching two cablegrams. I opened them and was completely
surprised and thrilled to read, to a cheering audience –

*Please convey to the seven blind climbers who
reached the summit of Kilimanjaro my warm
congratulations on their splendid achievement.*
                                        Elizabeth R.

I opened the other cablegram – it was from *Lord Hunt*, leader of the first successful ascent of Mount Everest.

> *We are all thrilled to hear that you have reached
> the summit. Congratulations.*

There were more cheers and the seven young heroes were carried around the camp shoulder-high, convinced of the enormity of their achievement for the blind people of Africa – indeed for the blind people of the world.

Chapter Fourteen

The Kilimanjaro episode had been demanding in both a physical and mental sense. Perhaps it added a new dimension to our work. At least this was the opinion of the planning teams in London and Nairobi. Though at first I questioned this claim, on reflection I found that the cold crisp mountain snows, the ice fields, quite staggering scenery and the utter isolation on the 'roof' of Africa had left me a therapeutic legacy which, in its right context, was enormous and at times exhilarating. A few years later when the aftermath of this adventure was probably wearing thin, it was put to the test again. This time it was to be in Asia.

One of my assignments took me to the slums of Calcutta and Mother Theresa's hospice, then located in a vast warehouse in the busy city suburbs. It was gleamingly clean and hygienic. I travelled on a further one thousand miles and from Delhi took the Mussoorie express to North India and on to Rajpur. It was here, located on an elevated plateau on the edge of the Himalayas that a Church of England missionary, Miss Hewlett, who lost her sight after an attack of measles, founded the first school for the blind in India. This was in 1887. Her one helper, Annie Sharp, who had taken specialist training contracted cholera within ten days of her arrival at the school and died in a matter of hours. I found the school still thriving a hundred years after its courageous founder had established it. The original buildings remain. A few new ones have been added but the school depends entirely for its survival on voluntary contributions. Those early pioneers had tremendous faith. Some years after Annie Sharp died her sister Dr Maria Sharp came to reside at the school. She arrived on 2nd June 1917, but on 10th June died suddenly of cholera – an almost exact repeat of the circumstances surrounding her sister's death in April 1903. The story of the Sharp sisters, now forgotten and largely unknown heroines, makes one feel very humble but as Margaret Ross, the Head of the Rajpur School, said to me as I left for

the Bay of Bengal, "there is no turning back, the fight must go on".
She was right.

I left Rajpur on my journey southward with Lal Advani,
intellectually a giant of a man, a senior civil servant who, though
totally blind, is the Indian Government's respected adviser on all
matters relating to blind welfare and education. After leaving the cool
air of the Himalayan foothills we parted company at Delhi and I
travelled alone across the vast sun-baked terrain to the Ganges delta
and on to Bangladesh.

It was a Bangladesh of the early Seventies. A poverty-stricken
land born out of the aftermath of war with Pakistan. A country which
is natural prey to the disasters of plague, famine, tidal waves and
storm which for centuries have wreaked havoc with the lives of both
cultured and peasant communities bordering the Bay of Bengal and its
hinterland. My travel-stained log book reminded me of those grey
days. I came across a passage which made me pause. They told me
about people and places I had almost forgotten. "Yesterday," ran one
entry, "the death toll was one hundred and thirty-seven, a slight
improvement on previous days." I recalled that these were the exact
impassive words of a pale-faced nun who with a handful of equally
courageous helpers, mainly Bangladeshi, had been running the refugee
camp I had just visited some twenty miles from Dhaka. The
impressions of that one horrendous day, albeit to be followed by many
quite as harrowing, remain with me today as stark and as naked as
many of the poor wretches that valiant little company were trying to
look after. Perhaps it is as well that nature in its wisdom can indelibly
etch on one's subconscious mind the trials and tribulations we can
sometimes forget when we live in the comfort, often luxury, of
modern society!

The camp was discreetly hidden away between two low folds of
hills, well camouflaged with palm trees and some twelve miles from
Dhaka, the capital of Bangladesh. There were dried out paddy fields,
lying bare and baked with not a wisp of life. A dozen vultures circled
lazily above two dying water buffalo who lay on the edge of the track
with ribs protruding and eyes glazed. It was a forerunner of things to
come. It was with some trepidation that I entered the huge
high-fenced compound encircled with coils of barbed-wire: left-overs
from the recent war I was told. Armed guards were placed at
strategic intervals along the perimeter fence, "to keep the inmates in

and to keep the wild dacoits out, away from the camp's meagre food store", my guide advised me when he realised that I thought the presence of the military out of place in such a setting. It was here in this one barren camp with little shelter that over nine thousand souls existed in various stages of disintegration. The incarcerated included beggars, the blind, the mentally and physically disabled and deformed, the diseased, the carriers of typhoid, of cholera and dysentery, of leprosy and a varied caseload of tropical ailments.

"All part of the daily scene," said the wistful nun who hailed from a small hamlet somewhere in a Bavarian mountain village.

"It is almost unbelievable," I remember muttering to myself.

"You have seen nothing yet, wait until you get out to the islands in the Bay," said my companion nun as if reading my thoughts.

The hospice run by Mother Theresa in Calcutta was, by comparison, a palace. I thought of the misery of famine I had seen around the plains of Dodoma in East Africa and now that seemed almost innocuous in its severity but of course it wasn't. The guards languidly paced the perimeter fence in the humid afternoon sun. Apart from the noise of their boots on the sun-baked earth road there was an almost ghostly silence, broken for a moment by faint spasmodic groans and distant wailing. I remember at the time it all appeared frightfully reminiscent of the Nazi death camps I had seen in 1945. There was the same fatalistic air of futility, the same stench and lingering odour and, curiously, almost the same regimented rows of the diseased lying prone on boards: but in the cases of those I saw in the Reich they were on the bare ground. There were the same thin soiled rags but the Nazis, sticklers for uniformity, even in the dying days of the Reich issued a pyjama-style uniform garb with grotesque black stripes. But there were more cogent differences. The poor wretches I saw dying in the camp near Dhaka were the victims of nature, not of man. It was the typhoons floods and their aftermath in the train of which followed famine and disease with all their consequences which killed people at one stage in hundreds of thousands.

The Nazi killing camps were more discriminating and better organised. They had been in existence since the late Thirties but curiously it was not until the winter of 1942, at a top-rank Nazi gathering near Berlin, that organised murder was given a formal blessing. The Nazi extermination camps I saw were run by highly disciplined units where the organisation was exact and demanding. My Bangladeshi friends could not afford the luxury of concentrating their thoughts on administrative matters whilst waging a losing battle against disease. Unlike the strait jacketed SS gaolers they could not find the time to record the names of the dead whom they buried each day. But the Nazi did. The SS 'minders' were disciplined to the last. In the Mauthausen camp with meticulous care they neatly wrote in the Death Register (which was bound in vellum) the names, prison number and causes of death, (usually heart failure) of the poor inoffensive creatures they had gassed that morning and this with approaching British troops only hours away. How does one explain the vicissitudes of nature in Bangladesh with the exactitudes of the Nazis and their campaign of mass extermination? The incinerators working continuously at Belsen and Mauthausen, their low chimney stacks pouring out a grey sickly smelling smoke – gold fillings were meticulously checked in the office. (They had been extracted from corpses before they were cremated.) And, most sinister of all, human hair was neatly stacked away in dozens of sacks for reasons which have never been explained.

The camp I was visiting that morning near Dhaka with its team of helpers was incredibly worse off than Mauthausen. It was bereft of the most elementary medical requirements, including disinfectant. Supplies had arrived at Dhaka airport the previous week but, "Formalities", said my Bangladeshi guide, "had prevented them being cleared quickly through Customs and consequently they were lost." I soon discovered as did many other aid workers that the place to find 'lost' medical supplies, which often included some of the most sophisticated and expensive drugs sent from Europe, was in the squalor of the local bazaar. Probably things have changed since those harrowing days but one of the jobs with which I had been designated was to make sure that the supplies sent out by a group of European voluntary organisations reached the people who needed them most. It was just part of an interesting and sometimes nerve-wracking assignment. Success might mean that an aggrieved party might approach a minister and ask for one's deportation[1]. Such were the complexities of local corruption when people lay dying by the thousand. I made three extended visits to Bangladesh and each time it

---

[1]The author was accused of being a CIA agent when an application was made for his deportation.

was to be in the aftermath of natural calamity. Perhaps after thirty years I had thought I was immune from the traumatic shocks of famine and disease. How wrong I was!

Traditionally Bangladesh, because of its fertile flat hinterland, had been known as 'Golden Bengal' (Sonar Bangla), but this only gave one side of the picture. The life-giving waters of the Ganges, the Brahmaputra and the hundreds of streams flowing from the Himalayas, form a vast delta which supports a population approaching ninety million. In the capital, Dhaka, there are a further two million, a city teeming with poverty, squalor and filth yet paradoxically beneath this sordid exterior one can find many gems of culture, rich tradition and rare intellects. Curiously, one of its most precious commodities is a cultured professional class which has become its main export. This group, a minority of whom refrain from leaving their homeland mainly for Britain, are badly needed to cope with the social and medical problems which overwhelm their country.

My first visit was just after an appalling typhoon which had swept in on 12th November 1970, and was followed by a vast tidal wave. This wall of water swept in from the Bay of Bengal covering hundreds of low lying islands and rolled up to the foothills three hundred miles inland. The official death toll was estimated to be around three hundred thousand, but in fact it was much more. (Some reliable authorities state that it was nearer a million.) Nine thousand fishing boats were destroyed and most of the forty-six thousand fishermen manning them drowned. Crops and houses were flattened. The wind speed of the cyclone was at least one hundred and thirty miles per hour and the wave height nearly thirty feet. One of the tragedies of this disaster was that the population was not alerted even though as early as 8th November, four days before the cyclone struck, the full gravity of the situation was known to the authorities. (The Pakistan Government was still in control of the country and its storm warning radar installations.)

Things have now changed for the better. There were three cyclones in 1973 and these were tracked from three radar stations, one near Dhaka, another at Rhepupara and one on the coast near Chittagong. The advent of Automatic Picture Transmission through weather satellites means that the actual formation of cyclones can be witnessed. The Bay of Bengal, which is funnel shaped, provides an ideal breeding ground for hurricane storms. Many of the worst storms including the one in 1970 and the ferocious cyclone on 8th December 1973, originated far out near the Andaman Islands. Significantly this last storm which could have extracted a toll equal to that of its 1970 predecessor inflicted comparatively light casualties because of early warnings. Nevertheless it was serious enough. One of the most appalling features after the 1970 storm was that it was a full two days before the Government authorities realised the enormous damage and casualties which had occurred. Some observers consider that it was this alleged indifference on the part of the Pakistan Government which ultimately led to the downfall of the Pakistan regime and the independence of Bangladesh.

Putting matters into perspective, the really serious cyclones which have devastated the country, apart from the horrendous 1970 storm, are fairly light in respect of fatalities. In October 1960, there were a total of eight thousand deaths. In 1973 thanks to utilising the early warning systems they were down to one hundred and eighty-three. The two worst storms recorded, apart from the cyclone of 1970, occurred in 1584. (This is written up in the ancient *Ain e Akbar* papers and affected the Barisal area.) In 1876 about two hundred thousand people died and the storm wave was estimated to be at least forty feet. It was estimated that in 1891 there were one hundred and thirty-five severe cyclones formed in the Bay of Bengal.

In the aftermath of the storm came the spectre of famine, disease and homelessness. My introduction to it was immediate. It was on a Sunday night when I arrived by air from London and was taken from the bomb-cratered airport along the river-front where half a dozen ships lay half submerged after an air raid. We went straight into the seedy steamy squalor of the city where the one hotel the Probani, was still functioning. There on the pavement a few feet away from the hotel main entrance, lay an untidy pile of ragged beggars, men, women and children, many terribly deformed, one or two limbless, some blind, and some too ill to move. Amongst them was the wraith of a young woman breast-feeding an infant a few days old. When I left early the next morning to go to a Government office, the woman lay dead and the child was alive clinging to her breasts. I suspect that she had been dead for a few hours. The busy throng hastening to work largely ignored her though a few may have given an impassive glance. By good fortune I spotted a bored looking official in a creased grubby uniform leaning against the hotel doorway smoking a cigarette.

He came over when I hailed him. He languidly looked at the tragic heap of humanity. A crowd had now gathered so my uninspiring policeman seemed suddenly goaded into action and with a mighty blast on his whistle and simultaneously waving his short white cane hailed a cycle rickshaw. Without further ado both corpse and infant were whisked away in a style which indicated that they were more an affront to society than a condemnation of it!

In those days I made a habit of walking each morning to the Ministry office in Dhaka with which I was in liaison. It was a revealing experience. As the clusters of cycle rickshaws weaved their way through the crowded streets a staid cart drawn by a buffalo wended its way leisurely along the streets to collect those who had died during the night. One morning I counted a load of nine bodies, but perhaps the reports I sent to the RCSB in England may help fill in the gaps of this tragic episode better. They were made in the midst of this carnage, not a decade later when the wounds have healed.

One extract read,

> This report is written against a catalogue of human suffering and misery which, even by local experience and living standards presents dimensions which may sometimes seem incredible. No humanitarian organisation however specialised its functions, can or would wish to remain detached from the consequences of the widespread famine and accompanying epidemics which now ravage Bangladesh. Infants lie dying in the streets, city slums are congested with emaciated people clinging to life, some relief camps have no suitable food for the under-twos who are then left to die – all this after many of the disabled have been removed from the city streets to up country areas to avoid embarrassing the authorities even more. The infected, whether by smallpox, leprosy, or cholera, can still be found lying or mingling in market places. The starving queue day after day at gruel kitchens often to be turned away unfed when supplies are exhausted. Around them are open ditches filled with filth and sometimes foetid human waste as well. Exposed watering places remain unprotected against contamination. Such things

ensure that this cycle of despair and human misery will continue.

This then is the background to our work in Bangladesh today – an unavoidable picture personally witnessed daily and adequately confirmed in discussions with medical and other relief workers attached to voluntary or Government organisations. Closely linked with all this is the fact that for many people in this country a disaster greater than blindness or potential blindness seems inevitable. The RCSB has worked in famine conditions before but it is doubtful if it has experienced anything quite like this. Famine we know is endemic to this region and something which has to be accepted otherwise sight-saving and social projects for the blind would never be launched but the present disaster has compelled us to join in the common cause of relief and rescue.

A visit to the Mirpur Relief Camp suggested that the standard of feeding has kept eye disease fairly low but in other camps up country there is serious concern at the state of many children's eyes. Medical authorities consider that xerophthalmia in all its progressive stages from xerosis to irreversible scarring of the cornea and partial or total leucoma is present.

The mechanics of relief in an organisation which is normally selective in medical and social services has demonstrated the adaptable role of an organisation like the RCSB. Once funding of a feeding scheme was available, in a matter of hours preparations had been made for food, cooks, vitamins and their distribution. Certainly there have been and still are problems. We could feed thousands, not a hundred, desperately hungry children. We are only able to do so much. It is for this reason that we have concentrated on the young and narrowed the field down further by giving priority to the blind, then other handicapped children and finally those who are in the most desperate need. We turn hungry children away every day, it is unavoidable. With the onset of the cold season within the next few weeks the child death rate will soar. It is for this reason that a cabled request was made to England for used children's clothing. Most of the children we help are naked. Although we have departed from our normal routine, it is not presumptuous to say that the RCSB aid and action is already saving lives and our intervention is almost certain to contribute in some degree to preventing xerophthalmia amongst at least some children if only we can maintain the service we have started until the crisis is over.

Now years later there is a new dimension to all this, thanks to the emergence of the eye camps strategy which now penetrates into the villages and isolated communities of Bangladesh, bringing new hope and, in numerous cases, saving sight. This movement which had its origins in Bangladesh was conceived by John Wilson as an original commando-type answer to a devastating problem. Its concept has been followed in most regions where funds and skilled resources are limited and blindness an endemic part of the landscape.

I met in those early years ophthalmic surgeons like Dr Rabual Hussein and Dr Dass, both of Chittagong, who pioneered the scheme giving freely of their time and skills. An 'eye camp' trek was a hardy experience for both staff and patients. Work started at first light. The people in the queues which formed had, in some cases, been waiting days in the immediate area where the camp was to be set up. Conditions were exceedingly primitive but they worked and, at the conclusion of each camp, it was safe to say that sight-saving operations had been performed not on dozens but on hundreds of people. This is how it all started. In 1987 this pioneer movement which had spread through nearly all the developing countries under the direct or indirect initiative of the RCSB treated nearly seven hundred thousand cases, performed nine thousand four hundred and fifty-five minor eye operations and restored sight to fifty-seven thousand five hundred and ninety-two men, women and children. Eye care is now concentrated in under-developed areas on eliminating trachoma, a fly-borne disease prevalent in areas where water is scarce, and paradoxically onchocerciasis (river blindness) which between them account for seven million blind in the world. But the chief causes in Bangladesh are cataract and blinding corneal malnutrition.

It is as well to remember that river blindness is much more widely distributed than originally suspected. Areas of Africa have been the focal points of attack whilst Asia has to contend with widespread Vitamin A deficiencies and trachoma which induce high concentrations of blindness. The good news about river blindness is that the research conducted since 1952 by RCSB (and more recently supported by regional governments and other international agencies), has made a series of important breakthroughs. In the mid-Fifties the simulium fly was proved to transmit river blindness. It does this by injecting parasitic worms under the skin. The females produce larvae, (micro-filariae) which invade the tissues of the skin and eyes. The vital parts of the eye, the cornea, iris, and eventually the optic nerve become inflamed and ultimately useless.

In Mali, (as in many other parts of West Africa) whole villages have been destroyed by the disease because the streams and rivers on which they are located are the breeding grounds of the simulium fly. The fly lays its eggs under water and so the cycle leading to loss of sight starts. People living in the villages I visited accept that by the age of thirty five they will become blind. The incidence amongst children in hyper-exposed areas is enormous and medical authorities in Kayes consider that their life expectancy, allowing for other factors as well is not more than nine years. The most encouraging developments following years of painstaking work is that the RCSB control programmes – the eradication of the simulium fly – have created large infection free zones. For those already infected the introduction of ivermectin, a drug which appears to have minimal side effects, can stop the disease spreading. One treatment appears to give protection for about a year. At last RCSB seems poised with its helpers to win a battle which has received little publicity but one which must have tremendous social consequences: meanwhile in Bangladesh medical research teams have other priorities.

The eye camps remove cataracts by the score each day. I saw the joy on the face of a wizened old peasant woman who had been blind for twenty years as she stepped out of the tent which served as a ward and gave a cry of delight as she saw faces and trees. She then symbolically flung away her white stick. These are the kinds of scenes which the eye camp heroes and heroines take for granted, but to you and me the message may be of greater significance. The

Kayes Region in the Republic of Mali

ONCHOCERCIASIS (River Blindness) ZONES

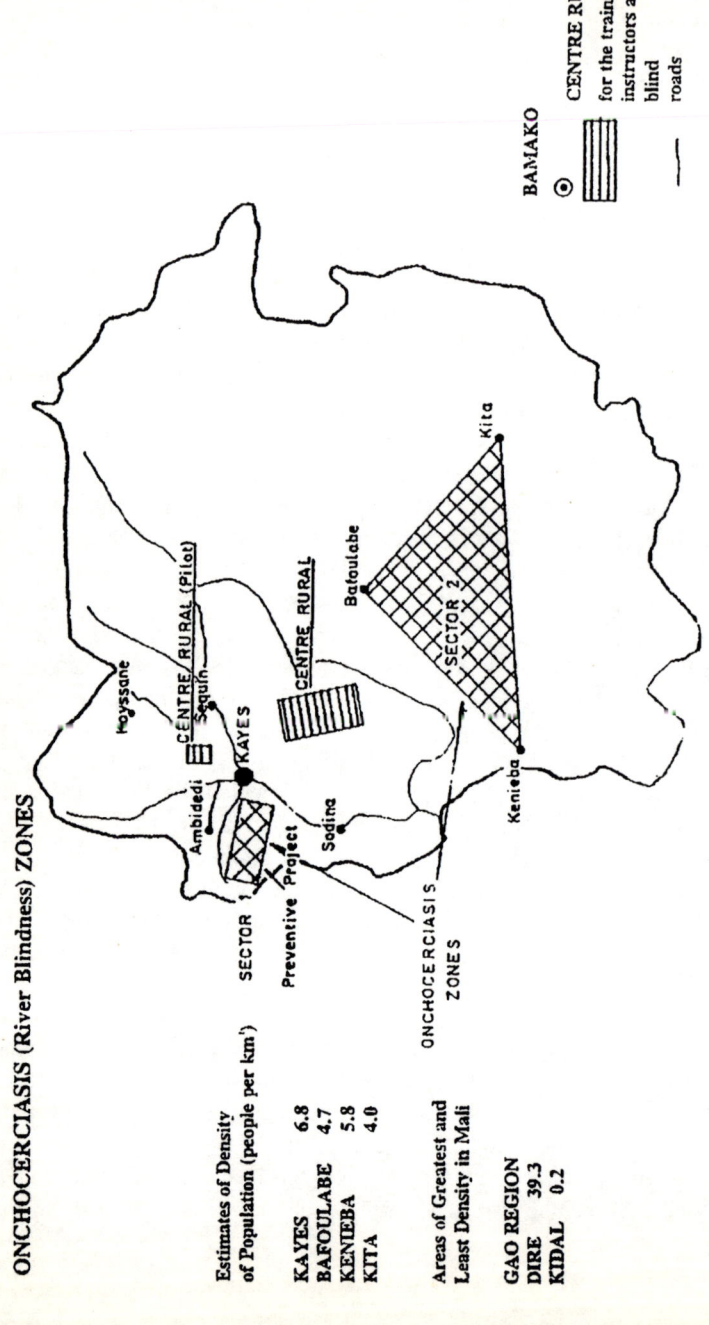

Estimates of Density
of Population (people per km')

KAYES	6.8
BAFOULABE	4.7
KENIEBA	5.8
KITA	4.0

Areas of Greatest and
Least Density in Mali

GAO REGION	
DIRE	39.3
KIDAL	0.2

BAMAKO ⊙

CENTRE RURAL
for the training of
instructors and the
blind
roads

Satellite eye hospitals:
1. Dinajpur
2. Sirajganj
3. Khulna
4. Mymensingh
5. Dhaka
6. Chandpur
7. Chittagong – base hospital

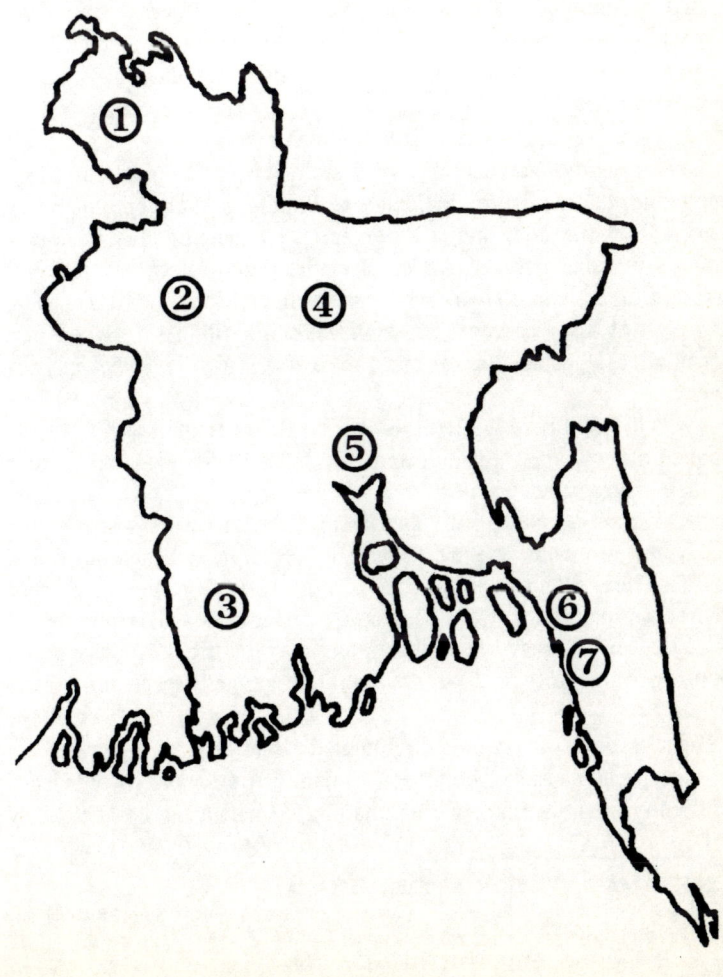

unknown war, the silent conflict against the scourge of blindness, is one war which is worth fighting.

Ironically enough it is sometimes forgotten that this work was largely one of the rare blessings and gifts which emerge from conflict. In the immediate aftermath of the last World War a quietly slumbering British Colonial Office department aroused itself to investigate the fate of ex-service men who had lost their sight. Their findings which were presented to Parliament in a White Paper were quite horrific. Their work was instrumental in uncovering tragedies of monolithic proportions amongst the civilian population. It was from this far-reaching document that the principles of a two-pronged thrust, prevention and treatment, plus care and training for those irrevocably blind emerged. Years later the WHO came on the scene and its surveys have confirmed the RCSB findings made many years earlier, that over eighty percent of the blindness in tropical areas is preventable, that whilst the incidence of blindness in Europe may vary between 0.05 per cent and 0.2 percent the concentrations of severe blindness in some parts of Africa is in the region of twenty percent. In certain areas where river blindness is endemic the incidence could be as high as sixty percent. In Mali, in some villages I visited in a river blindness pocket, the official figure I was given was seventy-six percent.

It was the RCSB which led this type of field research and for years ploughed a very lonely furrow, and it was the RCSB who, on its own initiative, introduced training and welfare schemes for those whose blindness could not be cured. The lesson from this work seems to be: identify the problems and then prove by example and demonstration that there are effective solutions. It is only then that a diverse selection of international agencies and governments will support you. For years the RCSB worked largely alone in this field. Today it has support and respect right across the international spectrum for its work.

The eye care programme in Bangladesh is now concentrated on two widespread causes of blindness. Vitamin A deficiency – this leads to blinding malnutrition (Xerophthalmia),[1] which is combated by

---

[1]BLINDING MALNUTRITION (XEROPHTHALMIA)
This is one of the world's largest destroyers of children's eyes. Xerophthalmia is a complication of malnutrition linked to a deficiency of Vitamin A in the diet of the youngest children and in Africa it is especially allied with measles. In India and

introducing the appropriate vitamin balance capsules and vegetables into the diet. There is also a fly-borne disease – trachoma. The eye camp is now an integral part of the sight-saving campaigns in Bangladesh, indeed in Asia and Africa as well. The camps work closely in liaison with rural health centres and Government clinics. The Bangladesh scene of the mid-Seventies was just one face of the timeless conflict against the scourge of blinding, disease and natural disaster. These challenges will always be present. The patterns of disease and misery which inflict countries like Bangladesh may vary, but their impact will last for decades to come. I firmly believe that this is a young people's war – one where tenacity and courage will always shine through the gloom. For me the modern day heroes and heroines are the youngsters who keep the flag of humanity and concern flying in places like the Delta lands of the Bay of Bengal or in the harrowing isolation of the lonely little school in the Himalayan foothills near Rajpur.

Bangladesh over forty thousand children go blind every year, due to this preventable disease.

Epilogue

The very days are too full fraught,
The very age of man has changed,
The way they live, the things they do
And life flits by like a moment
There's no return of days or months or hours or years
They fleet like water flowing from a Spring.

Alcuin (735-804)[1]

The haunting tragedies of Bangladesh, of Mali and other far-flung lands were still fresh in my mind when I landed at Heathrow after a final tour of duty overseas. Such calamities I reasoned had to be seen in perspective, at least they were natural phenomena, a far cry from the man-made variety of the last war which had swept some of my French Resistance friends into the gas chambers or in front of the firing squads. This outlook was shared by a female colleague from those distant days who met me in Paris later. In the steamy days of 1944 when network after network was being infiltrated and betrayed she had saved my life. In doing so she narrowly missed elimination in Dachau. Her father, an experienced intelligence officer was not so fortunate and perished alone in Neuengamme on August 26th of that year.

My companion considered that a society capable of organising the destruction of thousands of people every day and one which found time to conduct grotesque medical experiments on its victims was, at the end of the day more terrifying and unpredictable than the floods and disease which stalked parts of Africa and Asia. Be that as it may, the survivors of the reign of terror in 1944, which, in our minute sector eliminated six hundred and forty four men, women and children, are becoming fewer each year. Like them, I see the things

---

[1]Translation from Latin by Helen Wadell, *More Latin Lyrics*.

which happened through the eyes of a youngster for some of us were just out of our teens. Recrimination and brooding on the wrongs of that era is not helpful. I prefer to remember those who helped us in our hour of need – many of whom perished – as courageous people and commend them to history with our deepest gratitude.

We are living in an age when the aftermath of famine, floods and plague can be witnessed almost daily, in millions of homes on TV. Equally we can be armchair observers of the killings taking place in contemporary conflicts taking place throughout the world. I suspect that the 'TV culture syndrome' may have anaesthetised or conditioned our emotions into insensitivity.

How then can we expect young people to understand the traumas of the Nazi extermination camps, the Dresden affair, and the sadistic fate of Flight Lieutenant West at the hands of the Japanese? A man who was executed a day after being shot down and his flesh, including his liver, served up at a 'festive dinner' by Major Mataba for his 'honoured guest', Admiral Mori, (see page 114). Quite incredible but utterly true. The mists of time distance ourselves from the memories of such appalling obscenities; perhaps they should, or, perhaps they should serve as a timely warning of what can happen when depraved people are let loose on society. We should not forget that the tragedies in Northern Ireland have been compounded by almost equal obscenities.

This epilogue, indeed this book, seeks to keep the memories green and fresh of all the willing helpers, who in the last war assisted people like myself in occupied Europe, and the many largely unknown volunteers who have suffered and sometimes perished in the timeless war which is going on in Asia and Africa, to alleviate the plight of the handicapped and starving. Our gratitude to these 'unknowns' in these two contrasting types of wars does not grow cold.

I hope historians of this period will have the capacity to understand the role of our helpers be it the tensions of the last war or now, in the steamy jungles and sandy wastes of the tropics. For me this message of gratitude and thanks has been exemplified in two spheres. Firstly, one of serving in both these conflicts and surviving. I can now fully appreciate the sanity and tranquility of life in an enclave of rural Ireland. Secondly, I recall in more dramatic circumstances, the spirit of reconciliation at a unique ceremony for those who had suffered grievously and, in so doing had saved many others from death.

It was 21st June 1981, the first day of summer, the place: the crypt of St Clement Danes church in the Strand, London; and the occasion: dedication of a sculptured memorial plaque to commemorate those who had died or suffered grievously in rescuing British and Commonwealth airmen who had been shot down over enemy territory during the last war. It was a deeply moving ceremony. Gathered together on that sunny day in the three hundred year-old church, built by Sir Christopher Wren, were Service and civilian VIPs representatives of the Diplomatic Corps, and well over a hundred Helpers from every country in continental Europe where aircrews had received assistance. The youngest Helper was in his late fifties and the eldest fast approaching ninety! They represented every strata of society who had lived through those troublesome times.

The words of Elizabeth Lucas-Harrison caught the mood and the sensitivity of the occasion. "On that day," she said, "listening to the words and music, one was very much aware of those who had not returned, aware of the – to us – countless unknown names and unknown faces which were, at that very moment, on the minds of helpers in our midst. The weather was glorious and at times in the little church filled to capacity the only movement accompanying the prayers and the songs was the constant caress of the leaves of the plane trees outside, gently playing on the beautiful stained glass windows above the altar, somehow soothing, as though partaking in the memory, the grief, the anguish, the pride of the shared history... that little church was filled to overflowing with love and gratitude."

As memories swept across that unique gathering, sometimes of physical and mental torture, sometimes of those who 'disappeared' and have no known grave, there were some tears but shining through them a great spirit of comradeship, of unity and, yes, of reconciliation as well for those who were once our enemies.

The plaque which was unveiled that morning is starkly realistic and conveys the atmosphere of those dark days. It is made in solid bronze and measures about thirty-six inches by twenty-six inches. The scene it depicts is that of an aircrew member in full flying kit being dragged from the scene of a crash-landing by a middle-aged man, assisted by a young girl, whose furtive looks convey the urgency of the situation. There are a number of aircraft flying overhead. A parachute is coming down and the familiar pattern of searchlights in the background adds to the sense of danger in this ominous position. A short text details the story of the Royal Air Force Escaping Society and the persecution which threatened to engulf anyone who even contemplated assisting an Allied airman. Significantly, at precisely the same time that the service was being held in London, Australian members of the RAFES held a special memorial service at 7 p.m. on Hunter's Hill, in New South Wales.

On that June morning in London, the Rev. Bruce Lyons, the Chaplain of the Society, gave the address. To most of those present his words will always be remembered. They were simple yet full of dignity and drew aside for a brief moment the curtains of time so that everyone could catch a fleeting glimpse of the people we admired and the motives which inspired them. "Who were our helpers?" he asked. "Brave people – yes. Imaginative people, yes, beyond that," he said, "I think they were ordinary men and women who wanted to be free, who did what they could to bring others to freedom. They were people who knew little about glory, little of romance, just day to day worries and the harsh smell of fear. Just the usual hopes of people who knew what they had to do if they were to keep faith with what they believed in; people who knew that they could not face the future, could not look themselves in the mirror if they betrayed their ideals or if they failed to fight with every weapon at their disposal so that a tyrannous threat might be destroyed. This plaque," he concluded, "implies the struggle towards freedom with courage. *It proclaims that memory and gratitude have not grown dim after all these years.* Its presence in this church says that victory was gained under the hand of God."

The dedication of this memorial represented a small but significant token of appreciation which would record for posterity the contribution of the men and women of the Resistance movements who helped former RAF and Commonwealth airmen escape to fight another day, a task which for these underground members entailed terrible risks. Each year the number of those who 'helped' and those who 'escaped' or 'evaded' grows less, but from the day the war ended, the flyers who were saved formed the RAF Escaping Society, a unique charity run literally on a pittance. From Day one, it built up its funds and with these limited resources has helped those who were widowed, orphaned, wounded or maltreated because they rendered assistance to Allied airmen.

*

The ceremony which had taken place on that lovely June morning was a timely reminder to me not only of our indebtedness to those marvellous partisans, our helpers, but that living closely with them had proved to be an invaluable training and preparation for the civilian career which I was eventually destined to follow; a career which had involved tramping through the African bush sometimes trekking across the foothills and valleys of the Himalayas and, most formidable of all, bracing one's inner self to alleviate in some small way the scourges of disability which stalked those distant lands in its many malevolent forms. These days youngsters are trained in school and with youth organisations to combine outdoor pursuits and social service work as an integral part of their formative education. They take such things in their stride, but for the sheer willpower and motive force which operational flying and Maquis work had instilled in me, I would have been at a serious disadvantage when it came to living in one of those villages decimated by the simulium fly in Mali, or living where plague and famine have, from time immemorial been endemic.

I suppose that it was thoughts such as these, mingled with the ceremony in St Clement Danes, which were passing through my mind when I arrived back at my Irish home Roscahill, after my last and final trip abroad. It had been a testing journey – West Africa, Bombay, Calcutta, back up to my base – Delhi, and then away from the throbbing teeming steamy squalor of city life to the far away Dehra Dun and on to the snow-clad Garhwal Himalayas. It was this kind of life, especially when I was in central Africa, which oddly enough had induced some form of perspective into my work. Memories of those mystic days with Maquis *dizaines* lay well behind me reposing, even hibernating in the recesses of my mind after the full and busy life I had been leading overseas. I was lucky – I could switch off. There were others who were unable to do so as far as some aspects of their Maquis adventures were concerned. The horrific shadows of the elimination camps, "with", as one mental wreck confided in me, "the corpses stacked up so neatly just like cords of forest firewood ready for collection, meticulous organisation to the last," he sighed. I suppose all this is a legacy of a way of life which many today cannot believe ever existed. Even after five decades or more there are some of my Maquis friends whose sudden recollections of the familiar, long, low black Citroen cars used by the Gestapo (whose presence were normally the harbingers of trouble for some unfortunate person), still send a shiver or a nasty mental twinge through one's body.

On my arrival at Roscahill, it was the correspondence which was awaiting me which rapidly unlocked the frontiers of the past. There were precious memories in some of those letters from Simone and others but there were specks of poison as well in a French newspaper article recalling incidents which had long passed us by. I decided that I would reply to most of my friends within the next few days. There was one friendly correspondent who I thought deserved to wait a little longer, an individual who suggested that I should set down the recollections of my life in the Forest de Courton on paper immediately, "before", as he thoughtfully put it, "time sweeps you away from us!" There was in the same letter a paragraph about the fate of the old Gestapo headquarters in Rheims and something about ghostly Chantereine. For a moment I trembled.

I locked the correspondence in my desk. Somebody else wanted my attention – my three Yorkshire terriers, all with Irish names – Grainne, Tiree and Ossian the puppy, were impatiently reminding me that I had been away from home for several weeks and that the least they expected from me was their evening walk along the seashore. Yorkies have an endearing habit of getting their own way! That evening as we set off it was sultry and humid, not a breath of wind or a ripple on the water. We ambled along slowly over the shingle and eventually reached 'the point' – a landmark half a mile from the house. This is where the channel of the inlet narrows to less than a hundred yards and then opens out into the entire magnificence of Clew Bay with the towering sacred mountain of Croagh Patrick overshadowing the sea with its numerous islands.

I remember the evening well for that was the night one of those devastating storms swept in from the Atlantic. The sea had been silent and sullen for most of the day, hardly a ripple disturbed its mirror-like surface. According to the old folk whose homes were dotted around the shoreline, this could be a sign of troublesome times ahead. They knew nature's moods better than most of us and could read her warning signs with uncanny accuracy.

On our return we met old Brodie who lived in one of those delightful white thatched cottages which now have largely disappeared from the rural scene. His home bordered the strand but, for protection from the winter gales, it had been almost burrowed into the low hillside. This was the custom in the days when these ancient homesteads were built. There was no cement, with luck a little lime and seashore sand, and quite frequently just patient toil and quite brilliant skilled stone masonry work and little else. The gaps in the walls were stuffed with dry turf sods yet on a wintry night their homes were warm and cosy with a good fire burning on the hearth.

Brodie welcomed me back to Roscahill. There were too many "going foreign these days", he said with a hint of disapproval. He cast an experienced eye over the sea and glanced at the distant horizon and a black cloud hanging low over the huge mountains. "See over on yon mountain," he said, "it looks bad, the wind will be gusting from the Sou' west' he added grimly, "a storm could be in the offing. It is time," he went on, casting another anxious eye over the western sky, "to batten down the hatches and secure the ties on the thatch. The women," he continued with just a faint glimmer of a mischievous smile, "will need their rosary beads tonight." Brodie was the local historian and the ancient and respected patriarch of the hamlet. Ask him a question about the local past and he would have an answer. Few would care to contradict him even though he was not our only local – historian there were one or two neighbours with crystal-clear memories as well. Brodie could sometimes be scathing if the veracity of his stories was questioned. He had scant respect for authority which usually meant politicians. The medical fraternity fared little better, though, at the end of the day he may have prolonged his ebbing life for another year or two had he deigned to take advice and go into hospital. Such places he said were not for him. In his opinion they equated with the old poor law system – he would die at home. Until a few days before his death he struggled down to the shoreline to "look at the tide". He would rest for a few moments on the stone seat he had fashioned for himself and gaze across the narrow channel to Rossmindle, our sister hamlet, and then on to the gaunt ruins of the ancient castle, formerly one of the outposts of the Sea Queen pirate Grainne Ulaile, a female who terrorised the locality four hundred years ago. History and nature blend well together in this lonely creek.

Although the end of May was fast approaching, the sea had, as Brodie put it, "a constant troubled look". It was the deceptive calm which caused concern. It brought back the old folk memories of the 'great wind' of the mid-nineteenth century and evoked more recent recollections of the hurricane of the early 1960s which devastated much of the west. The sea trembled as dark ceilings of cloud came in with the evening tide. Small uneven wave patterns criss-crossed each other – tidal currents which can be exceedingly treacherous to the unwary – the kind which can give a small time sailor like myself some anxious moments.

Darkness descended that night at least an hour earlier than usual, but there was enough of a fragile twilight to witness the awesome approach of the tempest. The sea, now restless and uneasy first frothed and foamed and then quite suddenly our landlocked inlet became, it seemed, a boiling cauldron. The storm had struck.

It was one of those swirling Atlantic gales which strike fear into the hearts of the most hardened coastal watchers. It is the time when haystacks are lifted, roofs disintegrate, (as they did a few miles along the coast) and ships drag their moorings. I watched from the comparative safety of my house. I saw the black venomous squalls, the dread of all sailors race across the bay, the kind old Brodie had warned me about. "They will flatten you within seconds. There is no second chance. One mistake and you are gone," he had told me earlier as he sat on his pile of stones watching the tide. "Mark my words," he said, "I know," and with the air of one of authority he calmly filled his pipe. Brodie was right. I watched those frightening gusts sweep in over the low hills into the inlet. They came from the raging Atlantic with the dull roaring crescendo of an express train and hit the waters of the bay with a thunderous crack whirling across the confined lagoon and picking up sheets of salty sea.

This was the west of Ireland at its magnificent 'best', but also at its wanton worst as well – its most frightening. Each year on this wild Mayo coast-line the sea, like a pagan deity seems to demand its age-old human dues and usually receives them.

The gale reached its peak in the early morning hours, the tall sycamore trees which border my garden were almost bent in two. The fresh foliage, only a few weeks old (it had been a late spring) had clothed them in a delicate green mantle but within a few minutes the wild gusts had stripped them bare and torn them asunder. The long-legged cranes and herons which I had watched the previous evening on our walk to 'the point' had, retired much earlier than usual from their favourite feeding grounds opposite the house. They had made for the inland marshes and lakes. The sea swept across our humble coast road and came up to the garden gate. Would it ever stop? That early morning I watched a squall pick up a mighty sheet of water, a misty cloud, and race with it across the inlet onto the salt burnt Rossmindle hillsides.

By late morning the storm was spent. Shreds of leaves littered the lawns and pathways. Autumn seemed to have arrived already. The trees were quite bare, the road covered in seaweed but the sun was shining, the wind had dropped and the sea was a deep Mediterranean steel blue. The herons and cranes who fed on the islet opposite the house were back feeding as though nothing had happened. The air was still and chilly but as the sun gained more strength it seemed that soon we would be back into a calm summer day and nature's damage wounds from the previous night would soon be healed.

One of my neighbours, Sean Kelly, saw me bailing out my sailing dinghy. He enquired about the state of the boat and when I told him it was sound, still somewhat amazed he enquired about the state of my health! Another neighbour passing by, told me about the storm damage in the neighbouring bay, Rosmoney, fine boats dragging their moorings and one smashed against the seawall. With a sigh he concluded, "we have our moments sitting out here on the edge of Europe." I agreed with him.

"A raging force ten," I replied, "coming in from the open ocean does not pass over one lightly." He nodded his head in agreement, "The door to eternity seemed ajar last night for those unfortunate enough to be out on the sea," he reflected. He went his way.

In the perspectives of the previous night, his remarks had not been far off the mark. Lives had been lost but not on the Mayo coastline this time, but just around the southern corner off Connemara. I suspect that this part of the far west of Ireland had been inured over the years to hardships and tragedies, periodic famine, the curse of evictions from often worthless land and disease and storm. Yet, such adversities seemed to have brought out the best in many people; an indomitable spirit of courage, warmth and the ability to enjoy life in the most difficult of circumstances. How could it have been otherwise? The traditional wit, humour, songs and dancing had seen their forefathers through some of the most terrible social trials and tribulations.

We in Roscahill and Rossmindle are living in the midst of history and legend. Something we are not allowed to forget. There are 'fairy forts', another fort nearby of Viking origins. The same inlet which today shelters a dozen pleasure and fishing boats, sheltered four hundred years ago the pirate Queen's aggressive fleet. Castle Affey, the fortress which guarded our inlet has seen many violent days, especially in the sixteenth Century. This was the time when Tiboid, Grainne Ulaile, the Sea Queen's son was implicated with David Bourke, his cousin, in the seizure of a large vessel carrying a rich cargo from Scotland! The captain and all the crew were murdered. All this happened a few miles outside our little creek. There must have been prolonged celebrations at Castle Affey (where Tiboid lived) over this successful raid, but as one wit cheerfully remarked when I was discussing this episode with him 'We had to wait another four hundred years for the next party of equal stature.' He was referring to the occasion when neighbours from across the bay celebrated the wedding of their daughter on Rossmindle Hill. It was a night to be remembered. I am sure the old Sea Queen would have agreed. She probably graced, in spirit at least, that happy and memorable occasion when the old and the young in these two minute seaside hamlets joined the wedding party at Rossmindle.

The morning after the storm was blessed with a light westerly breeze which mopped up the pools left by the deluge of the previous night. The shore was littered with debris but the sea had taken on its characteristic steely blue. The air was soft and balmy, the birds were singing but the coast road was deep in seaweed. There was plenty of movement about, rosy faced youngsters on their way to school, the island boat, the *Clynis Lass* with Pat Gavin at the helm chugged towards the slipway leaving a wide white wake. Our cheerful postman, struggled up the drive with more letters and a mischievous reminder that my good neighbour was probably still abed and would I have a word with him.

*

The post keeps us in touch with the outside world and its arrival on that morning reminded me of the letters I had set aside in the bureau the previous evening to await another day. It was, I realised, somewhat guiltily, my cowardly way of 'escaping' news which I may not want to hear, or which would probably bring a surge of memories which I may not always welcome to the forefront of my mind. I suppose, at the end of the day, this explained why I had left the staid English countryside and sought refuge in the depths of the African bush away from these haunting wraiths. That day there was to be no escape – I could not let down those who after all these years still wished to reminisce with me about the past. "Did you know", enquired one elderly correspondent, "Madame Maria Andrée, who lived in la Rue Lenoir in Rheims?" I think back for a moment.

"Yes." A tall distinguished lady with sad eyes and greying hair, something of a recluse. I did not know her well. She was one of the 'unknowns' who abhorred publicity and decorations. My correspondent had described Madame Andrée as, "shy and retiring, somewhat eccentric." Yet for years she foiled the best brains in the Gestapo headquarters in the rue Jeanne d'Arc. She had died wrote my friend at the age of eighty-one, her Resistance work still a closely guarded secret. (Ironically she died following an accident with a car driven by an English tourist.) Madame Andrée's career would merit a book in its own right. The story was that when her husband died just before the last war she had then withdrawn from all social life and lived behind shuttered windows rarely ever going out, yet her secluded home was vital in the evasion and intelligence system. Allied flyers hid in her attic, those who were wounded she never turned away. Almost every night she went to the bottom of her garden where in an old chicken shed she manned a secret radio, picking up messages from London and from vital regions of France. She kept an impressive supply of arms for the partisans. On the dawn of liberation it was reported that neighbours were scandalised to see a young man leaving her house; he was one of the Allied airmen she had saved! The passing of Madame Maria Andrée into the shadows on that damp August morning meant that another bit of real history, another unknown but worthy heroine had left on the long journey.

There was a long charming letter from Paul Poittevin's wife, Jacqueline, beautifully written and very much to the point. Jacqueline was one of *les jeunes femmes* of 1944, vivacious, attractive, cool and confident. She writes mostly about her granddaughters of whom she is very proud. Her letter concludes with a lengthy postscript. "We have", she writes, "a dynamic young Mayor in our village. He is twinning our community with one in Germany. Now what do you think of that?" I wrote back to her a few days later and wished the Mayor's initiative good luck and added, "we could do with a few more people like that around, who are prepared to forgive and even forget!" I almost added – will Irish society with its prolonged hang-ups and penchant for vituperation ever come round during our lifetime to a saner way of conducting its affairs, learning to agree to disagree! There were other indications that ordinary French society was prepared to overlook the blatant wrongs of the war years. There was an extract from L'Union (the local paper) in one letter indicating that the city municipality in Rheims had agreed after a lengthy debate to demolish that House of Horrors, used by the Gestapo, eighteen, Rue Jeanne d'Arc. I think it was a controversial decision but as it was clearly an embarrassment to German friends, a municipality committee decided by a narrow majority that the place should be levelled. It has been replaced by a garden of remembrance.

From the day when Rheims was liberated to March 1986 the former Gestapo headquarters had remained a derelict building which had eventually become quite unsafe. The only token of recognition it received was that each year a service was held to commemorate those who died within its precincts and the men and women who, after interrogation, were sent to concentration camps never to return. Prior to the Gestapo requisitioning the building in 1941 it had been one of the status houses of the city. It was a fairly large mansion with well proportioned spacious airy rooms with high ceilings. (They needed to be airy). In those same rooms some of the most frightful tortures and crimes imaginable were committed under the supervision of Josef Weisensee. Whilst he and his deputies, Ruchti and Stollreiter, were formally accused of war crimes and sentenced to death (they all pleaded mitigation on the grounds that they were acting on instructions from higher authority), two of their comrades whose reputations were just as sinister were not so fortunate. They were apprehended at the end of August, or very early in September 1944 by a Maquis *diziane* and promptly despatched. (I believe their names were Ochs and Muller). It was rough justice – at least Josef Weisensee appealed against his sentence on grounds of diminished responsibility, but with the memories of recent massacres still fresh in most of our minds, the Maquis-type of 'justice' was certainly not uncommon – *franc tireurs* could not be bothered with preserving the lives of some of these individuals so that justice could pursue its cumbersome way!

The approach to rue Jeanne d'Arc was along a cobbled driveway with high walls on either side. The passage was quite escape-proof and well protected from partisan attack as well. There was a large impressive front door with an empty alcove on either side of the doorway let into the stone work. These neat little alcoves had each housed small statues of saints, but apparently they had been removed early after the Gestapo took over the building – perhaps as being incompatible with the use of the mansion! The passageway from the street was claustrophobic. Over the huge solid porch was the insignia of the Eagle, the Teutonic emblem. The hall was cold, even clammy, but large. It was suitably adorned with Nazi regalia, including a large picture of the Fuhrer looking down on the wretched victims. The room for preliminary documentation and interrogation was on the right. It was large with the usual high ceilings and a French window opening onto a balcony and leading to an extensive lawn at the rear of the building. Opposite this room there was another large office with high windows again reaching almost down to ground level. This was not the kind of place most people would associate with systematic torture and murder, but these were only preliminary settings – worse was to come. The Lacombe family, for example, when under interrogation for hiding an American airman, were first subjected to the 'two room treatment'. Monsieur Lacombe had been arrested the previous day and apparently had not been very co-operative. Madame Lacombe was arrested the next day "to help her husband's memory", as one thug put it.

"We have ways of making you talk," observed Captain Weisensee to the poor woman. "It is useless," he observed smoothly, "covering up for your husband who has been sabotaging locomotives and hiding allied parachutists."

Weisensee was always calm, but behind this calmness was a depth of cynical cruelty which has never been forgotten by people who fell into his clutches and survived. Madame Lacombe thought the interview was about to finish when suddenly she heard the most frightful shrieks from the room opposite with the large French windows. Weisensee did not flicker an eyelid. There were more screams followed by howls of somebody in utter pain which degenerated into long moans and groans. Weisensee, a 'gentleman' to the last it seemed, excused himself and left the door half open so that Madame Lacombe could see across the hallway to the opposite room.

From the hall he called to her, "Look," he said, "your husband is coming," and at the same time he left a ferocious Alsatian dog to guard her. "Have a good look," the Gestapo Chief called out. She did. Her husband crawled out of the opposite room, his face bloody and a mass of meaty pulp, his jaw she learnt later had been fractured, his clothes were in shreds and one of his tormentors, Ochs, kicked the wretched man and then flung him down a flight of steps to the cellars below. "This is where the real business begins," Weisensee told her. "Have you decided to talk yet?" he asked.

What happened afterwards to Monsieur Lacombe I never found out. What I do know is that the rooms or cellars below were specially equipped to deal with recalcitrant individuals. It housed a variety of torture instruments. There was an innocent wooden bath tub in which prisoners were either drowned or half-drowned as the Gestapo thought fit. There was a hand press for crushing bones and even for crushing the life out of victims so one person claimed. There was an assortment of clubs, whips, even a supply of piano wire for suspending victims and sometimes hanging them. On a table was an assortment of electrical gadgets for increasing by degrees the strength of electrical shocks. There was supposed to be a short rubber hose which, when forced up the anus of a victim and the tap was turned on, had the most appalling results imaginable. (Proof that this was actually used in Rheims never came my way, but in some Gestapo establishments it was 'standard' equipment and regularly used.)

I look again at those extracts from L'Union confirming that instead of making 'The Den of the Executioners' a museum as was the original intention, the plan has now been approved to level the building and replace it with a discreet public garden and a small study centre.

Now, years later I see that the annual commemoration ceremony has again been held at Chantereine. I see as well that in the little village of Oeuilly a few kilometres from the Forest de Courton and quite near the Champagne town of Epernay, the five British airmen who were killed on the night of 3rd May 1944 and now lie buried in the village cemetery, are remembered by the community. They were the crew of Lancaster 586 which was returning to England after a successful raid on a large German troop concentration. They were caught by night fighters, two of the crew were killed immediately and the plane, in the words of one witness, "raced across the town of

Epernay like a flaming torch." Only two men escaped, significantly one was sent to a concentration camp – Buchenwald. (He had been found hiding with the Maquis.) Each year children help tend the graves of those who died. This September, at a touching service of remembrance, they placed bunches of red, white and blue carnations on the graves.

*

So what does one make of all this now that we are nearing the end of the twentieth century? Was it all worth it? Regretfully, as the Nazi's Pandora Box was levered open with its bent on genocide, from 1936 to 1945, the methodical murder of thousands, no millions of innocents, in retrospect, this one reason alone seems to me to justify that appalling war. Where would it all have ended and what kind of society would be surrounding us if, in 1940, Britain had been subdued and America in December 1941 had failed to join the struggle?

These are the imponderables, when civilisation was at the cross roads, perhaps some aspects of it on the brink of extinction, maybe almost as much then as it is today, precariously riding the nuclear tiger! But there is a cheerful side to all this; mature people and mature nations are coming to terms with the past. It is *reconciliation* not *recrimination* which seems to be the modus operandi which is permeating the lives and attitudes of people and powers who a few decades ago, sought to eliminate each other. Perhaps Africa and Asia are finding the transition from the past difficult but, in their own way, the inner calm and sage philosophy of the East and paradoxically the tranquillity of life in Africa, away from the bright lights, a tranquillity which incredibly exists for those who care to seek it, points the way to saner times.

It is the histrionics of the fanatical and the psychopaths, motivated by hate, psychological hang-ups and sometimes an out-dated nationalism, which seems to be the real threat which can shock and soil many a fair and peaceful land. Ireland seems unable or unwilling to sort out the vile monster which lurks in its midst, a monster which is committed to anarchy and the overthrow of democracy. This perverted legacy left over from history runs deep. Is this why past delusions still seem more congenial to contemplate than present realities? Perhaps the Irish future is not so bleak after all! I think the younger generation are better informed, more widely travelled and certainly better educated in the broader sense of the word. They are not likely to be fooled by some pygmy politicians for much longer. Some will tell you that there will never be peace in Ireland until the country is united. Others maintain that the only time Ireland was ever effectively united was under Britain and that in any case the implications of EEC membership has overtaken events. The realists will point out that there are more people of direct Irish descent in Britain today than the existing population of the Republic. Whatever the rights and wrongs of such statements, the key to the future must surely lie in cultivating tolerance rather than provocation. Whilst discrimination is now much diminishing in the North, few, in the South have the courage to point out that the Republic with its mere two per cent Protestant population is in essence a discriminatory environment. These ambivalent and hypocritical attitudes do not encourage a pluralist society. Meanwhile it is one of the ironic facts of life whether it be in Africa or the turmoil of Ireland, that the weak and those who strive to upgrade the quality of life are the first to suffer when the blood wagons of 'freedom fighters', however well intentioned, start to roll. Innocents are the first to fall. Anglican missionaries like Marjorie and Tarka Savory, close friends of mine from Eastern Nigerian days, were needlessly slain on the banks of the Oji river.

At the other end of the murder spectrum men like Airey Neave[2] did so much to establish rapport with a former enemy, assisted the wrecks of humanity that had escaped the gas chambers and made sure that a humanitarian service went to those who had risked their lives for the allied cause and whose need was greatest. He was assassinated by cowardly thugs, people one supposes whose horizons are blighted by delusions of criminal grandeur and infantile fantasies. Commenting on the destruction of people like Airey Neave and the Savorys, I recall again the words of Bruce Lyons:

We live it is said in an age of tolerance. May we not be blinded by our own propriety and tolerance to the fact that there are many parts of the world which are not tolerant... never will be tolerant of any ideas which question their own... Airey-Neave and others like

---

[2]Airey-Neave was instrumental in setting up the RAFES and with others, making sure that those who needed help received it.

him, who had the goal of a free and tolerant society before them all their lives would not have died if society had been right.

So where do we go from here? Can we pause and hope that even in the shrivelled stony hearts of the Enniskillen[3] killers and their friends, one might yet find a glimmer of compassion and humanity? Or, must we accept that these dark cold blooded murderers, tacitly approved of by a small but vocal minority in Ireland, are impervious to logic and decency? I suppose we must. One of the seasoned killers in the Gestapo Headquarters in Rheims had a fleeting moment of revulsion and remorse after one bout of executions. Do the killers in Ireland who regularly foul the fair countryside they claim to love, have feelings of guilt as well when reason momentarily penetrates the veil of fantasy which cocoons their lives? Sometimes in this context I think of Eleanor Cheramy (Pat was her war time code name) who was recruited in June 1942 by MI9. After a stormy eight month period she was captured in dramatic circumstances. She suffered terribly at the hands of the Gestapo and never fully recovered her former fit and energetic self. When liberated from Mauthausen, (where she had been sent to be eliminated) she weighed less than three and a half stone[4]. She died in 1985 at the age of eighty still carrying the mental and physical scars of the past. One cannot of course compare the killers in Ireland with girls like Eleanor Cheramy who stuck it out alone in dreaded Fresnes, Ravensbrueck and finally Mauthausen. It is the contrasts which linger. At one extreme the totally obscene and at the other pillars of decency. It was Eleanor Cheramy's contention that for every sadistic horror story which emerges from the Europe of today and yesterday there are countless tales of courage and commitment which surround us if we are prepared to seek them out.

Perhaps she was right. I think of two personalities I came to know quite well, both shy and retiring, whose subsequent ordeals originated from widely differing circumstances. One was Dr Isobel Grant who, in middle age lost her sight but undaunted, describing herself as a "citizen of the world", tramped through the highways and byways of

---

[3]See Appendix III

[4] Tom Groome, another MI9 colleague who worked closely with 'Pat' was caught red-handed by the Gestapo transmitting to London. At gunpoint he was told to finish the message or die. Tom completed the transmission but left out the pre-arranged key letter thus warning room 900 at MI9 headquarters that he was operating under duress.

Africa and Asia determined to help others with her cheerfulness and fortitude. Long will she be remembered as a genuine friend of the destitute and handicapped. But Dr Fernand Braudel was also made in the same mould. Of him it was said with some truth that national boundaries had no meaning. Yet another victim of Mauthausen (who somehow managed to survive) his brilliant intellect helped to reshape and form the thinking of many modern historians. He could be utterly scathing about what he termed, "the sneaking, sniffling psychopaths who use cowardly murders to promote parochial forms of nationalism which should long ago have been consigned to history." Both Isobel and Fernand Braudel refused to dwell on the darker doings of humanity. Isobel had her message for the down and outs in the slums of Bombay, one of support for the grieving parents of a child condemned to die in the African bush and, for the numerous fellow blind she met in her wanderings through inhospitable terrains, a shining example of courage and fortitude. But Fernand Braudel had a message as well for those thirsting for revenge in the aftermath of war, for the angry and frustrated youth, and one for an Ireland living in the past, an Ireland unable or unwilling to forgive.

"I commend to you," he once said with an air of detachment but with much sincerity, "the words of Tom Paine",

The world is my country
All mankind are my brethren,
And, to do good is my religion.

I think these sentiments would have suited Isobel Grant's simple and humble attitude to life. When I asked her why she continued to risk her health (and sometimes her life) in far-flung lands at an age when most people had retired, her reply was illuminating. "My blindness," she said, "has compelled me to explore every crevice of life. It helps me to continue to wonder and not to take the world for granted. Each one of us", she continued, "carries a handicap which we try to conceal or smuggle into society as though we claimed perfection. In my blindness I have learnt to find that the world is a wonderful place. I think of the words of William Blake, the mid-eighteenth century poet, he says it all for me in just one verse."

To see a world in a grain of sand
And a heaven in a wild flower,
Hold infinity in the palm of your hand,
And eternity in an hour.

Appendix I

In the aftermath of World War II the transition from war to peace was difficult for some men and women. A few from both sides of the warring factions sought to channel the lessons they had learnt, self-discipline, initiative, and tenacity into the war against disability, both at home and abroad.

Amongst this unusual fraternity were people like the late Group Captain Cheshire VC whose international homes are now well known and are a lifeline for many disabled youngsters. There have been many others who took on incredible challenges. They include two former SS officers with whom the author worked in Asia, a Luftwaffe pilot who became a teacher of the blind in Hanover, and Daniel Mancier of the Arder Vallée Resistance *dizaine* who founded a clinic for the severely disabled in Rheims which is now a focal point for 'care' for both physical and psychological conditions. (Daniel and his Maquis is well remembered by the author who was held prisoner in his house as a suspect Nazi agent.)

Often overlooked has been the fascinating role of women in the war and their subsequent service to the badly handicapped and deprived. The name of Andrée de Jongh is known only to a few yet, this beautiful courageous girl took over the entire Comete Escape system after her father had been betrayed and executed. (She was awarded the George Cross.) Her story, like so many other girls of that era seems stranger than fiction. A trained nurse she spent years working in Leper settlements in Zaire and Ethiopia, "Not", she said, "to hide from the past but to take up challenges in a timeless war." The challenge aspect is probably the catalyst which motivated the majority of these ex-service characters, though one suspects, that some may have had memories they wished to bury.

Mary Lindell, who after being captured twice by the Gestapo, escaped to England. She was recruited by SOE and landed secretly in

France in October 21st 1942 with instructions to build up a network in the Limoges area. Like so many other SOE girls she was betrayed and joined Andrée de Jongh in the Ravensbruck elimination camp. Both were freed in the nick of time by the advancing forces and both were desperately ill. Mary Lindell survived until the mid-Eighties and died at the age of ninety-two whilst Andrée lived quietly in retirement near Brussels. Mary, a distinguished lady in both war and peace, had trained as a nurse, a profession she used to good effect in post-war years. A colleague described Mary Lindell as having "a very strong personality". I suspect she showed this during her nursing training as she is reputed to have flung a bed pan at a bad-tempered matron and survived! Her war work brought her an MBE.

And now, poignantly, who could forget once you had met her, a lady working under the shadow of Kilimanjaro in 1969 at the Outward Bound Mountain School looking after young people with 'special needs'. Her charges were blind and could not see her mutilated fingers. [They had been broken and the nails torn out.] "Did you ever hear of Fresnes?" she asked me, "and the Gestapo, they did it and more." Another of the SOE girls who preferred to remain anonymous but who would never forget.

But these forgotten heroines and heroes are only a fraction of this unique fraternity who fought in two types of war, one of destruction and the other to restore a semblance of humanity in its aftermath.

Appendix II

The demise of Dr Petiot overshadowed the even more heinous activities of Colonel Lois Brunner, a former commandant of Drancy concentration camp located just north of Paris. The macabre record of this SS officer has never received the wide spread publicity and revulsion, (except in France,) which it would seem to merit.

Lois Brunner was more fortunate than Petiot who, it seems may have collaborated with him. Brunner was twice sentenced to death by French courts but escaped capture thanks to the Organisation der SS Angehrigen, a group of former Nazis who provided escape routes to South America for senior war time criminals and, for some of the smaller 'fry', to neutral countries like The Irish Republic.

The author has vivid recollections of Brunner's activities. Two of his Maquis colleagues ended up in Drancy and after torture were never heard of again. Drancy was also a 'staging post' for sending Jews and captured Resistance workers to the death camps in Germany. On July 31st 1944, as the Allied advance from the Normandy beach head gained momentum the last train load of prisoners destined for Auschwitz wended its way through the countryside of eastern France. It was delayed due to Allied air attacks on the rail line in a siding. Two Maquis agents reported hearing the cries of children coming from the cattle trucks in which the prisoners were being conveyed. Little did they realise that Brunner had included 241 children between the ages of two and eighteen in this journey to almost certain death. Most of them were Jewish, some were handicapped, and others orphans from the Paris area[1].

Brunner is alleged to have been directly responsible for the deaths of at least one hundred and fifty thousand people. The irony of all this is that Brunner who during the war years was known to be 'a great lover of life' survived, according to some sources, until at least

---

[1] Subsequent research suggests that only thirty-two children survived.

August 1992. In 1947 prior to fleeing to Argentina Brunner was recruited by the Americans to serve in an intelligence unit but he left along the SS escape route to Bolivia and then onto Argentina. In the late Fifties he was working with the Syrian Government reorganising their intelligence service. The Syrians treated him well and always rejected French attempts to extradite him. One intelligence source does not accept that Brunner is dead and quite recently stated that he was living in the north of Argentina. If he is alive he will be eighty-eight. Brunner's wife and daughter still live in Vienna, Brunner's birth place. (The daughter was born in 1945.) Both daughter and wife kept in touch with him and this led to his location in Damascus in 1988. There were two attempts on his life, when he lost an eye and the fingers of one hand.

Appendix III

It was just after quarter to eleven on Sunday November 8th, 1987. Crowds were gathering under the shadow of the Enniskillen War Memorial to hold a service of Remembrance when, without warning, a massive bomb planted by the Provisional IRA exploded. It killed eleven people and injured sixty-three. The aftermath of this incident has been far-reaching. Its immediate effect was to bring together (for the time being at any rate,) the religious factions in this charming historic town, the central point of the Fermanagh Lakelands and its lush farming lands. The bomb alienated many overseas observers who at the time were sympathetic to the Republican cause. The worldwide intensity of disgust and revulsion were instrumental in making the political wing of the Provisional IRA, Sinn Fein quick to reverse its claim that the Provisionals had committed this atrocity. Its claim that it was a British 'plot' was simply not credible. Probably a Fermanagh unit of the IRA may have mounted this attack without, so it is alleged, the authority from its headquarters.

Years after this episode two personalities who were its victims rise above the carnage. One, Gordon Wilson whose daughter, Maria, died by his side will never be forgotten. Despite being seriously injured himself, and witnessing the suffering of Maria, a trained nurse, he devoted his time to healing the wounds of the past. When he died recently he left behind a legacy of the spirit of forgiveness, tolerance, and reconciliation. (In his book, *Maria,* these qualities are poignantly linked with the reactions to his daughter's murder.)

Amongst the other heroes and heroines of that tragic day are Mrs Noreen Hill and her husband Ronnie. Ronnie was headmaster of the Enniskillen High School. He survived the blast of the bomb but has been left in a sustained coma. Ronnie Hill spent the first four years in his now comatosed state in the local hospital where devoted nursing and the unstinting daily care and attention of his wife Noreen have helped him survive the wounds and traumas he suffered. For the last four years he has been cared for in a residential home managed by Mrs Hill. He is quite helpless, unable to communicate through speech, but from time to time seems sometimes to understand and to recognise the voices of those close to him. The tragedy of Ronnie Hill may be in danger of being forgotten. I hope it will remain as a symbol of decency and respect for all those victims on that Remembrance Sunday. In this context two articles written by Lily Dane in *The Impartial Reporter* of 2nd November, 1995 give a marvellous insight into the lives of a few survivors from that tragic morning. The way in which the Hill family adjusted to the sudden change of circumstances is typical of the courage demonstrated in this region.

Sadly in the midst of a prosperous tourist season in July, 1996 Enniskillen was hit again by, it is alleged, a Provisional IRA unit. Its famous lakeside hotel was largely destroyed. This at a time when apparently all but one political party, Sinn Fein, had renounced violence as a means of resolving the problems in Northern Ireland.

Bibliography

Northern Historical Journals,	Rhodes-Livingstone Museum, Livingstone, Zambia
Nyasaland Historical Journals,	The Society of Malawi, (Historical & Scientific Section) Zomba
Travelling Blind	John Wilson, Hutchinson (Century Press)
They Came to Northern Rhodesia	Richard Sampson, Government Publications, Lusaka
The Great North Road	G.L. Green, H. Timmins, Cape Town
Notes on Botswana Pharmacopoeia	G.H. Teichle, E.A. Medical Journal, Nairobi
Tanganyika Year Book, (1957)	John Moffatt, Tanzanian Information Service, Dar es Salaam
African Giant	S. Cloete, Collins
Nswana – The Heir	Dr Monica Fisher, Mission Press, Ndola

The German Achievement in East Africa	Richard Eberlie, Tanzania Historical Society, Dar es Salaam
RAF Escaping Society Journal	Elizabeth Lucas-Harrison, RAFES, London
'Andy, My Handicapped Brother'	Mary O'Malley-Medoc, *Western Care News*
Open Education	G.E. Salisbury, British Council and Royal Commonwealth Society for the Blind
Other sources included:	Foreign and Commonwealth Office St Helena Administrative Service and *The Impartial Reporter*, Northern Ireland, (ref. article by Ms Lily Dane) Mountain Medical Centre St Bartholomew's Hospital, London Dr Charles Clarke

Index

A

Acoranthea, 143
Addis Ababa, 34, 35
Africa, 151, 152, 177, 239
Afrikaans, 83, 91
Ain e Akbar papers, 245
Air Ministry, 50
Airey Neave, 269
Alcuin, 254
Aldenham School, 43
Allied Intelligence, xxv, 114
Amboseli, game reserve, 226
Amin, Idi, 168
Andrée, Mme Maria, 264
Ascension Island, 77, 79
Athlone school, 83

B

Babanau, Ronnie, 69, 71, 75, 188, 190
Bagamoya, 161, 185
Bangladesh, xiii, xviii, 111, 189, 212, 241, 243–249, 252–254
Bantu, 82, 83, 91, 133, 210
Barbados, 85
Barda, Mallam, 92
Barisal, 245

Barotseland, 125, 126, 128, 137, 200
Bastogne, 41
Batagarawa, 211
Beaufighter, 38, 45
Belgium, 33, 42
Belsen, 243
Bengal, Bay of, xxvi, 241, 244, 245, 253
Bentley Priory, 41–46, 49–51
Berlin, xxv, 42, 242
Berwick, D., 106
Biét Bridge, 87
Birkett, Dr, 168
Biss, Mrs B., vi
Blake, 220, 271
Blantyre, 199
Blaxell, Rev., 86
Boer War, 79
Bombay, 207, 258, 271
Botswana, 83, 99, 143, 144, 207
Bowshill, Mr, 106
Braemar, 76
Brahmaputra, 244
Braille, xiv, 66, 83, 104, 129, 132, 160, 177
Braudel, 271
Bristol, xiii, 51, 53, 63–65, 68, 69, 80, 205, 224
British Embassy (Paris), 48

Buchenwald, 217, 268
Buigiri, 184
Bujuku, river, 234
Bulawayo, 76
Burnham-on-Sea, 38, 39, 61, 62, 159
Burton, 183
Burtonwood, 52
Bushey Heath, 43
Bushmen, 82, 83, 92, 143
Bwana Mkubwa, 71, 75, 106, 108, 113, 116, 117, 123, 125, 128–131, 133, 135, 138, 143–146, 152, 157, 159, 173, 176, 182, 191

C

Calcott, Dr, 168
Calcutta, 207, 240, 242, 258
Cape Times, 84
Cape Town, 76, 80, 81, 83
Castle Affey, 263
Cathedral School, ix, 46, 57, 58, 61
Cathleen, Salisbury, 63
Chad, 92, 98, 210
Chali, Chiengi, xxiii, 147
Champagne, Region of, 31, 267
Chantereine, 214, 215, 259, 267
Chepkucia, 162, 163, 165
Cheramy, ('Pat') Eleanor, 270
Cheshire Foundation, 35
Cheshire Homes, 35, 203
Cheshire, G Capt VC DSO DFC, 35, 273
Chibemba, 73, 74, 100, 108, 113, 125, 131
Chiengi, 104–107, 147, 149, 154
Chifunauli, 154
Chikwawa, 146, 147
Chingwala, E., 195
Chipili, 109

Chitimukulu, 137, 138
Chittagong, 244, 248, 251
Chulya Mts, 225
Clapp, Douglas, 60
Clarke, C., 235, 280
Clichy, 47
Clostermann, P., 45
Cofitula, 122
Coillard, F., 137
Colchester, 59
Collier, B., 152
Cologne, 41
Colonial Office, 69, 70, 252
Commonwealth Secretariat, 63, 212
Corcoran, Agnes, viii, 214
Cotting, Father, 119
Courton, Forest de, 259, 267
Creil, Mr & Mrs, 197
Crimmins, Mr, 37
Crisp, Dr Geoffrey, 69, 75
Croagh Patrick, 259
Crocodiles, 73, 85, 89, 105, 106, 135, 137
Cults, 112, 135, 146, 164, 165
Cyclones, 244, 245

D

Dachau, v, xxv, 254
Dar es Salaam, 160, 161, 170, 175, 176, 186, 188, 191, 224
Darling, Anna, 89
Dass, Dr, 248
datura, 143
Davison, Tom, 148
Davison, *Yangwe*, 82, 118, 119, 126, 134, 136, 138, 142, 155–157, 174
D-Day, 33
Dehra Dun, 258
Delhi, 240, 241, 258

Dini-Ya-Msambwa, 162, 163. *See* Cults
Dodoma, 179, 184, 242
Dominic, Father, 123, 124
Douglas, Sir W., 85
Dowding, Lord, 41
Down's Syndrome, vi, xvi, 188, 199, 200, 205, 214, 217, 218
Drancy, v, 275
Dunn, 35, 36
Durban, 76, 83–85
Durham, 118

E

Egoji, 161
Ehrlich, Dr, 173
Elgon, 161, 163, 234
Elizabeth II, Queen, xv, 81, 147, 238
Entebbe, 168
Epernay, 267, 268
Equator, xxi, 74, 83, 221, 231, 235
Everett, Capt, 137
Eye Camps, xxv, 111, 189, 248, 249

F

Faleme, xxiv
Fighter Command, (RAF), 41, 42, 44–46, 57, 61
Fisher, Dr Monica, v, 88, 106
Fort Jameson (Chipata), 107, 148
Fort Portal, 161, 169, 234
Fort Victoria, 203, 204
French Resistance, 32, 37, 46, 48, 217, 254, 257, 264, 273, 275. *See* Maquis
Fresnes, 270, 274
Friedman, Dorothea, 107
Fulani, 92, 93, 98

Fundikira, S., 224

G

Gailanga, M., 237
Gambia, 85
Ganges, 241, 244
Garhwal, Mts, 233, 258
Geddes, 43
German Colonial Policy, 160, 170, 173–175, 185, 235, 280
German Counter-Intelligence, ix, 31
Gestapo, ix, xxii, xxv, 29, 32, 48, 214, 259, 264–267, 270, 273, 274
Gillies, Alou, 81, 83
Grainne Ulaile, 260, 263
Gramson, P/O, 36, 47
Grant, Dr Isobel, 270, 271
Graves, Pointe de, 45
Grenier, Père, 47
Groome, T., 270
Guedj, J.Max, 45
Gwaza, Bereston, 150, 151

H

Hall, F/L, 114
Halter, Sgt, 47, 50
Hanover, 212, 216, 273
Harrington, *Chiana*, 134, 148, 149, 150, 153–155
Harris, Professor J., 180
Hausa, 98, 112
Haywards Heath, viii, 189
Heinkel III, 52
Henderson, I., 167
Henessey, Mr, 168
Hewlett, Miss, 240
Hill, Ronnie, 277, 278
Himalayas, 233, 240, 244, 258
Hiroshima, 50

HMS *London*, 183
Holme, 35, 36
Humansdorp, 83
Hunt, Lord J. KG CBE DSO, vi, xii, 216, 224, 239
Hussein, Dr Rabual, 248

I

Ibadan, 93
Iganga, Teacher Training Centre, 169
Ilala, 196
Impact, Organisation for Prevention of Blindness, 71
Impashi Ants, 96, 97
Imperial Airways, 51
India, xiii, xvi, 170, 189, 206, 212, 233, 240
Ionides, John, 179
Itigi, 184
Ivermectin, 249
Iverson, D., 36
Ivory Coast, 212

J

Jacob's Ladder, 78, 80
Jamestown, viii, 77–79
Japanese Army, 113
Jeffrey's Bay, 83
Jemma, 34
Jennings, Flight Lieutenant, 51, 54
Johnson Falls, 107, 108
Jones, Arthur, 33, 36
JU 88 Night Fighter, 52
Juma, 124, 188, 192

K

Kachasu, 122, 142
Kalahari Desert, 82, 91–93, 143
Kaloko, 117

Kalunguishi, river, 99, 103, 150, 153
Kampala, 159, 168, 224
Kanamuri, Lieutenant, 114
Kano, 92, 210
Kasama, 143, 149
Kasembe, Chief, xxi, xxiii, 73, 90, 99–103, 108, 128, 150
Katanga, 122, 141
Katema Island, 105, 106
Katsina, 92, 93, 200, 210–212
Kawambwa, 74, 96, 103, 109, 150
Kayambi, 138
Kazima, 171–210
Kelly, Sean, 262
Kelsey, Mr, 137
Kent, 42
Kenya, xviii, 147, 159, 164, 165, 167, 168, 179, 221, 224, 233, 235, 237, 238
Mt Kenya, 161, 234
Keppel, Capt, 83
Khondowe, 196
Kibo, Mt, 235
Kikuyu Tribe, 136, 164, 165, 166, 167, 174
Kilimanjaro, Mt, v, x, xi, xv, xvi, xxv, 220–223, 225, 226, 228, 229, 233–235, 238, 274
Operation Kilimanjaro, 216, 222–224, 240
Kimathi, Dedan, 167
King's College, Taunton, ix, 55–58, 61
Kipkoech, 162
Kirk range mountains, 113
Kisaka, John, 228, 231, 237
Koch, Dr, 173
Kwihara, 183

L

Lacerda, Dr Jose, 151

Lacombe Family, 266, 267
Ladysmith, 76, 86
Lagos, 190
Lake Mweru, ix, xiii, xxi, 73, 74, 90, 98, 102, 104, 110, 137, 153, 160, 189
Lake Nyasa, 122, 153, 174
Lake Tanganyika, 107, 160, 183, 184
Lake Victoria, 159, 160, 185
Lal Advani, 241
Lala Tribespeople, 133, 143, 155, 156
Lammond, Willie, 82, 102, 107–109, 110, 111
Lapature, Peter de, 195
Leigh-Mallory, C.-in-C., 44
Leprosy, xxiii, 106, 242, 246
Lesueur, Rue, 48, 49
Limbe, 150, 197
Limpopo, river, 87
Liverpool School for the Blind, 63
Livingstone, xxiii, 88, 99, 150, 151, 183, 279
Livingstonia Mission, 195, 196
Lobatsi, 207
Loitokitok, 179, 225, 226, 229, 235, 238
Lowe, Sir Hudson, 79
Luapula Valley, xxiii, 73, 75, 87, 102, 106, 109, 111, 125, 128, 133, 135, 139, 144, 146–148, 150, 157, 186, 192. *See* Valley of the Blind
Luapula River, xxi, 73, 98, 108, 155
Lubega, James, 221, 232
Lubega, John, 236
Lucas-Harrison, Elizabeth, 256, 280
Lucien, Brother, 113, 119, 125, 142
Luftwaffe, 52, 273

Lugard, 100
Luka, Chief, 166
Lunda Tribespeople, xxi, 75, 89, 122, 147, 154
Luputa, 137
Lusaka, viii, 121, 167, 181, 206, 207, 279

M

Mackay, Alex, 69, 225
Mackenzie, Sir Clutha, 69, 190
Maclean, Cape, 195
Maji Maji Uprising, 173, 174, 176
Makafi, 127, 210
Malawi, xviii, 100, 109, 113, 135, 177, 192, 195, 197, 206
Lake Malawi, 195, 199
Mali, ix, xviii, xxiv, xxvi, 98, 212, 249, 250, 252, 254, 258
Malindi, 161
Mambalina, 98
Mancier, Christine, 31
Mancier, D., 31, 273
Maquis, ix, xxii, 30, 36, 54, 56, 214, 258, 265, 268, 273, 275. *See* French Resistance
Margaret, Princess, 183
Margherita, Mt, 234
Masai Tribespeople, 235
Masinde, 162, 165
matlakanye, 143
Matoba, Major, 114
Mau Mau, 159, 164—169, 171, 178, 191
Mau Mau Oaths, 165
Mau Mau Uprising, 94, 136, 162, 164–166, 174
Mauthausen, 243, 270, 271
Mayo, xxvii, 218, 261, 262
Mbala, xxiii, 151
Mbereshi, 74, 90, 94, 103, 107, 146, 200

Mbona, 196, 197, 198
McKinnon, Mr, 138
ME 110, 52
Menelik, King, 235
Metz, xxiii
Meurice, Hotel, 29
Meyer, Dr, 235
Mganga, 112, 134–137, 140–142, 146, 154, 155
MI 9, 29, 32, 37, 270
Milice, 32, 45
Mills, E.C., 138
Mirpur Relief Camp, 247
Mlanje, 192, 194–198, 233
Mobuku, river, 234
Mochudi Mission, 144
Moffatt, John, 171, 279
Mokambo, 94
Mombasa, xxiii, 147, 161
Mongu, 157
Monze, Fort, 152
Morekuru, 145
Mori, Admiral, 114, 255
Mosquito a/c, 35, 42, 45
Mountains of the Moon, 234. *See* Ruwenzori Mts
Mporokosa, 107, 147–149, 151
Mubita, Mr, 131
Munday, John, 133
Munkunglwe, river, 118
Mununga Village, 106, 149
Mununga, Chief, 103, 104, 107, 128, 147, 194
Musango, 94
Mussoorie, 240
Mustangs a/c, 51
Mutie, M., 237
Mwa, Robinson, 138–140, 141, 142
Mwansaswe, 137
Mwinilunga, 90, 122

N

Nagasaki, 50
Napoleon, 77–80
Nazi, v, xxv, xxvi, xxvii, 39, 45, 217, 218, 242, 243, 255, 266, 268, 275
Ndirago, 167
Ndola, 117, 121, 140–142, 155
Nelson, Lord, 43
Neuengamme, v, 254
New Africa Hotel, 170
Ngagenga, 235
Nigeria, xiii, xiv, 71, 98, 113, 127, 135, 180, 210
Niodougou, xxiv
Nkata Bay, 196
Norfolk Hotel, 225
Nyamwezi, 143, 177
Nyasaland Times, 146
Nyerere, Julius, 171, 177, 191

O

O'Malley, A., 218, 280
O'Malley-Medoc, Mary, 218, 280
Ochs, 265, 267
Oeuilly, 267
Oji, river, 180, 269
Onchocerciasis, xxiv, 248
Oost, Father van, 137
Open Education, xiv, 71, 92, 190, 211, 280
Operational flying, 51, 258
Opio, J., 231, 237
Opiya, Ennos, 225, 229
Outward Bound Mountain School, 179, 238, 274
Owen, Edna, 75

P

Packer, Bev, 96, 99

Packer, Margaret, 101, 107
Paine, Thomas, 271
Pakistan, 241–45
Palais de Justice, 48, 49
parachuteage, 31
Paris, 29, 31, 34, 36, 47, 48, 51,
    56, 254, 275
    Paris Mission, 137
Pearson, Sir A., 64
Peters, Dr K., 175
Peterson, 59
Petiot, Dr Marcel, 48, 49, 275
Pettit, Catherine, 208
Phillips, Dr Malcolm, 109–111
Plymouth Brethren, 107, 108
Poittevin, J. & P., 31, 264
Pont, Monsignor du, 137
Pouncey, Mr, 59
Poupart, Family, vi, 31, 47
Pretoria, 81, 86, 87, 111
Probani Hotel, 245
Puta Village
    Chief Puta, 189
Python, 73, 89, 103

Q

Quantock Hills, 56

R

RAF, 36, 37, 41, 46, 48, 51, 54,
    56, 75, 257
RAFES, vi, 32, 257, 280
Rajpur, 240, 241, 253
Rattray, 29
Ravensbruck, v, 215, 274
RCSB, xxv, 70–72, 75, 76, 125,
    161–164, 168, 169, 184, 188–
    190, 246–249, 252
Reader, Mrs, 151, 200
Rebenmann, 235
Reich, xxv, xxvi, 49, 242

Remlinger, J., 45
retrolental, 87
Rheims, v, 32, 36, 47, 59, 259,
    264, 265, 267, 270, 273
Rhepupara, 244
Rhodesia, 87, 144, 175, 176, 203,
    223
    Northern, 73, 81, 88, 127, 133,
        200, 279
    Southern Rhodesia, 76
Riebeeck, van Jan, 82
Rigby, F., 177, 192
Ritchie, Canon, 57, 58, 60, 61
Robb, DFC A/M, 44
Roodepoort, 86
Roscahill, 258–260, 263
Rossmindle, 260, 262, 263
Ruchti, 265
Rudolf, Brother, 197
Russell, Lord, 114
Ruwenzori Mts, 161, 234, 235.
    See Mountains of the Moon

S

Saddiku, 211
Saernambala, L., 237, 238
Sakabe, 114
Salima, 109, 199
Salisbury, Cathleen, vi, 35, 74,
    122
Salisbury, Harare, 144, 153
Samburu, 226, 233
Sampson, Richard, 200, 279
Sarcy, 47
Savory, 'Tarka' & Marjorie, 269
Seble, Princess, 34
Sefula, 137, 200
Selassie, Haile, 34
SHAEF, 44
Sharks, 83–87
Sharp, Annie, 240
Sharp, Dr Maria, 240

Shifta Tribespeople, 161
Shinyanga, 180
Shropshire, viii, 37
Simulium Fly, xxv, 69, 108, 112,
   249, 258
Singidia, 112
slave traders (Arab), xxiii, 100,
   107, 126, 153, 156, 160, 175
Smorenburg, Commandant, 79
Sokoto, 92
Solomon
   Family, 77, 79
   King, 170, 235
Somerset, 39, 56, 59, 159, 169,
   204
   Old Somerset and Dorset
      Railway, 39
Spitfire, 43, 50
Squadron No.76 (RAF), 35
Squires, Herbert, 106, 160
St Clement Danes, 256, 258
St Helena, viii, 77, 79, 80
St James, 78, 80
Stanley, Morton, 183, 234
Stanmore, 41, 43
Stellenbosch, 82
Stevenson, *Chirapula*, 82, 134,
   150, 153, 155, 156
Stollreiter, 265
Suk Tribespeople, 94, 161–169,
   174, 234
Suliman, Nasoro bin, xxvii, 153
Sunken Lake, 117

T

Tabora, xxiii, 160, 167, 171, 176,
   182–185, 191, 206, 224
Tachibaba, General, 114
TAF, 42
Tanzania, xiii, xiv, xvii, 71, 83,
   104, 112, 143, 159, 168, 170,
   171, 173, 174, 182, 184, 186,
   204, 221, 224, 230, 231, 237,
   280
Tayetch, Woizero, 34
Teichler, Dr, 144, 145, 154
Tembezeka, 194–98
Theresa, Mother, 240, 242
Thika, 165–167
Tiboid, 263
Tofida, 227
Toft S/L, 50
Trachoma, xxiv, 71, 108, 159,
   162, 168, 189, 248, 249, 253
Treblinka, xxv, 217
Treloar's Hospital, 62, 63
Tsavo, 147
Tzitzikama forest, 84

U

Uganda, 159, 162, 168, 169, 176,
   190, 221, 227, 233, 234, 237,
   238. *See* Salima
Uganda National Museum, 233
Ujama Villages, 177
UN, 203
UNESCO, xiv
UNICEF, 72
University
   of Bristol, 51
   of Newcastle, 180
University Air Squadron, 51–53
Unmack, Mr, 56, 61
USAF, 52

V

V1, 37, 46
V2, 37, 42, 46, 50
Valery, Captain, 48
Valley of the Blind, ix, xxiii, xxiv,
   xxvi, 73, 77, 87, 93, 109, 111,
   112, 157, 189. *See* Luapula
   Valley

Victoria Falls, 88, 200
Victoria, Queen, 235
Viper, Gaboon, 179, 182, 183

W

WAAF, 43, 45, 46, 49, 50, 57, 61
Wagogo Tribespeople, 177
Wannsee, xxv
    Directive, xxvi, xxvii
Wanyangwe, 169
Warwick Castle, 170
Weighgill, S/L, 50, 51
Weisensee, Capt, xxii, 265–267
West, F/L, 51, 255
White Fathers, 108, 137, 138, 143,
    151
White, 'Chalky', 62
WHO, 71, 72, 252
Wijenjie, Tom, v, 223
Wilhelm II, 235
Wilson CBE, Sir John, v, vi, xv,
    64, 69–72, 75, 82, 106, 110,
    111, 159, 189, 222, 224, 248,
    279

Wren, Sir Christopher, 256

X

Xerophthalmia, 71, 247, 248, 252

Y

Yorkshire, 35, 118

Z

Zaire, xxi, 73, 113, 170, 234, 273
Zambezi, 88–90, 137, 155
Zambia, viii, xiii, xviii, xxi, xxvi,
    73, 83, 88, 113, 125, 137, 147,
    155, 163, 164, 168, 194, 200,
    279
Zanzibar, 107, 170, 191
Zieuwerts, R., 82
Zimbabwe, 83
Zomba, 150, 151, 279
Zyl, Piet van der, 84–86

By the Same Author

What the critics say about *Yesterday's Flight Path*...

...The Gestapo accepted him as a half-witted oaf from Luxembourg: actually Geoffrey Salisbury was a downed RAF airman sheltered by French hosts and fighting on in the Resistance movement... Yesterday's Flight Path *is a chastening and exciting set of memoirs.*

The Daily Mail

There are few books which capture so vividly what life was like in occupied France and fewer still which pay tribute to the French Resistance...

    It is a book which the young of today should read as well as those who denigrate the French Resistance.

Imperial War Museum News

In years to come this book may well become a classic. It is the best one I have read which puts across what Occupation really meant. Authoritative and unbiased.

Group Captain Frank Griffiths DFC
(former Flight Commander of 138, Special Duties Squadron)

A book that does one good to read.

The Pennant